ReFocus: The Films of Kim Ki-young

ReFocus: The International Directors Series

Series Editors: Robert Singer, Stefanie Van de Peer and Gary D. Rhodes

Board of advisors:
Lizelle Bisschoff (Glasgow University)
Stephanie Hemelryck Donald (University of Lincoln)
Anna Misiak (Falmouth University)
Des O'Rawe (Queen's University Belfast)

ReFocus is a series of contemporary methodological and theoretical approaches to the interdisciplinary analyses and interpretations of international film directors, from the celebrated to the ignored, in direct relationship to their respective culture – its myths, values, and historical precepts – and the broader parameters of international film history and theory.

Titles in the series include:

Susanne Bier Edited by Missy Molloy, Mimi Nielsen and Meryl Shriver-Rice

Francis Veber Keith Corson

Jia Zhangke Maureen Turim

Xavier Dolan Edited by Andrée Lafontaine

Pedro Costa Nuno Barradas Jorge

Sohrab Shahid Saless Edited by Azadeh Fatehrad

Pablo Larraín Edited by Laura Hatry

Michel Gondry Edited by Marcelline Block and Jennifer Kirby

Rachid Bouchareb Edited by Michael Gott and Leslie Kealhofer-Kemp

Andrei Tarkovsky Edited by Sergey Toymentsev

Paul Leni Edited by Erica Tortolani and Martin F. Norden

Rakhshan Banietemad Edited by Maryam Ghorbankarimi

Jocelyn Saab Edited by Mathilde Rouxel and Stefanie Van de Peer

François Ozon Edited by Loïc Bourdeau

Teuvo Tulio Henry Bacon, Kimmo Laine and Jaakko Seppälä

João Pedro Rodrigues and João Rui Guerra da Mata Edited by José Duarte and Filipa Rosário

Lucrecia Martel Edited by Natalia Christofoletti Barrenha, Julia Kratje and Paul Merchant

Shyam Benegal Edited by Sneha Kar Chaudhuri and Ramit Samaddar

Denis Villeneuve Edited by Jeri English and Marie Pascal

Antoinetta Angelidi Edited by Penny Bouska and Sotiris Petridis

Kim Ki-young Edited by Chung-kang Kim

edinburghuniversitypress.com/series/refocint

ReFocus:
The Films of Kim Ki-young

Edited by Chung-kang Kim

EDINBURGH
University Press

Edinburgh University Press is one of the leading university presses in the UK. We publish academic books and journals in our selected subject areas across the humanities and social sciences, combining cutting-edge scholarship with high editorial and production values to produce academic works of lasting importance. For more information visit our website: edinburghuniversitypress.com

© editorial matter and organisation Chung-kang Kim, 2023, 2024
© the chapters their several authors, 2023, 2024

Edinburgh University Press Ltd
13 Infirmary Street, Edinburgh, EH1 1LT

First published in hardback by Edinburgh University Press 2023

Typeset in 11/13 Ehrhardt MT by
IDSUK (DataConnection) Ltd

A CIP record for this book is available from the British Library

ISBN 978 1 3995 1294 7 (hardback)
ISBN 978 1 3995 1295 4 (paperback)
ISBN 978 1 3995 1296 1 (webready PDF)
ISBN 978 1 3995 1297 8 (epub)

The right of Chung-kang Kim to be identified as editor of this work has been asserted in accordance with the Copyright, Designs and Patents Act 1988 and the Copyright and Related Rights Regulations 2003 (SI No. 2498).

Contents

List of Figures	vii
Notes on Film Titles, Romanization of Korean Names and Film Festival	viii
Notes on Contributors	x
Acknowledgements	xiii

    Introduction: Kim Ki-young, The First Global South Korean Auteur   1
    Chung-kang Kim

Part 1 Beyond the Border: Transnational/Hybridity/Border-Crossing

1 Kim Ki-young at the Intersection of Cold War Alliance, National Reconstruction and the Artistic Impulse   17
    Han Sang Kim

2 "We Shall All Need That Basket/A-Frame Carrier": A Comparative Analysis of *Goryeojang* (1963) and *Ballad of Narayama* (1958/1983)   34
    Kyu Hyun Kim

3 Love Thy Enemy: Kim Ki-young's Exploration of Korean-Japanese Romance in *The Sea Knows* (1961)   51
    Russell Edwards

Part 2 Beyond the Norm: Psychology, Biopolitics and Sexuality

4 Refiguring *The Housemaid*'s Singularity: from Dualism to Triadism Based on the Lacanian Perspective   73
    Kim Sohyoun

5 Men, Women and the Electric Household: Kim Ki-young's Housemaid Films   91
    Steve Choe

6 To Speak and To Be Spoken For: Deafness, Stuttering and the Women in the Films of Kim Ki-young   107
    Ariel Schudson

Part 3 Becoming an (Global) Auteur

7 The Intersection of Authorship and Film Regulation During the Period of Military Rule: An Analysis of Kim Ki-young's National Policy Films, *Soil* (1978) and *Water Lady* (1979) 129
Molly Kim

8 Rediscovering Kim Ki-young: The Rise of the South Korean Auteur on the Film Festival Circuit 146
Jason Bechervaise

Appendix 162
Index 169

Figures

I.1	Kim Ki-young at his home office (Courtesy of Korean Film Archive)	1
I.2	Kim Ki-young's wife, Kim Yu-bong, and Kim Ki-young "The Wife of an Artist: Kim Yu-bong discusses Kim Ki-young's film, *Geumbyeonmae*," *Donga ilbo*. (November 27, 1973)	7
I.3	Scene from *The Housemaid* (Courtesy of Korean Film Archive)	9
I.4	Scene from *Goryeojang* (Courtesy of Korean Film Archive)	10
1.1	The narrator's fainting in *Diary of Three Sailors* (c1955)	24
1.2	Pak Chi-sam's first appearance in *Boxes of Death* (1955)	26
1.3	A candle-light scene in *Boxes of Death*	27
3.1	In front of a hinakazari doll display Hideko dances for Aroun while he beats a drum	59
3.2	While US bombs fall, Aroun and Hideko's romance advances.	61
3.3	Aroun and Hideko leave the horror of (Japanese) war behind them.	66
6.1	Scene from *Water Lady*	115
6.2	Scene from *Water Lady*	116
6.3	Scene from *Neumi*	120
7.1	Opening shot of *Water Lady*	138
7.2	A tryst in the bamboo forest	139
7.3	A tryst in the bamboo forest	140

Notes on Film Titles, Romanization of Korean Names and Film Festival

1. *ReFocus: The Films of Kim Ki-young* uses the translation of Kim Ki-young's films as below. To prevent any confusion due to the various different translations of his film titles into English, the original Korean titles are indicated.

Ward of Affection (*Sarang ui byeongsil*, 1953)
I Am a Truck (*Na neun teureogida*, c1954)
Diary of Three Sailors (*Subyeon ui ilgi*, c1955)
Boxes of Death (*Jugeom ui sangja*, 1955)
Yangsan Province (*Yangsando*, 1955)
A Touch-me-not (*Bongseonhwa*, 1956)
A Defiance of Teenager (*Sipdae ui banhang*, 1959)
The Housemaid (*Hanyeo*, 1960)
The Sea Knows (*Hyeonhaetan eun algoitta*, 1961)
Goryeojang (*Goryeojang*, 1963)
Elegy of Ren (*Ren ui aega*, 1969)
Woman of Fire (*Hwanyeo*, 1971)
Insect Woman (*Chungnyeo*, 1972)
Transgression (*Pagye*, 1974)
Promise of the Flesh (*Yukche ui yaksok*, 1975)
Love of Blood Relations (*Hyeoryugae*, 1976)
Ieo Island (*Ieodo*, 1977)
Killer Butterfly (*Sarin nabi reul jjotneun yeoja*, 1978)
Soil (*Heuk*, 1978)
Water Lady (*Sunyeo*, 1979)
Neumi (*Neumi*, 1980)
Ban Geum-ryeon (*Ban Geum-ryeon*, 1974/1981)

Woman of Fire '82 (*Hwanyeo '82*, 1982)
Carnivorous Animals (*Yuksik dongmul*, 1984)
An Experience to Die For (*Jugeodo joeun gyeongheom*, 1990)

2. Korean names are romanized following the Revised Romanization System. The Korean family name comes before the individual's given name/forename, unless the author is known by their first name-last name order in Anglophone academia. The names of Korean directors recorded in the IMDb follow the spelling used with the IMDb. The names of other directors not known in IMDb are romanized following the Revised Romanization System.

3. The Busan International Film Festival (BIFF) changed its official title spelling from the Pusan International Film Festival (PIFF) to the Busan International Film Festival. To avoid confusion, this volume uses the Busan International Film Festival (BIFF) throughout.

Notes on Contributors

Jason Bechervaise is an academic and film critic based in Seoul where he has taught Korean Cinema at Korea University and at other universities. His Ph.D thesis, titled *Bong Joon-ho and the Korean Film Industry: The National and Transnational Cinema Intersection*, was completed at Hanyang University, Seoul Korea (2017). He is the author of several articles including "*Parasite* Forges New Paradigm on Transnational and National Cinema Intersection"(2020), "Inter-Korean Relations Remain Precarious: *The Spy Gone North, Illang: The Wolf Brigade, Swing Kids* and *Take Point* – trends in Korean Cinema in 2018" (2019), in *Contemporary Cinema Studies*, Contemporary Cinema Research Institute. He is currently featured on KBS World Radio as a film critic, and regularly writes film criticism in *The Korea Times* and *Screen International*.

Steve Choe is Associate Professor of Critical Studies in the School of Cinema at San Francisco State University. He is the author of *Afterlives: Allegories of Film and Mortality in Early Weimar Germany* (2014), *Sovereign Violence: Ethics and South Korean Cinema in the New Millennium* (2016), *ReFocus: The Films of William Friedkin* (2021), and is a co-editor of *Beyond Imperial Aesthetics: Theories of Art and Politics in East Asia* (2019).

Russell Edwards co-teaches Asian Cinemas at RMIT University in Melbourne, where he is currently researching representations of Japan in contemporary South Korean cinema. In the early 2000s, Russell was the founding Reviews Editor at *Empire(Australia)* (2001–3); covered film festivals for international trade publication *Variety* (2003–12); was President of The Film Critics Circle of Australia (2004-6); is a former advisor to the Busan International Film Festival and has given guest lectures at UNSW's School of Arts and Media, as well as Sydney's Korean Cultural Centre." Russell has also made short films, notably

The Agreement (2007), which played at several international film festivals including Sydney, Edinburgh, and Vladivostok and was screened on SBS-TV.

Chung-kang Kim is Associate Professor in the Department of Theater and Film at Hanyang University, Seoul, Korea. Her research considers the realms of Korean and East Asian cinema, cultural studies, gender, race, and sexuality studies, and (trans)national visual culture. She is now working on a book manuscript entitled *Entertaining the Nation: Politics of Popular Cinema in Trans-War Korea* (1937–79). She is a co-author of *Queer Korea* (2020), *Rediscovering Korean Cinema* (2019), *The Holy Nation: Gender and Sexuality in Law and Science* (2017), and *Orphans, People of No Heritage* (2014). Her articles appear in various journals including *Journal of the History of Sexuality*, *The Journal of Korean Studies*, *The Journal of Literature and Film*, and many other Korean journals.

Han Sang Kim is Associate Professor in the Department of Sociology at Ajou University, Suwon, South Korea. His teaching interests include visual sociology, qualitative methods, and the sociology of film and media. He has conducted research and written on the themes of film archives, ethics of photographic representation, post/colonial visual culture, and mobilities. His most recent book is *Cine-Mobility: Twentieth-Century Transformations in Korea's Film and Transportation* (2022) and traces the association between cinematic visuality and modern transportation mobility in forming a modern subjectivity in twentieth-century Korea. He has been concurrently working on his second book project based on his doctoral dissertation on US film propaganda activities towards South Korea from 1945 through 1972, putting on a self-reflexive critique of information-oriented archival approaches to film materials and expanding the project onto a methodological exploration. He has published essays in *The Journal of Asian Studies*, *Journal of Korean Studies*, *Inter-Asian Cultural Studies*, and several other journals in Korean. He was the inaugural programmer of the Cinematheque KOFA at the Korean Film Archive in Seoul and taught at UC San Diego, Boston University, and Rice University during his postdoctoral years.

Kyu Hyun Kim is Associate Professor of Japanese and Korean History at University of California, Davis. He received a PhD in History and East Asian Languages at Harvard University specializing in modern Japanese history. He is the author of *The Age of Visions and Arguments: Parliamentarianism and the National Public Sphere in Early Meiji Japan* (2008). His forthcoming book is entitled *Treasonous Patriots: War Mobilization, Colonial Modernity and the Problem of Korean Identity, 1931–45*. Kim has written numerous articles on modern Japanese and Korean history, Japanese popular culture and Korean cinema. He is Academic Adviser and Contributing Editor to www.koreanfilm.org, the oldest English-language website devoted to Korean cinema. His latest articles on Korean cinema are "The true colours of the 'Action Kid': Seung-wan Ryoo's

Urban Film Noir," in Chi-Yun Shin and Mark Gallagher, eds. *East Asian Film Noir* (2015) and "Don't Bother to Dispatch the FBI: Representations of serial Killers in New Korean Cinema," in Ken Provencher, Mark Dillon, eds. *Exploiting East Asian Cinemas: Genre, Circulation and Reception* (2018).

Molly Kim is a film scholar specializing in the history of 1970s Korean cinema, film censorship, and genre. Her doctoral research focused on the representation of women and sex labor in the 1970s Korean hostess films. She currently teaches at University of Suwon, Korea. Her latest publications include: "The Idealization of Prostitutes: Aesthetics and Discourse of South Korean Hostess Films" in *Prostitution and Sex work in Global Visual Media: New Takes on Fallen Women* (2018); "1970s Korean Cinema and Ha Gil-chong" (2019); "Women-made Horror in South Korean Cinema," in *Women Make Horror: Feminism, Filmmaking, Genre* (2020); and "Revolutionization of the Erotic Screen: The Films of Doris Wishman and Wakamatsu Koji" in *ReFocus: The Films of Doris Wishman* (Edinburgh University Press, 2021).

Sohyoun Kim is Senior Researcher, Center For Psychoanalysis of Korean Society, Konkuk University. She is an author of *Inside of Love: Seeing Kim Kiduk from the Eyes of Lacan* (2017), *Death of the Real: On the Transitional Reflexivity of Korean New Wave Cinema* (2008), and *Map of Fantasy: Questions against the Grain of Korean Cinema* (2008). She has written numerous articles including "Mirror Play or Subjectivization in *3 Iron*: Based on Lacan's Analysis of *Las Meninas* and His Political Model," in *Acta Koreana* (2014), "Immortal 'Realism' in Modern History of Korean Film Criticism," *Korean and Korean American Studies Bulletin* (2005), and many other Korean journals.

Ariel Schudson is an independent film scholar and moving image archivist. Contributing several articles to the Library of Congress website for their section on the National Film Preservation Board, she was also a regular columnist for several online film and media journals, most notably Quentin Tarantino's New Beverly Cinema publication. Her long-running podcast, Archivist's Alley, is known within the film preservation community for advocating inclusion of archivists from oppressed communities and pushing for greater attention to be paid to LGBTQI+/BIPOC/disabled moving image materials. She began writing about and researching Korean cinema in 2011, moving from Los Angeles to Seoul in 2019. Her research focuses on classic Korean cinema and women's representation, with a strong emphasis on disability theory, gender performativity, and sexual expression. She recently presented her work on Kim Su-yong, entitled "The Politics of Desire: Kim Su-yong's *Burning Mountain* and Women's Representation" at the Forgotten Popular Culture: Asian Cinema and Film History conference.

Acknowledgements

It is quite a coincidence that the start of the project of *ReFocus: The Films of Kim Ki-young* was with the news of South Korean film director, Bong Joon Ho's winning of the Palme D'or at Cannes Film Festival in 2019, and almost concluded with the news of Best Director Award for Park Chan-wook at Cannes in 2022. It is no exaggeration that South Korean cinema has enjoyed its international heyday over the past few years. At this moment, it is, therefore, probably equally important to remember the contemporary achievements of South Korean cinema were not made in one day. Long ago, South Korean cinema had its national 'Golden-Age' in the 1960s. Kim Ki-young was one of the key directors who led this remarkable period of South Korean cinematic history. And, it is therefore a great pleasure for me as a historian of South Korean cinema to present this important volume on Kim Ki-young, who has been such an inspiring figure to film scholars and filmmakers in Korea and the wider world.

In being able to bring together this book, I have become indebted to so many great people who made this volume possible. First of all, I would like to thank all the contributors who so enthusiastically engaged in this project and contributed significant and superb pieces on Kim Ki-young. As an editor, I enjoyed reading each chapter and soon came to realize the diversity of intellectual curiosity that Kim Ki-young's films inspired. My thanks go to the director of the Korean Film Archive, Kim Hong-joon, whose work was pioneering in compiling the visual and documentary materials in relation to Kim Ki-young's works. He gave me amazing feedback from the beginning of this project up to its completion. His willingness to answer many questions and assist our contributors enhanced the quality of each chapter to a significant degree. Kim Dong-yang, the son of director Kim Ki-young also helped and supported this project immensely. His help in figuring out the copyright of Kim Ki-young's work, and his willing permission to use Kim Ki-young's scripts and photos in our volume made this work even more valuable. I also thank Kim Seung-kyeong at the Korean Film Archive who provided us with such high-quality photographic materials. It was great to have my student, Song Won-jeong at Hanyang University, participate in the translation of the missing dialogue from *The Sea Knows*, and her wonderful translation of the original script is included in this volume as an appendix. Also crucially important to its completion, this project was partially funded by a generous grant from the department of Theater and Film at Hanyang University.

Finally, I thank wonderful editors of the *ReFocus* series at Edinburgh University Press, Robert Singer, Gary D. Rhodes and Stefanie Van de Peer. This project could not be completed without their encouragement and assistance. I thank the external academic reviewers of this project who guided this volume so usefully, and Luke Houston in particular, who provided immense help in the editorial process. Last but not least, I thank the staff at Edinburgh University Press who helped us so much to complete this project from beginning to end.

Seoul, January 2023
Chung-kang Kim

Introduction: Kim Ki-young, the First Global South Korean Auteur

Chung-kang Kim

Figure I.1 Kim Ki-young at his home office. (Courtesy of Korean Film Archive.)

KIM KI-YOUNG, THE FIRST GLOBAL SOUTH KOREAN AUTEUR

Over the thirty years of his career, Kim Ki-young (1919–98) produced and directed thirty-two feature films which are widely considered to be among the most sensual, grotesque, and provocative Korean cinematic works to have been created during the twentieth century. Although thirty-two is no small number of films to have directed, it is nonetheless difficult to say that Kim was particularly prolific in comparison to many of his South Korean contemporaries.[1] Twenty-nine of his productions were made before 1980, and so it could be said that his directorial output seriously declined after the 1970s. In the 1980s, Kim wrote seven scripts, though none of these scripts were made into films.[2] However, despite his relative lack of productivity in his later career, the unique thematic, stylistic and aesthetic character of the main body of Kim's work far exceeded the cultural and generic norms of the period, a legacy which renders him one of the most compelling directors in the history of South Korean cinema.

Despite the significance and unique nature of Kim Ki-young's oeuvre, it is notable that his work was largely forgotten by Korean and global audiences, only to be "rediscovered" through a retrospective program at the Second Busan International Film festival in 1997. As Chris Berry noted, when Kim Ki-young's films were brought back from the past and first presented to global audiences through this retrospective, the immediate appeal of his work to the international film community was that it offered something different to the idea of classic Asian cinema, as represented by the work of Ozu Yasujiro, Mijoguchi Kenji, and the Fifth Generation directors of China.[3] While the distinctive quality of Kim's work ("excessive" and "violent" in Berry's terms) rendered its stylistic and thematic categorization within the frame of "Asian art cinema" difficult, after the once forgotten director's films were widely welcomed by global audiences, his newly located oeuvre was immediately characterized as a "hidden Asian pearl."[4] Even domestically the retrieval of his lost directorial legacy came as something of a major critical surprise, and in relation to the success of the Busan retrospective one film writer even lamented that "the entire contemporary South Korean cinematic community during the 1990s [has] failed to produce any new works as interesting as the films of Kim Ki-young."[5]

Since his rediscovery, Kim's astonishingly refreshing visual style and consistent thematic concerns have been received passionately by national and global audiences as well as film scholars. One of Kim's most renowned films, *The Housemaid* (*Hanyeo*, 1960) has been invited nineteen times to various international film festivals.[6] *The Housemaid* has also been digitally restored and redistributed through the Criterion Classical Film Collection and is now widely regarded as a major canonical work within world cinema.[7] In South Korea, Kim's unpublished scripts were compiled into two edited volumes.[8] Three documentary films about the director have been made, and interest in his work has only heightened after his untimely death in 1998,[9] an event which tragically happened just few days before Kim was supposed to attend a major retrospective of his work at the Berlin International Film Festival.

One might ask the question of how Kim Ki-young, who had his heyday in the 1960s and 1970s, only became globally recognized as an "auteur" twenty years later, in the late 1990s. This was possible due to three factors. First, his critical rediscovery was initiated by many contemporary world-renowned Korean film directors, including Park Chan-wook and Bong Joon Ho, who were recognized as the emergent, young, ambitious, new directors of South Korean cinema in the late 1990s.[10] These directors grew up in the 1980s, a period culturally dictated by the harsh censorship of the South Korean military government. As young cinephiles they developed a "cult" interest in Kim Ki-young's films—which became widely available through VHS in the 1980s—and later came to cite him as being the most influential Korean director relative to the development of their work. Even today, the massive influence of Kim's legacy on South Korean cinema continues. For instance, *The Housemaid* was remade by Im Sang-soo in 2010, and Kim Jee-woon is currently making a film inspired by the director's life, titled *Spider House* (*Geomijib*, 2022).

Second, it is notable that many feminist critics, who began to form their own discourse of South Korean film history in the 1990s, also welcomed the re-emergence of Kim Ki-young's work. Although Kim's films are not precisely "feminist" works, they still provided a useful point of interest for feminist critics, not least because of the scarcity of South Korean woman directors.[11] Kim Ki-young's "The Housemaid" series of films frequently portrays powerful and ambiguous female characters and their sexuality. As Soyoung Kim notes, such features helped to open up the historical possibility of reading women's lives in South Korea from a feminist cinematic perspective.[12]

Finally, and perhaps most significantly, the critical recovery of Kim's oeuvre was closely related to the historical situation directly within South Korea at the time. In the late 1990s, after a decade of groundbreaking democratic rule, South Korea suffered the disaster of the notorious IMF financial crisis.[13] Korean filmmakers were not spared from this adversity and witnessed the extreme waning of the national film industry. "Globalization" and the creation of more "Korean-style blockbusters" were framed as the key ideas to help overcome the downturn suffered by national cinema, and enable it to compete with other international production hubs, primarily Hollywood.[14] Developing and boosting the Asian and South Korean "film circuit" was a crucial part of this globalization project, primarily based on the establishment of a "vernacular" South Korean international film festival that could compete for attention within the Western-centered international marketplace for arthouse cinema.[15] This is why several Korean international film festivals such as the Busan International Film Festival (1996–) and Bucheon International Fantastic Film Festival (1997–)

were created during this period. The timing of the introduction of Kim Ki-young as an "old" but "new" South Korean auteur onto the global cinematic stage within this climate was, therefore, no coincidence.

However, despite his now established international fame as the historical figure who inspired the celebrated South Korean film auteurs of the contemporary period, academic studies on the work of Kim Ki-young are practically stagnant, particularly in the Anglophone world. In South Korea, there have been four books published outlining the life of the director and his works since the beginning of millennium.[16] In English, only one such book has been published: *Korean Film Directors: Kim Ki-young*, published by Korean Film Council in 2006. As the editor Kim Hong-joon mentioned in the preface, this was primarily created to function as a "dossier for those interested in Kim Ki-young and his works." In other words, a reference text for specialist readers associated with film festivals and cinematheques, and generalist audiences who seek more factual information about the director.[17] Given this context, further academic studies in a complied volume on the director have been conspicuous only in their complete absence.

As the first comprehensive scholarly volume on the director in English, *ReFocus: The Films of Kim Ki-young* is, therefore, deliberately orientated to address his entire career and history of cinematic work, highlighting the thematic and stylistic singularity of his oeuvre, and discussing how this was created relative to the specific historical and cultural conditions of postwar South Korea. The contributors to this volume provide a wide range of fresh and nuanced perspectives on Kim Ki-young's films. Additionally, due to the significant and novel selection of discussion topics presented in each chapter, *ReFocus: The Films of Kim Ki-young* also provides an innovative departure point from which to explore the wider historical context of South Korean film relative to the history of world cinema, while simultaneously situating Kim's work within the broader fields of modern regional history, transnational cinema, cultural studies, pyscho-analysis and gender and sexuality studies.

To publish this volume on Kim Ki-young at this moment, when 'K-wave' drama and 'K-cinema' is of such interest to the wider world, is particularly meaningful. The current changes in film and media viewing practices, which have been facilitated by the massive expansion of digital streaming platforms (and intensified because of the COVID-19 pandemic over the past two years), mean that film audiences are increasingly, if not overwhelmingly, introduced to new material outside of the traditional site of the movie theater. In this respect, global audiences' ability to access an immense range of films through their personal digital devices has opened up an entirely new set of possibilities for watching rare and old movies that were previously out of reach.

In this current situation, the past difficulty overseas audiences have had in being able to access classic Korean films with English subtitles, something which was often only possible within a film festival screening, has been resolved to a meaningful degree. Thanks to Korean Film Archive's digitization project that began in 2007,[18] many South Korean classic films are now available with English and multiple language subtitles through the Archive's YouTube channel, "Korean Classic Film."[19] And many of Kim Ki-young's films that are dealt with in this book are also similarly available through this platform. With the rising interest in Korean film and this ease of accessibility, *ReFocus: The Films of Kim Ki-young* offers a substantive critical basis for new and old fans of Korean classic film in the Anglophone world to meaningfully expand their knowledge of the director's work, relative to the exciting, insightful, and diverse topics offered in the book.

"WAYS OF SEEING": KIM KI-YOUNG'S CINEMA IN A GLOBAL/TRANSNATIONAL PERSPECTIVE

The formation of the idea of the "global auteur," as created through the critical discourse that surrounds the international film festival circuit, has often functioned for global audiences to regard such auteurs and their work as representative of their distinct national cultures. However, this fixed "external" way of seeing or perceiving a given director relative to their domestic context is often misleading as to the wider significance of their work, both at home and abroad. In this case, such an approach directly hinders a useful understanding of Kim Ki-young's oeuvre, both due to the particular transnational orientation of his output, and the singular, "bizarre," "excessive," "extreme" aspects of his films which render his productions entirely unique within the wider context of South Korean cinema. As such, to meaningfully approach Kim Ki-young's work requires viewers to adopt a new critical lens, one which will allow them to also productively expand their view of South Korean history and culture.

Kim's films precisely resonate with the changing trajectories of modern Korean history, a path shaped by numerous layers of tumultuous transnational historical experience: Japanese colonial occupation (1910–45), national division by the USSR and USA (1945–8), the Korean War (1950–3), a short-lived democratic period after the April Revolution (1960–1), thirty years of military dictatorship (1961–87), and then democratization through student-led demonstration (1987). Of course, most of the Korean people that lived through these passages experienced parallel levels of personal transformation. However, Kim Ki-young is unique as a director because he sensitively observed these historical changes with unbiased perspective, and this process inspired him to express a range of related complicated concepts, perspectives, and psychological ideas in his cinema, the significance of which cannot be neatly narrated in a simple national formula. As film critic Kim Yeong-jin commented, it often seems as if the work of Kim Ki-young has sensitive visionary tentacles embedded within and beyond the historical era,[20] because his films uncover the intense elements of hybridity and transnationality that stretch beyond the immediate moment of national time and space depicted within the cinematic frame. Yi Yeon-ho discusses this distinctive aspect in terms of a "simultaneity of the non-simultaneous (citing Ernst Bloch),"[21] which is manifested within Kim's work and generates an uncanny response within viewers. For this reason, a useful understanding of the director's life and oeuvre cannot be maintained within a simple nationally orientated perspective, and "transnational" and "global" perhaps offer better keywords to frame an analysis of his work.

Kim Ki-young's personal history shows how mobile his own life trajectory was. Born in to an upper-middle class family in Seoul, his father, Kim Seok-jin was a school teacher and Kim and his two older sisters all showed talent in various arts. When his father was transferred to Pyeongyang (today the capital of North Korea), he moved there and attended Pyeongyang High School (1940–2). This educational establishment was celebrated as a cradle for modernist Korean culture, as many of the school's alumni were already famous artists, such as playwright O Yeong-jin (1916–1974). Thanks to the progressive ambience in Pyeongyang High School, Kim Ki-young left the institution fully imbued with an appreciation for modern Western and Japanese art and culture.

However, he did not immediately pursue a career in the creative arts. Instead, and as happened to most academically able upper-middle class children in Korea at the time, he followed social expectations and decided to become a doctor. But he failed to gain admission to Severance Medical School (today the Medical School of Yonsei University) and went to Japan in the middle of Asia Pacific War (1941–5). Later, Kim recounted that this experience living in Japan as a young man became the foundational force that developed his love for art. His candid expression of love for Japanese culture continued even after Korean liberation in 1945, a moment when most other intellectuals and artists hurriedly denied their own connections to colonial Japan in response to the fervent nationalism that was sweeping the country after independence. Thus, the "unfamiliarity" that prevails in Kim's work doubtless stems in part from his conscious and unconscious admiration for Japanese colonial culture and the revelation of this approbation in post-colonial time; an influence in South Korean post-colonial cinema which remains hidden in the work of most other directors, as Yi Hyo-in pointed out.[22]

Kim Ki-young's film career, nonetheless, was born under heavy American influence at the very outset of the Cold War. After the country's liberation from Japan, Kim Ki-young came back to Korea, and entered the medical school of Seoul National University to become a doctor. However, his interest in art made him to join a students' theatrical group, the National University Theater at SNU (1945–50) where he met his life-long companion, financial

Figure I.2 Kim Ki-young's wife, Kim Yu-bong, and Kim Ki-young "The Wife of an Artist: Kim Yu-bong discusses Kim Ki-young's film, *Geumbyeonmae*," *Donga ilbo*. (November 27, 1973)

supporter, and wife, Kim Yu-bong (1928–98). Within the group, Kim served as a stage director up until the outbreak of the Korean War in 1950. During the conflict he took refuge in Busan and worked as a doctor. There, he happened to meet an acquaintance from high school, the playwright O Yeong-jin, who was working for United States Army. He advised Kim to make newsreels for the United States Information Service (USIS), which was virtually the only organization supporting film production during the war. Then, through USIS, Kim began his directorial career by making several small documentary productions. Because he had to produce these films without any professional assistance, Kim was compelled to learn about the whole process of filmmaking, and this became the basis for the establishment of his independent production approach throughout his career. Kim's early documentary films such as *I Am a Truck* (*Na neun teureogida*, c1954) and the anti-communist narrative production *Boxes of Death* (*Jugeom ui sangja*, 1955) demonstrate how even his earliest endeavors in cinema were apparently marked by various stylistic experiments, a hybrid approach Kim learned by combining various trends he had seen within international cinema. Even though his early films were made to conform to the global Cold War political climate, his budding talent was usefully able to develop within the institutional system of USIS sponsorship.

After his commercial debut with *Boxes of Death*, Kim made eight productions in the 1950s. Unfortunately, the prints of these films do not survive today, except an incomplete version of *Yangsan Province* (*Yangsando*, 1955) and two rolls of *A Touch-me-not* (*Bongseonhwa*, 1956). But even at this early stage in his career, Kim's films seem to have been recognized for their particular style; his talent as an auteur was apparent, and so he became widely known within the film industry as a gifted director. For example, one of his films, *A Defiance of Teenager* (*Sipdae ui banhang*, 1959) received the Outstanding Korean Film Award (*Usu yeonghwasang*) and was sent to the San Francisco International Film Festival, where one of the performers, An Seong-gi, received a special award as a child actor. It is hard to know for sure what the stylistic character of this production was because there is no print of the film. But the general critical response was positive in Korea, acclaiming Kim's particular way of revealing the "reality" of the postwar Korean situation and the strong referencing of Italian neo-realism within the film. However, Kim Ki-young himself has always emphasized that he does not think his work ever followed any "ism" or stylistic movement, and by this point he would have certainly moved toward developing his own, unique approach which would fully bloom in the 1960s and 1970s.

In the 1960 and 70s, South Korea was governed under a dictatorship led by Park Chung Hee (Pak Jeong-hui, 1917–79), a former second lieutenant of the colonial Japanese army during the Asia Pacific War, who swept to political power through a military coup in 1961. Soon after this authoritarian seizure of political power, new legal and social systems were established by Park government in early 1960s, and cinema also fell under strict government control through the creation of a specific Film Law (1962). In this context, while the government encouraged the industrialization of the film industry, the freedom of the individual filmmaker was diminished, primarily through rigorous censorship. Controlling the depiction of sexuality was one of the key concerns of governmental control, and any portrayals that strayed from the prescribed social norms were unimaginable. In 1972, Park Chung Hee further intensified his dictatorial reach, implementing the so-called Yushin (restoration) constitution (1972–9). This totalitarian system was designed to regulate the entire body of South Korean society, and, as part of the Yushin reforms even the length of hair for men and women was strictly regulated. Given this restrictive legal environment, and the wider repressive social mood of the 1960s and 1970s, it is incredibly surprising that Kim Ki-young's films of the period were able to display their notable excess of sexual content and aesthetic focus on the grotesque.

Perhaps Kim Ki-young's most renowned films are those of *The Housemaid* series, which were primarily produced during this repressive period of military rule. This series consists of the productions *The Housemaid, Woman of Fire* (*Hwanyeo*, 1971), *Insect Woman* (*Chungnyeo*, 1972), *Woman of Fire 82* (*Hwanyeo*, 1982) and *Carnivorous Animals* (*Yuksikdongmul*, 1984). In these works, Kim repeats similar narrative structure: a housemaid is inserted into a stable middle-class family and proceeds to finally destroy everyone, including herself. The conventions of female/male iconography and the "norm" in many 1960s and 70s Korean film break down in these films. In them, he creates an expressive

Figure I.3 Scene from *The Housemaid*. (Courtesy of Korean Film Archive.)

atmosphere defined by the perverse or bestial sexual and reproductive desires of men and women, a focus which is often accompanied by direct analogies to animal life within the narrative, such as rats, chickens, and snakes. The unusual and transgressive nature of Kim's output also included representing people with physical disabilities and marginalized sexual identities, along with taboo subjects such as pedicide, cannibalism, and necrophilia. Perhaps the director's interest in Freudian psychology and his experience as a doctor imbued his artistic perspective with a complicated understanding of human body and mind; as if Kim considered himself an anthropologist or a physician who was able to diagnose the ills of both the human condition and contemporary Korean society through his cinema. His interest in providing this descriptive analytical commentary intensified in later productions such as *Ieo Island* (*Ieodo*, 1977), *Water Lady* (*Sunyeo*, 1979) and *Neumi* (*Neumi*, 1980). Such films provoked audiences of the time to rethink the social norms set up within a country in which the field of biopolitics was controlled by a brutal and draconian regime.

As exemplified by the narrative of *The Housemaid*, which focused on the story of an adulterous but repressed husband and a murderous young woman, one of Kim's favored themes was the (often deviant) expression of sexual desire. But even in his films that stray from this frequent interest, Kim's work can be still seen to consistently reflect his wider idiosyncratic aesthetic and conceptual concerns. The representation and portrayal of traditional Korean society in a grotesque, rather than sentimental or celebratory manner, for example, is another of

Figure I.4 Scene from *Goryeojang*. (Courtesy of Korean Film Archive.)

his repeated areas of interest. This can be seen in films such as *Yangsan Province* (*Yangsando*, 1955), *Goryeojang* (1963), *Transgression* (*Pagye*, 1974), and *Ieo Island* all of which are based on the reconstruction of Korean history not in terms of a self-orientalist nostalgia but as the site of a conflictual aggregation of culture and tradition. This is quite a different approach from the other celebrated Korean auteur, Im Kwon-taek, who came to international prominence in the late 1980s with his self-orientalistic view on Korean society focusing on beautifying the country's traditions and the national past. By way of a direct parallel, Kim's historical films such as *The Sea Knows* (*Hyeonhaetan eun algoitta*, 1961) and *Elegy of Ren* (*Ren ui aega*, 1969) tragically represent the colonial and post-colonial past of Korea, while still displaying the director's unique aesthetic concerns and his unbiased transnational perspective of national history.

As censorship became increasingly intensified within the 1970s Yushin System, the independent spirit of Kim Ki-young as an auteur was significantly affected. This circumstance is exemplified by the manifold changes enforced upon *Ban Geum-ryeon* (1974/1981). Initially made in 1974, and based on a traditional Chinese erotic story, the film included depictions of cannibalism, which resulted in its prohibition from screening. Eventually a heavily cut version of the film was screened in 1981, but this was without the permission of the director, because an exhausted and frustrated Kim had by this point completely given up his rights to his own film production company.[23] This situation of censorial repression was the direct reason that Kim then chose to make several "National Policy Film[s] (*gukcheak yeonghwa*)" to professionally survive the period. However, even the subsequent production of semi-propaganda films, such as *Water Lady* and *Soil* (*Heuk*, 1978), usefully testifies to the creative adaptability of Kim as an auteur, and the dedicated nature of his professional survival strategy under the oppressive censorship of the Yushin regime.

In considering the career path Kim Ki-young negotiated across the political vicissitudes of tumultuous post-war South Korean society, a final significant aspect of his oeuvre that demands to be critically emphasized is the relative "independence" he maintained in his filmmaking practice. In answering a question about how he would like to be known among younger film audiences prior to his landmark retrospective at the Second Busan International Film Festival in 1997, Kim replied that he wanted to be remembered as "the father of independent film" rather than as simply a "cult" director.[24] Kim's personal emphasis here on being able to work as an independent filmmaker is something that has been very much neglected in previous critical discussions of his work. From his 1956 film, *A Touch-Me-Not*, Kim Ki-young immediately set up Kim Ki-young Productions, which later became the Sinhan Munye Film (*Sinhan munye yeonghwasa*). For this venture his own house was used as a company office where all the props and necessary equipment for filmmaking were stored. While the unique manner of Kim's output (which first led to emergence of the director as "cult figure" in late 1980s South Korea) has always been justifiably central to any discussion of his work, it is equally significant that his films were created through an independent low-budget practice that was viable only because his wife, Kim Yu-bong, was a dentist who financially supported his artistic endeavors.[25] In this regard, Kim's consistent maintenance of his unique thematic and aesthetic oeuvre (which secured his status as an auteur), was only possible through his persistent adherence to his own independent filmmaking production philosophy; a practice that was compelled by his extremely limited access to mainstream financial resources and governmental restrictions. Kim's personally rigorous and total approach to his craft was far removed from that of other high-profile Korean film directors of the period, such as Yu Hyeon-mok (1925–2009) and Shin Sang-ok (1926–2006).[26] In sum, it could be stated that Kim's all-encompassing devotion to the sustenance of a long, consistent, and independent career can be considered as proof of his deserving status as the most distinctive "global auteur" to have emerged from South Korean during the pre-democratic period.

CHAPTER ARRANGEMENT

ReFocus: The Films of Kim Ki-young consists of eight chapters focused on separate aspects of his career, roughly arranged in chronological order. This collection of essays by different authors aims to introduce the broad oeuvre of Kim Ki-young to global audiences, from the very early stages of his career up until his rediscovery in the 1990s. Since Kim's career spans a period stretching from the Korean War to the turn of the century, these chapters naturally cover various transformations that occurred within Korean filmmaking parallel to this turbulent period of national history, and address precisely how the unique features of Kim's work as an auteur intersect with and reflect specific conditions within the country.

Each chapter in this volume speaks to the diverse themes interwoven within Kim Ki-young's work and career: such as gender and sexuality, disability studies, interethnic love, colonialism and post-colonialism, trans-Asian and transnational border-crossing, propaganda and censorship, bio-politics, replication and remaking, and the politics of film festivals. Thanks to this extensive exploration, a holistic engagement with these essays will enable the reader to firmly locate the position of Kim within the history of Korean and world cinema, while readers specifically interested in the more selected themes and topics surrounding his films will also be able to easily navigate the text.

NOTES

1. Many South Korean film directors active during a similar timeframe produced around a hundred films. For instance, Kim Su-yong (1928–) has 118 films in his filmography, and Im Kwon-taek (1934–) completed his hundredth film in 2006 and made two more films after that.
2. Seven scripts include: *Rain Tomorrow* (*Naeil eun bi*, 1985), *Orange Color Raincoat* (*Orenji bikkal ui ubi*, 1986), *The Station of the Heaven* (*Cheonguk ui yeok*, 1987), *A Woman with Deep Root* (*Gipeun ppuri ui yeoja*, 1988), *My Body is Diamond* (*Namom eun daiamondeu*, 1989), *Yangsan Province* (*Yangsando*, 1989: New Version of *Yangsando*), *Returned Woman* (*Hwanhyangnyeon*, 1989). Regarding the materials produced this period see Geum Dong-hyeon, "Kim Ki-young with New Materials (*Saeroun jaryo ro mannaneun Kim Ki-yeong*)," in Kim Ki-young Document Collection at Korean Film Archive, 2022.
3. Chris Berry, "'Introducing Mr. Monster': Kim Ki-young and the Critical Economy of the Globalized Art-House Cinema," in *Korean Film Directors: Kim Ki-young*, ed. Hong-joon Kim (Korean Film Commission, 2006), 54–5.
4. Rosi Braidotti mentioned this about Kim Ki-young's film when it was screened at the Berlin International Film Festival in 1998. Cited in a KBS documentary film, *An Anatomist of Film, Kim Ki-young* (*Pilleum ui haebuhakja, yeonghwa gamdok Kim Ki-young*, 1999), made in 1999 after Kim Ki-young's death. Accessed through Youtube at http://www.youtube.com/watch?v=7IVXdqWWf7A.
5. Jeong Jung-heon, "Why are South Korean Films in Crisis? [Hanguk yeonghwa wae wigiinga?," *Film Criticism* [*Yeonghwa pyeongnon*] (December 29, 1997).
6. Statistics from the Korean Film Commission website, https://www.kobis.or.kr/kobis/business/mast/mvie/searchMovieList.do.

7. David Scott Diffrient, "Secret Sunshine (2007): The Canon, the Criterion Collection, and the Question of Cinematic Religion," in *Rediscovering Korean Cinema*, ed. Sangjoon Lee (Ann Arbor: University of Michigan Press, 2019), 446–458.
8. Kim Ki-young, *Kim Ki-young Screenplay Collection I* [*Kim Ki-young sinario seonjib 1*] (Jimmundang, 1996); Kim Hong-joon, ed., *Kim Ki-young Screenplay Collection II* [*Kim Ki-young sinario seonjib 2*] (Korean Film Archive, 2008).
9. Kim Ki-young's house burned down in 1998. Kim Ki-young and his wife could not escape from the house and died. The documentaries about Kim Ki-young are: *Kim Ki-young and Yu Hyeon-mok* (*Kim Ki-young gwa Yu Hyeon-mok*, Kim Byeong-wuk, KBS, 1997); *An Anatomist of Film, Kim Ki-young; Two or Three Things We Know about Kim Ki-young* (*Gamdokdeul Kim Ki-young eul malhada*, Kim Hong-joon, 2006); *Actress Talks about Kim Ki-young* (*Yeobaeu Kim Ki-young eul malhada*, 2008).
10. Bong Joon Ho made his commercial debut film, *Barking Dogs Never Bite* (*Peullandaseu ui gae*, 2000). Park Chan-wook made his debut as a director in 1992, but *Joint Security Area* (*Gongdong gyeonbi guyeok*, 2000) was his first mega-hit, made in 2000. In this respect, the late 1990s and the early 2000s were certainly the time the idea of the South Korean film auteur began to be formed.
11. There were only four female directors active in South Korea before the late 1980s. They were Pak Nam-ok (1923–2017), Hong Eun-won (1922–1999), Choe Eun-hui (1926–2018), and Hwang Hye-mi (1936~).
12. Kim Soyoung points out the significance of considering the presence of the female audience in South Korean films from this period because male directors were so obviously conscious of them, even though images of women were mostly "man-made." In this respect, *The Housemaid* by Kim Ki-young has been exemplified as a filmic text that revealed the life of Korean women at the time. Kim Soyoung, "Questions of Woman's Film: The Maid, Madame freedom, and Women," in *Post-Colonial Classics of Korean Cinema*, ed. Chungmoo Choi (Irvine: Korean Film Festival Committee, University of California, 1998), 17.
13. The IMF crisis was a financial disaster that thwarted the positive mood of democratization and the economic success of South Korea (which has often been labelled as "the miracle of the Han river") in the 1990s. Due to the huge amount of national debt, the South Korean government was forced to ask for a bailout from the IMF in 1997, which resulted in the fundamental restructuring of the South Korean economic and social system.
14. This is why the 1990s is known as the period of the "South Korean Film Renaissance."
15. At the Busan International Film Festival Seminar held in 1996, the festival committee invited international film festival organizers such as Paul Yi, Wong Ain-Ling, and Tony Rayns to advise the Korean organizers on how to plan and manage an international film festival. And in this regard, the staging of an international film festival was widely perceived to offer a fresh start for South Korean cinema, and considered as representative of the great ambition to globalize the national film industry. "Proceedings of the Busan International Film Festival Seminar" (Busan International Film Festival Committee, 1996), 1–19.
16. Kim Soyoung's book *The Phantom of Modernity* [*Geundaeseong ui yuryeongdeul*] deals with Kim Ki-young's work as a significant element in discussing the development of South Korean modernity. Kim Soyoung, *The Phantom of Modernity* (Hyeonsil munhwa yeongu, 2000); Yi Hyo-in, *The Housemaids Raised Up!* [*Hanyeodeul bonggihada*] (Haneulare, 2002); Yi Yeon-ho, *The Legend and Stigma* [*Geonseol ui nagin*] (Korean Film Archive, 2007).
17. Hong-joon Kim, *Korean Film Directors: Kim Ki-young* (Korean Film Council, 2006), 5.

18. Cho So-yeon, *The Study of the Strategy for Developing Media Archives in the Digital Age* [Digiteol sidae ui yeongsang akaibeu baljeon bangan e kwanhan yeongu] (Master's thesis, Chung'ang University, 2009), 33–36.
19. https://www.youtube.com/c/KoreanFilm/featured.
20. Kim Yeong-jin's words in the brochure of the *Kim Ki-young Memorial Exhibition* held by the Korean Film Archive in 2018.
21. Yi, "Introduction," in Kim ed., *Korean Film Directors*, 12.
22. Yi, "The Housemaids Raised Up!," 14–25.
23. Ibid., 80.
24. Ibid., 83.
25. Ibid., 86.
26. Yu Hyeon-mok is well-known as a "realist" director who came to prominence and maintained a successful practice as an independent filmmaker. However, Yu once confessed that he could never produce his own films but rather preferred to remain focused on the role of director, because managing an independent film production was so difficult. Additionally, in comparison to Yu Hyeon-mok and Kim Ki-young, Shin Sang-ok was a contemporaneous director who was ambitious to replicate a local version of the Hollywood (studio) system in Korea. In short, it is perhaps no exaggeration to state that Kim Ki-young is the only celebrated director of the pre-democratic period in South Korea who managed to maintain a truly independent, low-budget approach throughout his career.

PART I

Beyond the Border: Transnational/ Hybridity/Border Crossing

CHAPTER 1

Kim Ki-young at the Intersection of Cold War Alliance, National Reconstruction and the Artistic Impulse

Han Sang Kim

Just as the issue of "Korean cinema" as a paradigmatic example of national cinema has been controversial, similarly the collective identity of Korean filmmakers has also remained difficult to define.[1] This is because this notion of a collective identity can hardly be posited in a coherent continuum when we consider Korea's modern historical and political trajectory, as the peninsula transitioned from being a colony of Japan to becoming two sovereign states. This historical complexity serves to frame Korean filmmakers' identity outside any single, solid category. The difficulty here derives from the several different possible approaches to defining "Korea" as a nation: one that follows transcendental boundaries, independent from the state-formation process, one that adheres to the frame of the established state system in consideration of legal rationality and legitimacy, and another that traces an ongoing dynamic in the formation of a collective consciousness as nationhood. On the other hand, this difficulty also stems from the ambiguity that exists in any definition of what is "national" in cinema. Controversies can emerge, such as whether one can attribute a film's nationality to that of its producers, whether one can firmly locate the nationality of a film which was made by producers from different countries, whether films from the colonial period should be registered as the products of the decolonized country or the former colonial power, and, beyond these legalistic issues, whether one can indeed ever definitively establish the national identity of a film that is both a work of collective creation and a medium through which audiences around the globe potentially share their experiences with one another. Therefore, it is inevitable to find heterogeneity, and even indefinability, in the notion of a collective identity that can be assigned to Korean filmmakers, especially that of those filmmakers who personally experienced a discontinuous sense of national belonging from the colonial period (1910–45) to the liberation and to the subsequent division of the nation in 1945.

This chapter examines such a contested identity of Korean filmmakers during the period of reconstruction after the Korean War, especially in the years between 1953 and 1955, by examining the case of director Kim Ki-young. As written in sound specialist Yi Gyeong-sun's memoir, cinematographer Yu Jang-san's oral statements, and film historian Yi Yeong-il's book,[2] South Korean filmmakers regarded themselves as nation-builders during and after the Korean War. This is consistent with Andrew Higson's proposition that the identification of a national cinema accompanies the recognition of a nation.[3] Since nation-building does not always designate the process of state formation, one should consider the long-term transition ranging from the fall of the pre-modern regime and the period of colonial rule through the establishment of an independent government and the (in)completion of a national identity, when examining the history of nation-building in Korea. Among those transitions, this chapter particularly explores the heterogeneous era in which state formation was combined with nation-building. Due to the inconsistent nature of nation-building in South Korea—its geopolitical particularities that led it to become the Far Eastern front of the "free world" bloc; a state competing with its own national other, North Korea, during the process of postcolonial state formation—the concept of national cinema cannot simply be applied to Korean cinema. Kim Ki-young and his early films show how such inconsistency and heterogeneity appeared in the identity formation of South Korean filmmakers.

USIS-KOREA'S MATERIAL RESOURCES AND THE CONDITIONS FOR SOUTH KOREAN FILMMAKERS

Before and after the Korean War, the US Information Service in Korea (hereafter USIS-Korea) functioned as an educator to Korean filmmakers. For USIS-Korea, the outbreak of the Korean War was a catalyst for many tremendous strides in film production. The organization was able to establish its own film studios, first in Jinhae and later, when it relocated, in Sangnam, both of which were positioned near the wartime capital, Busan. The film studios in Sangnam, active from 1952 to 1967, provided an exceptional environment for the development of both film technology and techniques. A considerable number of newsreels and documentaries were regularly produced in this studio, especially in the 1950s. USIS-Korea hired South Korean filmmakers to localize their propaganda filmmaking, which became an abundant source of material and technological supplies for those filmmakers.[4]

Over the course of the Korean War, however, key crew members of the USIS-Korea film production organization were replaced. A major replacement of personnel happened during the preparation for the relocation from Jinhae to Sangnam. Six Korean filmmakers, Yi Kyeong-sun, Kim Hyeong-geun, Kim Heung-man, Kim Bong-su, Jo Baek-bong, and Jeong Ju-yong, resigned from USIS-Korea, and set up their own recording and processing laboratory in August 1951.[5] It is worth noting that the reason for their resignation is remembered differently by these filmmakers and by the USIS Motion Picture Officer, William G. Ridgeway. According to the filmmakers, it was because they resented Ridgeway's refusal to lend the studio facilities for the ROK Army film unit's war film, *An Assault of Justice* (*Jeongui ui jingyeok*, 1951).[6] While USIS-Korea could afford to establish its own production studios during the Korean War, the ROK public information agencies had poor financial and technical conditions in place for their own film productions. Thus, Ridgeway's refusal was understood as a humiliation, and an affront to the pride of their nation. According to Kim Hyeong-geun, after a discussion, the six filmmakers decided to resign and establish their own laboratory:

> Ridgeway said, "This is not the ROK Government's property, but the US'. This is sponsored by the US Government with the US citizen's tax. It is impossible to let the ROK Army use it." He allowed [us] to use the facilities for a couple of times, and then didn't allow it. So, we said, "Well, drop it! We are Korean." To Ridgeway, we said "Goodbye! Sayonara!" Then six of us rented this Marine Corps building and built the laboratory.[7]

However, what Ridgeway remembered was considerably different from Kim's account.[8] According to Ridgeway, the advanced equipment of the Sangnam studios was perceived as a threat by these senior Korean film specialists, who were familiar with the old equipment which they had learned to use during the colonial period. Ridgeway recalled that, although a great number of the main staff members resigned simultaneously, better performance with the new equipment and facilities helped improve the quality of productions, and the assistant staff were able to successfully replace their predecessors:

> All of the lab chiefs went on strike when the new processing machine arrived. They thought they would lose face in not knowing how to operate it, so consequently they quit. I don't know what they really expected us to do, but anyhow I was able to train their assistants [on] the new machine. That was the end of the old lab chiefs and their strike. They all had their own special formulas which were closely guarded, even from each other. It was assumed we would be helpless without their know-how. The film that we processed by the old system was terrible. [. . .] So, finally, for the first time we were now able to turn out reasonably

good quality, consistent photographic material—and, best of all, at the same time, at a much greater pace. The new equipment included sound recording equipment that used magnetic film. [. . .] The staff absorbed the new techniques. [. . .] First of all, they followed instructions and didn't have to unlearn anything like some of the older movie people. A good two-thirds of the staff were originally contract employees.[9]

This contradiction of accounts shows the intricate identity of Korean filmmakers hired by USIS-Korea at that time. They were remembered as the builders of Korean national cinema according to their life histories and discourses. However, at the same time, they were wage earners during a period of wartime, who had to negotiate the most favorable terms for their work. Ridgeway's comments on "contract employees" is important in this regard. According to Yi Hyeong-pyo (who was also affiliated with USIS-Korea at that time), many Korean filmmakers were not permanently hired but worked in a sub-contractual relationship with USIS-Korea as an outsourcing production team. They actually preferred outsourced production because it was believed to guarantee a greater profit. This scenario caused a conflict of interest between them and Ridgeway, since Ridgeway wanted to reorganize the employment system into direct management.[10] The resignation of the old employees thus seems to have made way for the direct engagement of staff at USIS-Korea.

The filmmakers' reluctance to be employed directly by USIS-Korea reflects their understanding of their relationship with the US agency. They possibly considered their employment relationship with the US agency as an impermanent one. It is probable that they did not feel a sense of belonging to the foreign agency, nor a sense of ownership of the products they made for the agency, when pursuing serial single profitable projects from the ordering organization. Rather, they wanted to negotiate with the client to raise their market price. Ridgeway's prescription to acquire new machines and directly engage workers put their positions as skilled workers in jeopardy. Just at that moment, the wartime situation gave them many alternatives for employment since filmmaking skills were in high demand from various agencies, including the ROK Army, Navy, Air Forces, and the ROK Office of Public Information (hereafter OPI).[11] Their sense of having a shared or individual mission to build South Korean cinema, of course, might also have affected their final decision to leave USIS-Korea.

KIM KI-YOUNG, USIS AND THE "GERMINATING PERIOD OF THE KOREAN CINEMA"

The situation of the newcomers, including Kim Yeong-gwon and Kim Ki-young, was not remarkably different. Kim Ki-young was a playwright and theater director who became a screenwriter while taking refuge in Busan during the war. The first films he directed were initial issues of *Daehan News*, the official newsreel series of OPI, using equipment borrowed from USIS-Korea.[12] Shortly thereafter, he was hired by USIS-Korea to make its own newsreel series, *Liberty News*. While there is no accurate literature regarding the date of his departure from OPI, since *Liberty News* was launched in May 1952 and *Daehan News* in 1953, Kim must have started working for USIS-Korea in 1953.[13] Four of Kim Ki-young's USIS films are housed in the US National Archives and Records Administration (hereafter NARA): his first commercial feature, *Boxes of Death* (*Jugeom ui sangja*, 1955), and three short films, *Ward of Affection* (*Sarang ui byeongsil*, 1953), *I Am a Truck* (*Na neun teureogida*, 1954), and *Diary of Three Sailors* (*Subyeong ui ilgi*, c.1955). *Ward of Affection* was the first documentary produced by USIS-Korea after setting up the Sangnam studio,[14] *I Am a Truck* was released on March 26, 1954,[15] and *Diary of Three Sailors* was transported to the United States Information Agency (hereafter USIA)'s New York film laboratory on June 22, 1955 although its release date is not known.[16] *Boxes of Death* was approved for screening on June 11, 1955 and was released around July 1st.[17] After *Boxes of Death*, Kim received an offer from a private film production company and started to work as a commercial director in making his second feature film, *Yangsan Province* (*Yangsando*, 1955).[18]

Two aspects of the South Korean film industry during Kim's career in USIS-Korea are worth noting: one is the relationship between South Korean filmmakers and the USIS-Korea film units, which came about as a result of negotiations. Kim Ki-young started earning 50,000 won a month when he was scouted from OPI to the Liberty Production, a salary far higher than the average of 3,500 won earned by physicians in Korea at the time.[19] This kind of headhunting shows the rivalry between the ROK and US agencies. Since the state used wartime newsreels to organize and mobilize the population, there was a considerable degree of competition and tension between the South Korean nation-building and the US-led "free world" bloc-building forces.[20] Interestingly, Kim Ki-young viewed his USIS years as merely a period of the privity of contract by virtue of his own ability, and stressed his creativity as an auteur which had remained free from the hirer's purpose of propaganda.[21]

However, working as production agents in an American public information organization meant that these individuals could not conduct their activities from their own "Korean" perspectives. Although their films were made for the Korean audience, they clearly had an American voice. Their aim was to create a favorable environment to have an American subject speak to the Korean people. The format of *Liberty News*, a core staple of Liberty Productions from 1952 through 1967, was similar to that of wartime American newsreels, such as *The Paramount News* and *The March of Time*. By inserting the dubbed *Hearst Metrotone News* section, the newsreel was more informative than South Korean newsreels. The voiceover narrations were recorded in stiff formal tones and the opening credit, "USIS-Korea Presents," showed its provenance. Hence, an American sentiment was expressed, but in the Korean language.

Another interesting aspect is the subsequent historical discourse on South Korean cinema that emerged in the late 1960s. South Korean academia did not entertain a historical interest in film until 1969, when Yi Yeong-il published *The Complete History of Korean Cinema* (*Hanguk yeonghwa jeonsa*).[22] In that book, Yi Yeong-il considers the years from the mid-1950s to the mid-1960s as "the golden age of Korean cinema."[23] Yi argued that Korean cinema was able to establish its own substance as both an industry and an art form during this golden age. According to him, Kim Ki-young, Shin Sang-ok, Yu Hyeon-mok, and Yi Man-hui were the leading directors of the golden age, who beforehand had established the aesthetics of national cinema during the "germinating period of Korean cinema."[24] As Yi Sun-jin explains, "the critical discourses on Korean film history have mainly been generated by the two thematic impulses—realism and authorship" since Yi Yeong-il in 1969.[25] In the center of this group of auteurs were those directors who had been highly exposed to Hollywood and European cinematic aesthetics. Kim Ki-young, who started his film career as a USIS-Korea employee, and Shin Sang-ok, who learned film from USIS-Korea's outsourcing of production,[26] cause us to further consider the role of this American propaganda agency, something which has not yet been addressed in detail within the history of Korean national cinema.

TRANSLATION, MIMICRY AND SIGNATURE OF THE AUTEUR

Kim Ki-young's USIS short films, *I Am a Truck* and *Diary of Three Sailors*, demonstrate an interesting aspect of the film products made by USIS-affiliated Korean filmmakers, in terms of the tradition of American wartime documentaries. According to Cheon Hak-beom, who worked for the Motion Picture Department of USIS-Korea from 1948 to 1957, there were more than 8,000 American propaganda films with Korean dubbing, or subtitles, in USIS-Korea's film library in the 1950s.[27] While 8,000 seems an improbably high number, this statement indicates how large he thought the collection was. Bae Seok-in, who worked as a film director for Liberty Productions in the mid-1950s, also makes a similar claim.[28] Therefore, one can assume that Kim Ki-young could learn much from the film collection of USIS-Korea's library. For Kim, "a film buff" who tried to watch "every foreign masterpiece" and every newly released film he could,[29] the latest American documentaries housed in this library might have been must-see items. The tradition of wartime documentary and propaganda films began with World War I, and the US was one of the most successful countries in building up a large scale film propaganda system following the legacy of World War II. *The March of Time* and *This is America* series were typical examples of wartime propaganda.[30] Given that American wartime documentaries, such as *Fury in the Pacific* and *Justice*, had been imported and screened nation-wide in South Korea since 1946,[31] such films must have become models for war films during and after the Korean War.

Considering this premise, Kim Ki-young's 1954 film *I Am a Truck* is a work of considerable critical interest. This first-person documentary, narrated by a military truck, was probably influenced by a group of popular World War II American propaganda films. During World War II, a "talking Jeep" was featured in numerous children's books, and one of the Office of War Information (hereafter OWI) films, *Autobiography of a Jeep* (1943), appears to have been part of this trend.[32] In the film, the protagonist-Jeep's ability to cut through forests, navigate rivers, or board planes lends itself well to military purposes, and the film seems to set the goal of making people better understand military equipment by anthropomorphizing them. Kim's localized USIS film, *I Am a Truck*, also partakes of this practice. Kim's other short, *Diary of Three Sailors* (1955), also shows the influence of American war films. After March 1942 when the Signal Corps Photographic Center was activated, the US War Department launched a newsreel series, *Fighting Men*, narrated by "a soldier speaking typical soldier language." This is said to have been influenced by the speech of Lieutenant General Wesley McNair at the Army War College and the form of soldier self-narration that became popular thereafter.[33] Pare Lorentz's *Diary of a Sergeant* (1945), also produced by OWI, is a soldier's first-hand account of rehabilitation following the loss of his arms.[34] Kim's *Diary of Three Sailors* is very much in this tradition. A sailor, who entered the ROK Navy at age seventeen, recalls his days in boot camp.

Both of Kim's short films are not only examples of translation, adaptation, and mimicry, but also the director's self-conscious attempts to overcome a one-sided reception of the American war film tradition. *Diary of Three Sailors* basically well reflects the humorous and lively mood in American educational documentaries. However, in one unusual sequence, while sailors are undergoing metalwork training on a battleship, oblique-angle moving shots, high tension amplifying background music, and high-contrast lighting together call attention to the critical nature of the situation. The narrator-protagonist's fainting could be calculated to make the audience perceive his collapse as an accident (see Figure 1.1). Then this tension quickly disappears, and the film moves on to its next sequence using a stable long shot of the battleship against peaceful music. This urgent sequence is evocative of the signature approaches usually found in Kim's later works, such as *The Housemaid* (*Hanyeo*, 1960) and *Goryeojang* (1963). This sequence is in effect a self-conscious moment when

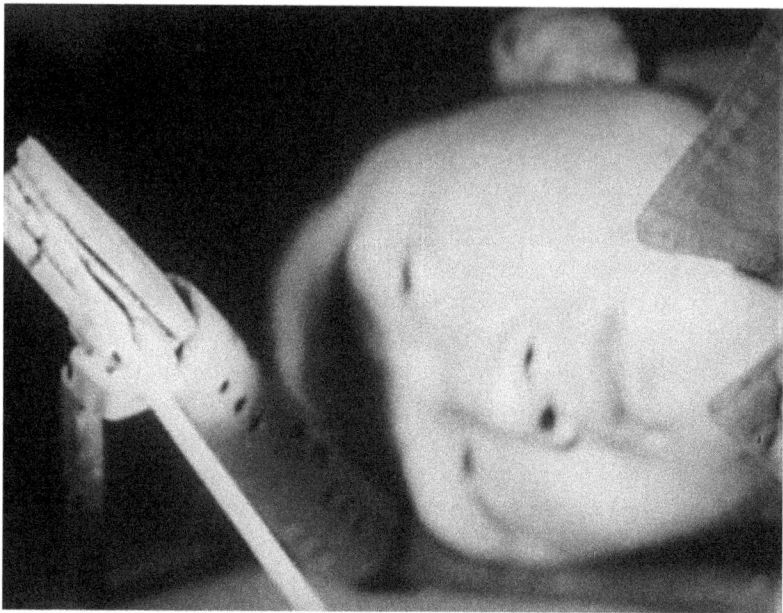

Figure 1.1 The narrator's fainting in *Diary of Three Sailors* (c1955).

the director refuses to be identified as merely a successor to American war documentaries, by seasoning the scenes of crisis with his unique expressions of darkness and anxiety. Such an intriguing moment of subjectivation is made possible by accepting some non-American thoughts and traditions. Interestingly, Kim himself rejected the label "Expressionist," and instead defined his works as "Freudian."[35] In other words, his fondness for high-contrast lighting and extreme angles was to express certain mental states identified in Freudian psychology. Regardless of whether this *ex post facto* interview forty years after the production date explains the film's original meaning or not, the stylistic unexpectedness of such a sequence shows a definite connection to the idea of the director as a free-willed auteur, as Kim tried to break free from the fixed conventions of typical American propaganda films.

I Am a Truck also demonstrates examples of Kim's auteurship. While its American counterpart, *Autobiography of a Jeep*, creates an intimacy between the military vehicle and the audience, this Koreanized film is more like a horror movie. After the sound of a car crash, the narration starts with scenes of a United Nations Army cemetery and a junkyard, which is "a cemetery of the dead cars." The narrator here is an old truck dumped in this yard. After passing through the ROK Army's recycling factory, this truck will reemerge as a useful vehicle. Lines like: "My rusty body showed much damage when it was disassembled," "At the end of that first day, I was completely taken apart," "I am now disassembled into tiny pieces," and "I was worried that I would not be rebuilt at all," are juxtaposed with the dark interior scenes of the factory and its high-contrast lightings, heavy factory machines, and dismal background music. The narrator's description of dismemberment here is rather grotesque and far from the usual upbeat nature of American propaganda.

These two cases demonstrate the gloomy sentiment during the period of reconstruction, using the stylistic legacies from American war documentaries. At the same time, it portrays a filmmaker who was conscious of the European notion of a "film auteur."[36] As Kim Soyoung points out, the sustenance of this aueurist impulse during the Cold War was made possible through the inseparable relationship that existed between war and cinema.[37]

BOXES OF DEATH: THE PRESENCE OF THE OTHER

Kim Ki-young's first full-length commercial film *Boxes of Death*[38] also resembles his early short films shown above, but it is more intricate. There are only a couple of cases that show the direct industrial link between USIS-Korea and South Korea's commercial film industry, the other case being *Bird of a Feather* (*Eokji bongjabi*, 1961), which starred a famous Korean comedic actor, Kim Huigap. Therefore, *Boxes of Death* occupies a unique position in the film production of USIS-Korea and builds interesting, even unique, bridges between USIS-Korea and the Korean commercial film market.

According to Ridgeway, this film's script was a product of the collaboration between Kim Ki-young and himself to show "a different approach in anticommunist propaganda" from that of the ROK government's naïve propaganda films depicting "the communist as a bloodthirsty monster."[39] While the film's sound is missing in NARA,[40] an analogical synopsis that I reconstructed from available film reviews published at that time is as follows:[41]

> The mother and sister of a South Korean soldier, Kim, who was killed in the Korean War, have been holding memorial rites in preparation for the Great Funeral in the third year. One day, a North Korean partisan army officer, visits their house and pretends that he was Kim's comrade, telling them that he is a discharged South Korean soldier, and that Kim is still alive in North Korea, having converted to communism. This helps him to use the house as a strategic position for his covert action. He persuades his comrades, who are staying in their hideout among the mountains, not to use armed force but to concentrate on political maneuvering like disturbing the hearts of people, manipulating prices and interrupting the local elections. Along the way, Jo Sun-taek, a police officer and boyfriend of Kim's sister Jeong-hui, happens to meet a discharged soldier who

brings Kim's ashes in a box. Realizing this, Park attacks them to escape detection. He holds Jo at gunpoint and drags him to his hideout. In the process, Jo secretly switches the ash box with a bomb. Finally, Jo blows up the hideout and the partisan soldiers, along with himself. After this heroic death, the bereaved mother and sister hold another memorial rite with the returned ash box.

The plot reflects a typical anti-communist narrative. However, this film also includes unnecessarily excessive moments of cinematic expression which can be seen as the auteur's signature. For instance, in the sequence of Park Chi-sam's first appearance, he helps Jeong-hui to cut a hen's throat and, at this moment, the camera switches to a close-up of his face underlit to illustrate Park's insidiousness (see Figure 1.2). A similar type of lighting also appears in the night scene when Jeong-hui goes for a walk with her lover, Jo (see Figure 1.3), an outdoor scene which contrasts the evening darkness with the light of a candle held by the actress, seeming to convey her mental state. Kim Ki-young states in an interview that he devised this high-contrast lighting after a brief demonstration by a lighting technician who had worked for the Toho Company during the colonial period.[42] However, the use of such signature techniques was not uniquely known to Kim. Film critics like Yu Du-yeon, who played a leading role in the discourse on cinema and introduced European aesthetic trends such as neo-realism, described the ways to catch "the spirit of a film auteur" in film.[43] This new authorial interest within film criticism resonated with the discourse of nation-building in general during the period of reconstruction,[44] in that the successful expression of such a spirit of auteurship was understood by critics to also require a clear recognition of "the urgent social situation in the postwar era."[45]

Although it was intended as an anti-communist work, the main issue with *Boxes of Death* for critics was its entertainment value. In a review on July 24, 1955, the film received bitter criticism from the poet Kim Jong-mun, who

Figure 1.2 Park Chi-sam's first appearance in *Boxes of Death* (1955).

Figure 1.3 A candle-light scene in *Boxes of Death*.

denouced the grotesque representation of the enemy and the use of communist characters simply to stimulate curiosity.⁴⁶ He concluded that it was a sensationalistic entertainment movie thus "dimming the prestige of the sixteen allies" and that the work was "a massive embarrassment as it was produced by the Liberty Production." He added that "For the sake of the Liberty Production and in order to deliver our truth to the outside world, I hope that this kind of work will no longer emerge and filmmakers will engage themselves in the creative business with a higher level of self-consciousness."⁴⁷ Here, Kim Jongmun was defining South Korea's geopolitical status in the Cold War system through film criticism, something made even clearer in the following excerpt from his review:

> Today, all the cultural activities we conduct must contribute to the fulfillment of a worldwide mission: anti-communism. It is because all cultural and artistic activities constitute "resistance" against the lack of freedom, which must be based on actual life, and because our national aim, furthermore the aim of all mankind, is summarized in a single thesis: anti-communism in the name of the liberty. Therefore, due to our special geographical condition that we are confronting the communist forces on the opposite sides of the demarcation line, there is no doubt that our cultural activities must be built on a strong anti-communist foundation.⁴⁸

For Kim, anti-communist films had an important mission to extol the honor of the sixteen allies,⁴⁹ and Liberty Productions was to be admired for its commitment to that mission.

Against this criticism, a scriptwriter, O Yeong-jin, offered a counter-argument on August 3 and 4.⁵⁰ He identified four categories of anti-communist films, using examples from American cinema: polished satires, such as *Ninotchka* (Ernst

Lubitsch, 1939); action dramas like *State Secret* (Sidney Gilliat, 1950); realistic docudramas like *Man on a Tightrope* (Elia Kazan, 1953); and war films like *The Bridges at Toko-Ri* (Mark Robson, 1954). Through this array of examples, he argued that the entertainment value of anti-communist film did not compromise its worth as a tool of enlightenment. For him, *Boxes of Death* was an attempt to "pioneer another *type* of anti-communist film" which could not be seen in foreign cinema since "they have only a small number of such films and the variety of certain types is poor."[51] Nevertheless, there was an underlying geopolitical argument, namely, that Korean cinema should be unconventional and experimental since it is located on the true front lines against global communism. It is interesting here that American films were presented as universal and mainstream. Thus, this controversy shows how producers of the discourse in Korean cinema recognized South Korean cinema's geopolitical location, and how this awareness encouraged these critics and filmmakers take a certain position regarding their aims.

Kim Jong-mun's criticism of *Boxes of Death* was similar to that of Hollywood films in general. Jo Sun-taek's chase scene follows Hollywood conventions, and Park Chi-sam's portrayal of the communist army infiltrator is similar to that of Cold War spies in Hollywood films. Hence, Kim Ki-young's insistence on using certain expressions reflects Hollywood's influence. At the same time, this film shows the general characteristics of American propaganda films. The way in which it calls attention to external enemies infiltrating a peaceful village is shared by many films produced by USIA, the homeland umbrella organization of each local USIS branch.

However, *Boxes of Death* also shows a connection with the tradition outside Hollywood and USIS-Korea. As discussed in Kim Ki-young's filmography, this film is a "psychological thriller,"[52] which borrows from the stylistic features of 1920s German Expressionist films. In several scenes that show Park Chi-sam's infiltration and covert actions, the film characters and their states of mind are magnified by high-contrast lighting, distinctive camera angles, and unexpected actions. By the same token, these characteristics can be understood as a result of the director's theatrical interests. In a documentary about his life and work, Kim Ki-young stated that the frequent use of provocative scenes in his films was an outgrowth of his involvement in theatre as a student. As he offered: "when I was at college, I looked through many theatrical plays. From old Greek plays through Ibsen and Eugene O'Neill, I searched a lot. So, if you read my scenarios, there are a great deal of desperate scenes."[53]

Several outdoor scenes using real locations also display the stylistic influence of Italian neo-realism. Kim remembers that there were certain social conditions in postwar South Korea that were similar to those that fostered Italian neo-realism after 1945.[54] However, the intellectual concerns of filmmakers at that time also seem to have influenced these stylistic approaches. As, in 1954, neo-realism was of topical interest to Korean film criticism.[55]

The remnants of Japanese colonialism are also noticeable in the film. The portrait of Jeong-hui's dead brother is said to have been prepared for the third year of the *daesang* (great funeral), while O's film review at that time points out that such a long funeral was extremely rare in Korean custom.[56] It reminds us of the Japanese home memorial, *kamidana* or *butsudan*, or the first scene of the wartime colonial Korean film, *Straits of Joseon* (*Joseon haehyeop*, 1943), depicting a portrait of a dead soldier. Moreover, the ending in which the officer Jo Sun-taek sacrifices himself and destroys the enemies' hiding place evokes the images of *junshoku* (death in the line of duty) films that were frequently produced in Japan during the Pacific War.[57] While the former elements are linked to Kim's consciousness as an auteur, the latter shows a distinct continuity between the culture of the colonial and a postcolonial society of Korea.

Still, the most important point is the lasting influence of America and USIS-Korea in the work of Kim Ki-young. As Kim Jong-mun points out, the film was a product of Liberty Production, part of a local branch of USIA, and this fact is significant among the discourses that surrounded Korean cinema. The same framework was shared by his critical interlocutor, O Yeong-jin, who supported this film based on the logic that it represented a remarkable achievement which even the headquarters in the US had been unable to accomplish. This film was understood to have a mission—to support the allies of the "free world." And it was this geopolitical recognition that entered the narrative of postwar South Korean national cinema.

Such geopolitical self-identification in attempting to constitute a new national cinema was caused by Korean filmmakers' self-awareness as being actual military units on the frontlines of the global Cold War, and the local "hot" conflict of the Korean War. At the same time, the self-identification was directly influenced by the strategic plans of the "free world" and its bloc-building agencies, supportive elements upon which the filmmakers depended, both technically and financially. According to the *Country Plan for Korea*, a report by the American Embassy in Busan to the US State Department in February 1953, Korea became "the vivid symbol of willingness to act knowing that forfeit to Communism in even remote lands promotes the Soviet technique of world conquest."[58] According to that report, "a campaign of positive propaganda production in Korea for use throughout the world and, of course, in Korea" is necessary, and USIS-Korea "should lay out a master production schedule and systematically begin production." At this point, especially for motion pictures, "extra manpower" was needed.[59] The plan to obtain extra manpower shows the conditions that allowed Liberty Productions and its filmmakers to build an advanced local filmmaking system. This also demonstrates that other propaganda activities in South Korea were made possible by their role in the strategic plans of the United States.

NATIONAL CINEMA AND ITS FILMMAKERS IN IDENTITY NEGOTIATIONS

From this perspective, Kim Ki-young, who was preparing his debut as a freelance director in the commercial film market, found himself in an entangled position. He was a Korean who had to speak for America. He wanted, however, to choose his own identity in the competition between nation-building and ideological bloc-building. He was one of those filmmakers who had been exposed to American film styles but, at the same time, he was an auteur who wanted to transform Hollywood and USIS conventions by drawing from his personal aesthetic concerns, which had been formed through his career in the theater and extensive film watching. He was eager to escape from such dilemmas. Therefore, his USIS-Korea films were a result of intense negotiations among those very contested identities. As we have seen, Kim's early career in association with USIS was instrumental in forming his later identity as an auteur. This realization raises the need for further investigation into his later works to trace out all possible elements of continuity and fully coherent account of his creative development.

South Korean filmmakers' deep involvement in American propaganda activities during the years of reconstruction is found not only in the case of Kim Ki-young. Foreign agencies like USIS-Korea and United Nations Korean Reconstruction Agency (UNKRA) intervened in the work of numerous Korean filmmakers to achieve "free world" bloc-building, and those filmmakers availed themselves of the resources of those agencies. The hybridity of subject formation in South Korean national cinema, therefore, was a shared characteristic of many filmmakers at that time.

ACKNOWLEDGMENT

A significant part of this chapter has been revised and developed from the author's original article: Han Sang Kim, "Cold War and the contested identity formation of Korean filmmakers: on *Boxes of Death* and Kim Ki-yŏng's USIS films," *Inter-Asia Cultural Studies* 14, no. 4 (2013): 551–63.

NOTES

1. Kim Han Sang, "Research on the Film's Nationality and the Institutionalization of the History of Korean National Cinema [Yeonghwaui gukjeok gwannyeomgwa gukga yeonghwasaui jedohwa yeongu]," *Society and History* [*Sahoe wa yeoksa*] 80 (2008): 257–86.
2. Yi Gyeong-sun, *The Creation of Sound* [*Sori ui changjo*] (Seoul: Goryeo chulpansa, 2000), 92–7; KRECA, (Korean National Research Center for Arts) ed., *Yi Yeong-il's Oral Testimony*

Collection for Korean Film History: Yu Jang-san et al [*Yi Yeong-il ui hanguk yeonghwasa reul wihan jeungeollok: Yu Jang-san oe*] (Seoul: Sodo, 2003), 30–71; Yi Yeong-il, *The Complete History of Korean Cinema* [*Hanguk yeonghwa jeonsa*] (Seoul: Sodo, 2004): 226–9.
3. Andrew Higson, "The Concept of National Cinema," in *The European Cinema Reader*, ed. Catherine Fowler (London and New York: Routledge, 2002), 133–4.
4. Such relationships between Korean filmmakers and American public information agencies were not entirely new. However, while USAMGIK and USAFIK outsourced almost all of the work to non-affiliated Korean filmmakers and production companies, USIS-Korea directly hired Koreans.
5. Yi, "The Creation of Sound," 92–7.
6. Yi, "The Creation of Sound," 92–7; KRECA, "Yi Yeong-il's Oral Testimony," 41–58; Kim Hyeong-geun, interview by Han Sang Kim, March 30, 2012.
7. Kim Hyeong-geun.
8. William G. Ridgeway, *Interview with William G. Ridgeway*. Interview by G. Lewis Schmidt, February 28, 1989. Oral History Records in US Library of Congress, The Foreign Affairs Oral History Collection of the Association for Diplomatic Studies and Training.
9. Ibid.
10. Yi Hyeong-pyo, "Yi Hyeong-pyo: The oral history of modern Korean arts, no. 69 [Yi Hyeong-pyo: 2005nyeondo hanguk geunhyeondae yesulsa gusul chaerok yeongu sirijeu 69]," November 29 and December 6, 2005, http://www.daarts.or.kr/.
11. Yi, "The Creation of Sound," 91.
12. Yi Hyo-in, *Thirteen South Korean Film Directors* [*Hangug ui yeonghwa gamdok sipsamin*] (Seoul: Yeollin chaekdeul, 1994), 368–71; Hong-joon Kim, ed., *Kim Ki-young* (Seoul: Seoul Selection, 2006), 65–87.
13. KBS (Korean Broadcasting System), *Catalogue of the Liberty News Film Collection, 1950–1967* [*Ribeoti nyuseu yeongsang jaryo mongnok (1950nyeon–1967nyeon)*] (Seoul: Korean Broadcasting System, 1992), 1–2.
14. J. R. Higgins, *USIS Film Program*, April 10, 1953, Textual Records in NARA, RG59 Department of State Decimal File, 1950–54, Box 2541.
15. Liberty Production, *I AM A TRUCK*, 1954, Textual Records in NARA, RG306 USIA, Movie Scripts, 1942–1965, Box 16.
16. Liberty Production, *DIARY OF THREE SAILORS*, 1955, Textual Records in NARA, RG306 USIA, Movie Scripts, 1942–1965, Box 9.
17. Heo Baek-nyeon, "Comments on Current Cinema—Two Topics [Yeonghwa sipyeong ije]," *Hanguk ilbo* (July 1, 1955): 4.
18. Hong-joon Kim, ed., "Kim Ki-young," 65–87.
19. Yi Hyo-in, "Thirteen South Korean Film Directors," 368–71. According to Kim Yeong-hui, this 50,000 won salary included extra pay for detached service. It seems that Jinhae and Sangnam were regarded as temporary placements during wartime. KOFA, *Talking about Korean Cinema: Renaissance of Korean Cinema*, Vol. 3 [*Hanguk yeonghwa reul malhanda*] (Seoul: Korean Film Archive, 2007), 9–67.
20. In fact, one can find concrete evidence in the history thereafter, which showed censorship conflict between USIS-Korea and the ROK government. Kim Won-sik, "Liberty News, Fifteen Years of Joy and Sorrow [Ribeoti nyuseu siponyeonui myeongam]," *Sindonga* (July 1967): 289–95.
21. Yu Ji-hyeong, *Conversation for Twenty-Four Years* [*Isipsanyeon ganui daehwa: Kim Ki-young gamdok inteobyujip*] (Seoul: Seon, 2006), 19–38.
22. Yi Hyo-in and Yi Sun-jin acknowledge that Yi Yeong-il's writing offered "the completion of the gigantic history of Korean cinema," covering "the entirety of Korean cinema."

Yi Sun-jin, "Current stage of Korean film studies [Hanguk yeonghwasa yeonguui hyeondangye]," *Journal of Popular Narrative* [*Daejung seosa yeongu*] 12 (2004): 187–224.
23. Yi, "The Complete History," 27.
24. Ibid., 25–7.
25. Yi, "Current stage."
26. Shin Sang-ok used to practice shooting with a Mitchell camera that was rented out from the USAFIK's OCI to Choe In-gyu's production, one of OCI's most frequent subcontractors. Kim Jong-won, *Dictionary of Korean Film Directors* [*Hanguk yeonghwa gamdok sajeon*] (Seoul: Gukak jaryowon, 2004), 318–22.
27. Cheon Hak-beom, "USIS Collected Public Opinions and Reported to the US Government [Mi gongbowon (USIS), minsim donghyang sujipae bonguge bogo]. *Ohmynews* (January 16, 2018).
28. KOFA, *Korean Film Oral History Series—Life History: Bae Seok-in* [*Hanguk yeonghwasa gusul chaerok yeongu sirijeu*] (Seoul: Korean Film Archive, 2009), 35–6.
29. Yi Yeon-ho, *The Legend and Stigma* [*Jeonseol ui nagin*] (Seoul: Korean Film Archive, 2007), 37–40, 145.
30. Richard Meran Barsam, ed., *Nonfiction Film: Theory and Criticism* (Toronto and Vancouver: Clarke, Irwin & Company Limited, 1976), 94–135.
31. SCAP, *Summation of United States Army Military Government Activities in Korea*, No. 8, May 1946. Textual Records in NARA, RG331 SCAP, Military and Non-Military Activities 1945–49, Box 8303.
32. NFPF (National Film Preservation Foundation), ed., *Treasures from American Film Archives: 50 Preserved Films* (San Francisco: Water Mark Press, 2000), 119–20.
33. Barsam, ed., "Nonfiction Film," 138.
34. Pare Lorentz is regarded as the leading figure of the American governmental documentary scene in the Roosevelt era. Patricia Aufderheide, *Documentary Film: A Very Short Introduction* (New York: Oxford University Press, 2007), 65–7.
35. Yi, "Thirteen South Korean Film Directors," 368–71.
36. In interviews, Kim says that he was highly keen on the new aesthetics of world cinema and always tried to catch up on the new trends. He also frequently talks about the influence of Italian neo-realism during the 1950s. Yi, "The Legend and Stigma"; Yu, "Conversation for Twenty-Four Years," 19–38.
37. Kim Soyoung, "Suspended Modernity: The State of Emergency and Critical Cinema [Yuyedwoen geundaeseong: bisang satae wa bipanjeok sinema]," in the proceedings of the symposium, *Re-screening the Social* (2012): 135.
38. Some secondary sources have recorded the film's Korean title as *Jugeom ui sangja* (*Box of Corpse*) or *Jugeom ui sangja* (*Box of Death*), and its English title as *Box of Death*. However, its official title in Korean is *Jugeom ui sangja* (an ambiguity between *Box of Corpse* and *Box of Death*) and that in English is *Boxes of Death*. USIS-Korea, *USIS Film Catalogue 1964*, 151.
39. Ridgeway, "Interview with William G. Ridgeway."
40. This film had been assumed to be missing until the author discovered all nine reels of negatives in NARA in July 2010; however, the film still lacks sound.
41. Kim Jong-mun, "Blind Points in Korean Anti-Communist Films [Guksan bangong yeonghwa ui maengjeom]," *Hanguk ilbo* (July 24, 1955): 3; O Yeong-jin, "Several Types of Anti-Communist Films–2 [Bangong yeonghwa ui myeot gaji hyeong (ha)]," *Hanguk ilbo* (August 4, 1955): 4.
42. Yi, "The Legend and Stigma," 129.
43. Yu Du-yeon, "A New Trend in Film Techniques: On Neo-Realism [Yeonghwa gibeob ui singyeonghyang, 'neo rieollijeum'e gwanhayeo]," *Chosun ilbo* (May 10, 1954): 4.

44. Pak Ji-yeong, "The Consciousness of Translators in the 1950s and their Cultural and Political Positions [1950nyeondae beonyeokga ui uisikgwa munhwa jeongchijeok wichi]," *Journal of Modern Korean Literature [Sangheohakbo]* 30 (2010): 351–96.
45. Yu, "A New Trend."
46. Kim, "Blind Points."
47. Ibid.
48. Ibid.
49. These sixteen combatant nations on the South Korean side included Australia, Belgium, Canada, Colombia, Ethiopia, France, Greece, Luxemburg, The Netherlands, New Zealand, the Philippines, the South African Republic, Thailand, Turkey, the UK, and the US.
50. O Yeong-jin, "Several Types of Anti-Communist Films–1"; "Several Types of Anti-Communist Films–2."
51. O, "Several Types of Anti-Communist Films–2."
52. Yi, "The Complete History," 247–8.
53. KOFA, *Film Director Kim Ki-young* [*Yeonghwa gamdok Kim Ki-young*] (Seoul: Korean Film Archive, 1997).
54. Kim, "Kim Ki-young," 69.
55. Yu, "A New Trend."
56. O, "Several Types of Anti-Communist Films–2."
57. Peter B High, *The Imperial Screen: Japanese Film Culture in the Fifteen Years' War 1931–1945* (Madison: University of Wisconsin Press, 2003), 381–421.
58. J. R. Higgins, *IIA: Country Plan* (May 12, 1953). Textual Records in NARA, RG59 Department of State, Decimal File, 1950–54, Box 2541.
59. Ibid.

CHAPTER 2

"We Shall All Need That Basket/ A-Frame Carrier": A Comparative Analysis of *Goryeojang* (1963) and *Ballad of Narayama* (1958/1983)

Kyu Hyun Kim

Goryeojang (1963) is one of Kim Ki-young's less talked-about films. Perhaps one of the reasons for this relative neglect is that it bears a series of unmistakable resemblances to Kinoshita Keisuke's renowned Japanese film *Ballad of Narayama* (*Narayamabushi-kō*, 1958). However, as we shall examine here, the former is anything but a copycat project, riding on the coat-tails of a more internationally successful Japanese film. A comparison of *Goryeojang* and the two cinematic adaptations of *Ballad of Narayama* by Kinoshita and Imamura Shōhei (1983) allows for a rare occasion through which we could observe three master filmmakers addressing a common subject matter but taking very different approaches in entirely distinctive historical and cultural contexts, analogous to the way the cinematic adaptations of Shakespeare's *Macbeth*, by Orson Welles, Roman Polanski, and Kurosawa Akira, are all strikingly distinctive from one another.

Goryeojang is situated in the filmography of Kim Ki-young as following on the heels of his acknowledged masterpiece *The Housemaid* (*Hanyeo*, 1960) and *The Sea Knows* (*Hyeonhaetan eun algoitta*, 1961), a powerful commentary on the Japanese colonial experience and the problematic (mis-)reckoning of its legacy in the postcolonial era. As Yi Yeon-ho ultimately admits after trying to construct a taxonomy of Kim's cinematic output, it is nearly impossible to find any auteurial coherence in the conventional sense in his films. Yi argues that Kim's works are instead marked by distinctive, aggressive manifestations of thematic, stylistic, and genre-traversing perversity, a sign of their refusal to conform and something especially remarkable under the restrictive and oppressive cultural conditions of the Park Chung Hee dictatorship.[1]

Instead of focusing on the ideological proclivities or political meanings of *Goryeojang*—Is the film a critique of modernity or capitalism? Is it sufficiently "progressive" or "populist" from the contemporary Korean viewer's point of view?—I would like to present an interpretation of this remarkable cinematic text through an extensive comparison with two Japanese versions of *Ballad of Narayama*. An avid follower of world cinematic trends as well as a connoisseur of Japanese theater and cinema, Kim Ki-young was clearly aware of Fukazawa Shichirō's (1914–87) novel, *Ballad of Narayama*, and its 1958 cinematic adaptation, which competed at the Venice International Film Festival and was the official selection for a Japanese entry for the category of Best Foreign Language Film in the thirty-first Academy Awards. In an interview, he acknowledged his awareness of the Japanese film but also indicated that his own work deliberately departed from the Japanese version:

> *Narayama bushikō* is a novel written by Fukazawa Shichirō based on a folk tale. We Koreans had a similar custom called *goryeojang*. [*Ballad of Narayama* and my film] tell the same story of abandoning the elderly in the mountains, but because the sentiments of the Japanese differ from ours [Koreans], you can see that the contents of the movies are also different from one another.[2]

Kim saw himself plugged in a discursive network of global cinematic production and consumption and was sufficiently stimulated by *Ballad of Narayama*'s international success to rework and rethink the latter's approach and aesthetic choices, creating a Korean film that bears the unmistakable stamp of his own authorship. I would argue that *Goryeojang* is an excellent example of how a talented popular cultural Korean artist of 1960s, laboring under restrictive political conditions and a severe lack of material resources, could reconfigure the foreign yet familiar (including the Japanese traits, imbued as they are with the asymmetrical cultural balance of power between the two nations as well as concrete legacies of colonialism) into something distinctively Korean yet (disturbingly) unfamiliar.[3] The unfamiliarity that results from Kim's modes of transfiguration and adaptation deviate from the kinds of (insufficiently) postcolonial tropes and symbolic capital that signify "Korean uniqueness" as well as the allegedly common traditions between Korean and Japanese cultures, such as the Confucian ethical norm of filial piety.

In other words, *Goryeojang* serves, in my reading, as a critical text that problematizes not only the essentialization of Korean, Japanese, and/or East Asian cultures in the dominant genealogies (in a Foucauldian sense) of the Japanese and Korean cinema, but also the very notion of "Japanese (foreign) influence" on Korean cinema. In many examples of modern Korean cultural products (and not just cinema), the Korean subjectivity is in fact manifested in the very process of the dialogical relationship with its Other ("foreign") counterparts. My position is analogous to that of Christina Klein, who considers that the "poaching" of Hollywood film conventions and styles by such 1950s Korean filmmakers, such as Han Hyeong-mo, was not a sign of subservience to American hegemony but a form of a counter-hegemonic power against the latter. Films such as Han's *Hand of Fate* (*Unmyeong ui son*, 1954) and *Madame Freedom* (*Jayu buin*, 1956) might have accorded with the ideological (anti-communist, pro-capitalist) objectives of the American Cold War propaganda apparatuses but were also distinctively "Korean" in the sense that they reflected the historicized subjectivity of the Korean culture producers, and not simply through superficial reasons such as that they feature ethnic Korean actors speaking Korean-language dialogue.[4]

In addition, I will argue below that despite being separated by two decades and their own distinctive, iconoclastic styles, Kim and Imamura's films share what I would like to call a "modernist" stance, problematizing and critiquing sublimity as an aesthetic device to evoke (as employed by Kinoshita in his version) the common-sense morality of Japanese and Korean communities, through the deployment of the iconic imagery of a Sacred Mother figure. Moreover, they also fully articulate modern subjects as their main characters. The latter are modern in terms of how they cope with the hypocritical, oppressive, or easily manipulated communal norms and religious-ideological orders, on the one hand, and "nature," on the other, as a force fundamentally hostile to humanity.

THE GERONTICIDAL NARRATIVE IN EAST ASIAN TRADITIONS

Before we begin analyses of Kim, Kinoshita, and Imamura's films, let us first take a look at the origins of the folk tales that served as the basis of these works, specifically those that deal with the killing by abandonment of the elderly (known as *giro seolhwa* 棄老説話 in Korean, *kirō setsuwa* in Japanese. For the sake of brevity, I will refer to these narratives as *giro* tales below). It has been established by scholars of folklore and cultural history that the *giro* tales have been told in various permutations at least since the early medieval period in China, Japan, and Korea. One of the prototypes for these tales was likely a Buddhist edification text that tells of a particular ancient nation identified by its custom of deserting the elderly (in Chinese designation, the name *Qilaoguo* 棄老国 was used), which reformed its practice by learning that the wisdom of the elderly was actually a valuable national asset.[5] This prototype *giro* narrative is identified by Kim Yong-ui as the "riddle" version. However, another variant of the geronticidal narrative exists, sometimes referred to as the "basket carrier" (*mokko*) or "A-frame carrier" (*jige*) version, that likely originated within an ancient Chinese compilation of stories promoting filial piety, and subsequently spread to both Korea and Japan.[6]

In this version, a man goes into the mountains accompanied by his young son, in order to abandon his elderly father according to the custom. Upon the man's departure from his father's would-be grave, the young son attempts to bring back the carrier used to carry the elderly father. When the man berates the son, the latter answers, "When you get old and I must bring you to this place, I will need that carrier." Struck by the son's answer, the man returns to retrieve his father, thus terminating the evil custom of abandoning the elderly. This is the archetypical *giro* tale that most Koreans are familiar with, and makes a brief, almost inconsequential appearance in *Goryeojang*.

According to Kim Yong-ui and Choe Gi-suk, there are quite a number of variants among the folk tales of Korea and Japan relating to the abandonment of the elderly, including one in which the discarded elderly outwit their children and manage to survive and even prosper, but all of them refute the custom of abandoning the elderly, from the moral and pragmatic standpoint of inculcating filial piety and respect for the elderly, and their wisdom.[7] It is more difficult to determine whether these tales have any basis in historical fact, that is, the actual customs of East Asian cultures. Here, I will stop by pointing out that the filmmakers discussed here treat the practice of abandonment of the elderly as a legend or a folk tradition completely unmoored from the concrete reality of historical space and time.[8]

Indeed, it is immediately apparent that neither version of *Ballad of Narayama* nor *Goryeojang* follow the prototypical idea of the narrative designed to reinforce or inculcate Buddhist or Confucian moral lessons. This refusal to uphold the values of filial piety, the wisdom of the elderly or other moral teachings was also initially evident in Fukazawa Shirō's source novel, originally published in the influential *Chūō kōron* magazine in 1956. It is worth noting that, even though the novel contains many referents to the dialect (known as *nayashi* dialect), customs and natural landscapes of today's Yamanashi Prefecture (although it is nominally set in the adjacent Shinshū region, today's Nagano Prefecture), Fukazawa deliberately de-historicized his narrative. Interestingly, the local folk tale transmitted in this region is identified not as an age-old custom but a decree by a domain lord during the Warring States period (sixteenth century). This folk tale is a variant of the "riddle" version, positing a filial farmer who refuses to abandon his mother, eventually compelling the domain lord to repent and rescind the decree. Fukazawa's novel, on the other hand, is only vaguely identified as taking place in the late Edo period (possibly early nineteenth century), and the involvement of political-legal authorities or details of the class system do not play any significant role in its narrative.[9] And in stark contrast to the folk tale, the custom of geronticide is not reversed or even critiqued (at least at face value) in the novel. The central protagonists, seventy-year-old Orin and her middle-aged son Tatsuhei, while obviously in a loving and caring relationship, entirely accept the practice of *obasute* (geronticide) as righteous and necessary.

However, it would be wrong to assume that Fukazawa eschewed the stance of historical reflection that brought forth certain parallels between the chronic poverty as well as sometimes cruel and inhuman customs of a hypothetical early modern mountain village and their modern, war-originated, state-enforced analogues during wartime Japan. Fukazawa himself indicated that he partly based the character of Orin on his own mother, who had suffered from liver cancer and frequently expressed her desire to die. He also noted that the *kamikaze* fighters and Sasuke in Tanizaki Jun'ichirō's *A Portrait of Shunkin* (1933), a character who willingly blinds himself to devote his life to the care of a samisen artist, served as further points of inspiration for Orin's character.[10]

In his subsequent work, *Fūryū mutan* (1960), Fukazawa deployed nonsensical satire as a prism through which he could refract and critically reflect on both the wartime totalitarian mentality and the excesses of political protest in the context of the post-Occupation Japanese democracy. His attempt badly backfired, however, stimulating outrage among right-wing ideologues, because it featured a (rather comical and slapstick) scene in which the imperial family was beheaded by an angry mob. This led to the home invasion and murder of the *Chūō kōron* magazine's president Shimanaka Hōji's housemaid by a seventeen-year-old right-wing youth. Instead of sympathizing with Shimanaka's stance of defending freedom of expression, public opinion turned critical of the magazine and Fukazawa, who had to issue a public apology for using "vulgar words" to depict the imperial family and retreat from the literary scene.[11] Fukazawa's unfortunate experience, however, serves to suggest that his *Narayama* was never intended to valorize the "sacrifice" made by Orin nor the communal traditions that enforced such sacrifice. Presenting his narrative as a folk tale or a legend stripped of most concrete historical referents allowed him to explore and present the unspeakable and inexplicable aspects of the wartime experience in an everyday setting "safely" removed from that of contemporary Japan, which in 1956 still retained vivid memories of the collective cruelties and dehumanizing conditions of the war.

TWO VERSIONS OF *BALLAD OF NARAYAMA*: SUBLIME SACRED MOTHER AND LABORING BODIES

Kinoshita Keisuke's *Ballad of Narayama* follows Fukazawa's strategy of dehistoricization. Kinoshita explicitly presents his film as a cinematic rendering of a *kabuki* or *bunraku* (puppet) play, removing from it any association with the socio-economic system or political conditions that might have, in real history, contributed to necessitation of the *obasute* custom. The film quite consciously takes place in a mythical realm, identifiable as a generic version of "old rural Japan" divorced from any historical specificities. In his narrative, Kinoshita specifically guides the viewers to accept Orin's death as a sublime moment. He achieves this by focusing on Orin as a resilient, strong and compassionate old woman, and valorizing her act of self-sacrifice for the good of her son, family, and community. Moreover, he frames this supreme act of sacrifice within the recognizable appurtenances of traditional Japanese performing arts, such as narrated songs that serve as commentaries on the character's psychology and external action, highly stylized renderings of "natural backgrounds," and exquisite color cinematography that deliberately reminds the viewers of the artifice of the imagery they are engaged with.

To be sure, the sublimity that Kinoshita seeks to inculcate at the end of his film is distinguished from the kind, for instance, that Ban Wang discusses in terms of the Communist and socialist realist arts, expressed as identification of the true Subject of History (often in the form of a heroic narrative).[12] Kinoshita takes care to decouple his film from the politically and ideologically narrated "histories," including modernization as well as Marxist-left-wing narratives that perceive the premodern past as "backward," "unenlightened," or something to be overcome. The mentalities, collective values, and unspoken or spoken communal norms of Orin and Tatsuhei's village are distinguished from those enforced or promoted by a legal–political order or an organized religion but are powerful and encompassing just the same. They are also seen to be profoundly internalized by the individuals, even those with strong personalities such as Orin, and Tatsuhei's considerate and hard-working new wife, Tama. Yet, these characters are also less "obedient" to these communal values and norms than they are actively compliant, fully aware that the latter sometimes disagree with their personal emotions and desires. These conflicts taking place internally in the characters, between the values and norms that they voluntarily accept, on the one hand, and their individualistic desires, on the other, are the main sources of the genteel but powerful pathos permeating the film.

I would like to propose that Kinoshita's film relies on a notion of "common-sense morality" (*tsūzoku dōtoku* 通俗道徳) as its organizing principle. Developed as a heuristic device of "people's history" by such Japanese historians as Yasumaru Yoshio, common-sense morality is constituted by the values, norms, and mentalities (*mentalités*) of a premodern Japanese community (*Gemeinschaft*) and voluntarily internalized by the members of such a community as discursive and somatic device of self-discipline and self-training. Often dismissed as "feudalistic" or "premodern," the common-sense morality, according to Yasumaru, ended up supporting the hegemonic political powers and socioeconomic systems from the ground up, but also could generate those forms of independence and autonomy ultimately resulting in articulations of "individualistic" subjectivity not quite identical to that of a modern rational subject. In Yasumaru's formulation, common-sense morality, rooted in the actual lives of families, villages, and specific regionalities, always had within itself a possibility of challenging and critiquing the dominant sociopolitical order.[13] While Orin, Tatsuhei, Tama, and other "good characters" in the film ultimately accept the moral legitimacy of deserting an old woman on an isolated mountain, their actions are still undergirded by subjectivity and colored by psychological conflicts based on conflicting desires and obligations. They are not "puppets," manipulated through the strings of fate by the *kuroko* (the black-clad puppeteers of a *bunraku* play), as seen in the similarly stylized *bunraku* adaption *Double Suicide* (1969) directed by Shinoda Masahiro.

Ultimately, however, Kinoshita tasks Orin and her sublime vista of self-sacrifice near the end (a passage through which she is explicitly portrayed in the manner of a Buddhist icon, perhaps a Boddhisatva) to suture the potential discordance between the majesty and righteousness of the *Gemeinschaft*'s common-sense morality and its inhumanity and cruelty. She comes to embody the Sacred Mother, a linchpin figure in several key wartime and postwar films directed by Kinoshita, including *Army* (1944) and *The Japanese Tragedy* (1953): the Sacred Mother is simultaneously the ultimate victim, the ultimate resilient survivor and the ultimate savior of the Japanese (national) community.[14]

It is not surprising that Imamura, a filmmaker whose works had been recognized and celebrated for their naturalistic, documentarian, and ethnographic approaches, was attracted to Fukazawa's novel. Imamura incorporated the characters and narratives from Fukazawa's other novel set in the same world as *Narayama*, *The Jinmu Emperors of Northeast* [*Tōhoku no zunmutachi*, 1957] into his film, but the main plot and central characters, namely Orin, Tatsuhei and Orin's grandson Kakekichi, remain anchored in the former narrative. Having noted this, however, it is also worth pointing out that Imamura is not really interested in mounting a historically faithful recreation of what it would have been like to live in a snowbound mountain village in nineteenth-century northeastern Japan. Likewise, Imamura's ethnographic research is not invested in capturing the "essential" qualities of being Japanese in the manner of a *Nihonjinron* or "theory of the Japanese."

As is the case with some of his other films set in contemporary Japan, Imamura seeks to access the "reality" often elided in "official" historical accounts as well as in "mythical," ahistorical, and essentialized representations of the Japanese past. The characters in Imamura's *Narayama* are not archetypes: you seldom wonder what they "do" outside of the filmic text. They are constantly working, grinding grains, feeding and caring for horses and livestock, hunting game, cooking gruel, tending to sick or infirm family members, and so on. They are first and foremost laboring bodies, who exist independently from the functions or roles assigned to them in the schematized narrative. In this they are markedly different from the corresponding characters in Kinoshita's film, whose main activities are communal and ritualistic, most importantly eating together as a family, and who do not have identifiable "lives" outside the hermetically self-contained world of the cinematic text. Orin in Imamura's version, while a resilient and resourceful character, is no Sacred Mother. Even Risuke, Tatsuhei's sexually frustrated younger brother, ostracized by the village community due to his disgusting body odor, is seen to be vigorously engaging in various activities of pursuing sexual gratification, which Imamura presents as a form of corporeal labor instead of an act of passive consumption. In contrast, one character marked in the film as a "consuming body" is Kakekichi's first common law wife Matsu, whose habit of stealing and eating the food from Orin/Tatsuhei's household eventually results in her being murdered, along with her family, as a village sanction against food thieves.

I would like to caution here that Imamura's propensity to get to the bottom of the "natural state" of humanity (and Japanese) does not necessarily lead to his embrace and valorization of the "naked" natural human either. Imamura in my view is agnostic toward nature, both "human nature," those elements undisciplined by social norms and uncamouflaged by cultural patterns, and the "nature" that exists in contradistinction to "humanity." I believe this attitude of his is illustrated in his depiction of various animals in *Narayama*, intercut with a wide range of human behaviors: sexual, predatory, peacefully in repose, and so on. He shows a disturbing sequence of a snake being gnawed and eaten by a pack of rats, obviously calling to the viewer's mind a parallel between his human characters and rats. However, he then later shows a snake swallowing a rat whole. The juxtaposition of rats to human beings, or a tendency to interpret these scenes as metaphors for nature–human or human–human relations, is not supported by these shots. Another interesting touch is the presence of serpents residing in a particular farmhouse, a reference to the Japanese folkloric designation of them as "lords of the house (*ie no nushi*)." When the thieving Amaya family are apprehended and massacred by the villagers, a serpent is seen to be slithering away from their house. Does this mean that Imamura is showing the viewers the "gods" condemning the Amayas for breaking the rules of the community? A more likely reading is that the "gods" (or "nature" if you prefer) are essentially indifferent to human desires and suffering: a lord of the house is ready to leave the house when it senses that the household can no longer provide for (in other words, properly worship) it.

GORYEOJANG: HUMANITY AND NATURE

Imamura's agnostic depiction of rats makes an interesting comparison to Kim Ki-young's treatment of them in *Goryeojang*. The Korean director starts his film with a prologue set in a studio recording session of a modern-day (early 1960s Korea) radio show, introducing the Malthusian view of humanity by explicitly likening them to rats, defined mainly by the parallel drive of both species toward reproduction and proliferation. One panel member of the show, to the thrill and amusement of the audience, notes that, when the rats are starved due to overpopulation, they will cannibalize one another in order to restore an ecological "balance." The imagery of rats as hungry, voracious animals singularly devoted to reproduction and proliferation is constantly evoked in the visual depiction of the famished slash-and-burn farmers, including malnourished and uncouth children, especially in their disturbingly predatory collective action to overwhelm the adults and take potatoes stored secretly by them.[15] When the young adult version of Guryong, the main protagonist, attempts to flirt with Gannan (the film's approximate equivalent of Tatsuhei's second wife, Tama, in *Narayama*) he likens a desirable human marriage to a coupling of rats:

> Guryong: I may be a cripple but have a house and lands of my own.
> Gannan: What about a wife?
> Guryong: I prefer a smaller woman. They say a cow may give birth to one calf, but a rat can give birth to ten in one litter.
> Gannan: Why don't you take a hen for your wife then? That way she can lay three hundred sixty-five children every year for you![16]

Although Imamura and Kim both draw parallels between humans and rats, the Korean director's view of his characters emphasizes more directly than Imamura's the biological (rather than "collective") impulses for sustenance, reproduction, and proliferation. Of course, this does not necessarily mean that Kim is more morally or politically judgmental toward the (rat-like) human characters of his film than the Japanese director.

A number of plot details are shared by his film and Fukazawa's novel as well as its 1958 cinematic adaptation, such as an old man in the neighborhood who, unlike Orin and Geum, the Korean film's equivalent character to Orin, refuses to accept his fate to be abandoned in the mountains, and the climatological changes that accompany Orin/Geum's deaths. However, the differences between Kim's film and the Japanese films are also glaring and remarkable. Kim almost entirely divests his dark, dank, and decrepit slash-and-burn farming community of any common-sense morality internalized as self-disciplinary principles by its constituents (except for the kind of starkly animalistic, an-eye-for-an-eye commandment that allows, for instance, Guryong's archenemies, his stepbrothers, to demand the killing of Guryong's mute wife who had killed one of them in an act of vengeance for their rape of her). In its place is a religious–legal order that presides over the villagers overseen by a shaman and materialized in the form of a gnarled totemic tree, which also serves as a hanging tree for publicly executing the village's "criminals." Likewise, the startlingly violent, almost ridiculously excessive but nonetheless cathartic ending of the Korean film radically departs from the pathos-filled, serene endings of both cinematic versions of *Narayama*. In the former, Guryong returns from the abandonment of his mother, Geum, only to find his second wife, Gannan, hanging dead from the shaman's tree. He unleashes his explosive rage, hacks to death most of his stepbrothers, the co-conspirators with the shaman, and then cuts down the old tree, crushing the shaman to death in the process.

Even though Kim Ki-young himself acknowledged the possibility of interpreting this sequence as a reference to the April 19 democratic uprising that had toppled the Syngman Rhee (1875–1965) dictatorship,[17] I doubt that the director had so much faith in the "public spirit" of the ordinary Koreans or, for that matter, humanity in general, that he felt compelled to make his film into an explicit allegory of the recent democratic transformation of South Korea. Guryong's fierce, apocalyptic rage unleashed against his stepbrothers and the shaman appears less an act of political justice than one of personal vengeance, or affective articulation of his *ressentiment* as a "cripple" (a derogatory Korean term for a disabled person is constantly used throughout the film), his disability, a limp leg, resulting from the harassment of his stepbrothers during his childhood.[18] All in all, there is little textual or contextual evidence that Kim intended his film to be critical of the geronticidal practice as either a premodern "evil" custom to be eliminated or a morally offensive behavior from a Buddhist or Confucian viewpoint.

This lack of commitment to either modernization drive or moralistic edification as the organizing principle of his film (the latter tendency still quite common among the popular period pieces of New Korean Cinema) accounts for a strangely tangential and lukewarm insertion of the "A-frame carrier" tale into the climactic sequence. One of Gannan's children, a young boy, Geon, accompanies Guryong in his trek across the mountains to abandon Geum, and it is this boy who states the line from the tale, "We must bring the carrier back home, so that I can then bring you here many years later." Guryong's response to this remark is a rather noncommittal acknowledgement of his own guilt, that he clearly "deserves" to be abandoned like his own mother by his (step)son, rather than an activation of internalized moral norms such as filial piety. This is how Kim Ki-young himself described the implied meaning of the ending to his film:

> What would be the task of slash-and-burn farmers after the movie had ended? To ensure that their children flourish, by protecting and farming the lands they have inherited from their ancestors. As time passes, children will grow up to be adults, and adults will become the elderly, and the latter will be buried in the valley of death through the practice of *goryeojang*. For [this cycle of life and death] to continue, they must plant the seeds and grow them. The seeds also mean the reproduction of children.[19]

As we can infer from this comment, Kim might have presented Guryong's final act as a rejection of the village's religious–legal order but not of the practice of *goryeojang* itself, which in his conception was akin to a representation of the natural cycle of life and death, just as the reproduction and proliferation of "children" by the human species is what he ultimately saw as "natural," and by implication, beyond the control or interference of social norms or religious–legal powers.

CLIMACTIC SEQUENCE: MOTHER AND SON

Let us, then, closely examine the climactic sequence in which the son (Tatsuhei/Guryong) physically carries the mother (Orin/Geum) to the place of her death in all three films. Yi Hyo-in rightly points out the relative significance of this sequence, in that it takes up approximately 25 percent (*Goryeojang* and Kinoshita's *Narayama*) to 30 percent (Imamura's *Narayama*) of the total running time in all the productions.[20]

As I suggested above, for Kinoshita, the sublimity of Orin's self-sacrifice is the most important feature of this sequence, in which Orin literally becomes a Buddhist icon, in a transliteration of a common Japanese term for death, "becoming a Buddha (*jōbutsu* 成仏)." Imamura at first glance appears to follow Kinoshita's view in presenting Orin's death as a sublime event. However, when you closely observe the sequence, it becomes evident that Imamura's Tatsuhei and Orin interact with one another at their final meeting place as two modern individuals, fully cognizant of their "natural impulses" without aestheticizing their emotions into theatrical representations. Perhaps this sequence in Imamura's film is so powerfully authentic and moving because the director places them much closer to the notion of "ordinary modern citizens," that is, the prospective contemporary viewers of this film (which was released more recently in 1983, rather than in the earlier era of 1958 or 1963), with their guilt, weaknesses, strengths, survival instincts, and love for one another.

In Imamura's conception, Orin is not admirable or "special" because she is a transcendental embodiment of sacrifice for the greater good of the family, community, or nation, but because she faces her death with courage and equanimity. Both Orin and Tatsuhei fully acknowledge, in the course of the film, their perpetration of and participation in unspeakable acts: Orin sending Matsu off to her family on an errand so that she would be killed by the villagers along with her other family members, and Tatsuhei murdering his own father after an argument over the latter's refusal to acquiesce to the custom of geronticide (this revelation, added by Imamura to the novel's original plot, reminds the Japanese viewers of the hypothetical conflicts between the younger generation of the wartime Japan of 1930s and 40s and their elders educated during the more liberal 1910s and 20s, and regarded by the former as decadent, irresponsible, and excessively Westernized). I argue that this awareness that they have committed these unspeakable acts makes them "modern" (unlike Kinoshita's characters, or those in the original geronticidal folk tales), vividly reminding the viewers (not necessarily Japanese, but any modern citizen living in a post–World War II world, and certainly including Koreans) of the hardship, pain, mortality suffered by themselves and their family members, as well as their own moral compromises and failures.

Kim Ki-young, like Imamura, situates the mother and the son in a space stripped of socially proscribed roles, and observes their "naked humanity," expressed in the unadorned desire to escape their destinies and go back to the primal relationship between a mother and a child. However, Kim then goes on to graphically depict Geum's death, never explicitly shown in either version of *Narayama*. Here the director designs her death as an expressionist horror set piece, negating any sense of conventional celebration of Geum's death as a noble self-sacrifice. Almost instantly after Guryong tearfully leaves his mother in the pit of skeletons, a large carrion buzzard, seemingly straight out of a classic Western, slaughters her and devours her body. Time appears to be dilated in this sequence, so that Geum's body appears to decompose in the matter of hours if not minutes, so that she is already reduced to a white-haired, seemingly decayed cadaver picked apart by carrion buzzards by the time Guryong reaches the base of the mountain and the prophesied downpour materializes. Kim emphasizes, again like Imamura, that nature is completely indifferent to human "goodness," utterly negating any sense of Neo-Confucian moral rigorism, including the conception of filial piety as a "natural" human trait (as in the adage that a person's moral commitment, say, to filial piety, "moves even Heaven"). The downpour metaphorically tied to Geum's death in the Korean film is also starkly different from the gentle snow that falls to cover Orin in both versions of *Narayama*, generating an atmosphere of "moral violence" that upends any sense of sublimity. Guryong's final destruction of the shaman might be construed as an assertion of a modernizing drive against "premodern customs,"[21] but the affective strategy behind the act is geared toward the negation of any religious or ideological authority, very probably including statism and nationalism in its scope.

GORYEOJANG AND THE MODERN SUBJECT

In this essay, I have sought to argue against those interpretations of *Goryeojang* and Imamura's *Narayama* that hold they are about atemporal, deeply structural, and collective "truths" about human existence. These films are, in my view, concerned with the idea that modern individual subjects are too "weak" (or perhaps too "human") to take full moral responsibility for their actions and the ways in which they navigate their oppressive and hypocritical societies and cultures, as well as the indifferent, often hostile "natural" environment. Imamura's film, in particular, has been subject to many conventional interpretations focused on the director's ethnographic proclivities. These views virtually ignore those elements in his text that, while eliding direct editorial interventions (his films seldom feature the director's "persona" or a representative "everyman/woman" serving as an easy point of identification or surrogate figure for the viewer), clearly speak to the presence of modern subjectivity. This quality is substantiated by the fact that the elements of "natural" mayhem portrayed within the film (the conflicts, sexual acts, and abject eruptions of violence including rape) are always presented through, and on behalf of, modern human beings, that is, his characters and the viewers.

Take, for instance, the horrifying sequence in which Amaya's entire family, including infants and young children, are massacred, screaming and pleading, by a group of villagers. Here, Imamura breaks from his usual editorial style in *Narayama* and continues to film for an extended time, from a medium-length distance, the villagers in workday clothes, hoes and shovels in hands, diligently piling masses of dirt on the squirming bodies of the Amaya family. The viewers who started watching in mid-sequence might legitimately think that the villagers are simply tilling the land after having just planted some seeds. The stark everydayness and ordinariness of their labor, with its physical, mechanical exertion unmarked by any outward display of remorse or hesitation, is deliberately captured by Imamura in an extended cut that accentuates its horror and cruelty. This passage also drives home the modern notion that, for mass murderers (who could of course be any number of "ordinary people" just "caught up in the moment" or "obliged to follow orders/a consensus decision otherwise their own lives would be threatened") an act of mass murder could be a form of everyday labor, not a particularized act of emotional or ideological violence. I submit that this sequence could be presented in such a deliberately distancing manner only because the filmmaker and the viewers are expected to be fully cognizant of the abject horror as well as mundanity of such an act.

Moreover, the Amaya family's mass murder as presented in *Narayama* might be over-interpreted by some critics to assume that this type of act used to be sanctioned, at least diegetically, by a communal norm inherited over many generations (the Japanese term is *shikitari*). However, as both cinematic versions of *Narayama* make it clear, the villagers who decide to massacre the entire family deliberately choose the cruelest and most annihilating means of punishment for the Amaya's transgression, rationalizing it with the argument that "there should be no loose ends (*kōkan*, 後患 in Korean, *huhwan*)," that is, there should be no grudge-bearing surviving descendants who could wreak vengeance on them or their descendants. Imamura succinctly but clearly shows how the decision to kill the entire family is made (he refuses to assign blame to a "bad apple," an instigator, among the villagers, as Kinoshita does), and how Tatsuhei and Orin are reluctantly but surely roped into the murderous scheme. The *shikitari* is always subject to human interpretation and manipulation, like any religion or ideology, and never "pure" nor necessarily just. The fact that Tatsuhei and Orin carry within themselves the guilt of having killed his father, even if accidentally, and of sending a young girl, Matsu, to her horrible, entirely unjustified death, respectively, is an essential component of their subjectivity, and meaningfully intercedes into their decision to comply with the geronticidal practice.[22]

Likewise, Kim Ki-young in *Goryeojang* implicates Guryong in a series of morally compromised acts, aside from his abandonment of his mother. He, albeit reluctantly, stabs with a knife and kills his first mute wife in an act of semi-assisted suicide, in acquiescence to the demands of his stepbrothers that the "an-eye-for-an-eye" injunction be carried out. Later, he allows Yeon, Gannan's young daughter with a pockmarked face and the most forthright and assertive female character in the entire film (with the exception of the villainous shaman), to be killed by the shaman in a disturbing ritual so that she could be spiritually enslaved by the latter to supernaturally prophesy the timing for the lifting of the drought. If there is any character who could be interpreted as a stand-in for the young student demonstrators "sacrificed" during the April Revolution, it is Yeon. In the denouement, Guryong acknowledges that the destruction of the old tree and the shaman has now "freed" the girl's spirit. I posit that Guryong's behavior and emotional outbursts in the conclusion of the film illustrate his awareness of his own participation in the religious–legal system that resulted in the deaths of his first wife, Gannan, Yeon, and Geum.

To reiterate, Kim Ki-young's *Goryeojang* and Imamura's *Narayama* are united in their skepticism toward any religious–legal order or "commonsense morality," in their rejection of sublimity as an aesthetic strategy to highlight heroism and moral values of their personages, and in their presentation of the central characters as modern subjects rather than cultural archetypes or the supposedly "natural" beings unencumbered by modern subjectivity.[23] In the Kinoshita version, Orin as Sacred Mother dominates the narrative. In the former two films, Tatsuhei/Guryong is the true protagonist. Tatsuhei's bifurcated self—torn between his psychological guilt and sense of love and responsibility toward his mother and family—is left without reconciliation or suturing at the end of the film. Similarly, Guryong destroys the shaman but he does not negate the practice of geronticide itself: what he destroys is a system of biopolitics that rationalizes such practices in the name of some "greater good." Kim makes the distinction between the practice of *goryeojang* as a synecdoche for the cycle of life and death, on the one hand, and as a "Korean tradition" subject to religious–ideological manipulation, on the other.

CONCLUSION

Many filmmakers—Korean, Japanese or other—making films about the premodern past, end up affirming conventional moralities as they think would have been prevalent in the era, or, worse, project to these films the dominant ideological agendas of their own era. They sometimes condemn "backward" customs and inhuman, ignorant behaviors of the premodern population, or "discover (in truth, invent)" democratic, humanist, nationalist, and other values and ideas in certain premodern figures, customs, and practices (portraying Admiral Yi Sun-sin as not only a super-heroic military figure but also a proto-democratic political leader, for instance). I hope that I have shown through this essay that Kim Ki-young, Imamura Shōhei, and to a lesser extent Kinoshita Keisuke all challenge this tendency through their mythical forms of filmmaking that profoundly critique the conventional understanding of the "historical past." Imamura has always fought against the "proper things" (*kireigoto* in a Japanese expression), including ideology, "culture," "tradition," moral conventions, and "humanistic values." Kim, while operating from an entirely different aesthetic, stylistic and philosophical angle, is a kindred spirit in this regard. Their films, the 1983 version of *Narayama* and *Goryeojang*, remain radically subversive and profoundly challenging even when seen from the viewpoint of the 2020s. In their daring to situate modern individuals in compelling, and ultimately powerfully moving dramas set in the distinctively mythical worlds of the premodern past, these films force us, the viewers, to see ourselves in these characters.

NOTES

1. Yi Yeon-ho, *The Legend and Stigma* [*Jeonseol ui nagin*] (Seoul: Korean Film Archive, 2007), 50–9.
2. Kim Ki-young interview, conducted by Yu Ji-hyeong, *Conversation for Twenty-Four Years* [*Isipsaneyongan ui daehwa*] (Seoul: Seon, 2006), 100, quoted in Yi Hyo-in (see note 20), 281.
3. On the controversy in 1960s Korea over the alleged plagiarism of Japanese cinema and the "bad Japanese influence" on Korean cinema, see Jin-soo An, *Parameters of Disavowal: Colonial Representation in South Korean Cinema* (Oakland: University of California Press, 2018), ch. 2, "Film and the *Waesaek* ["Japanese Color"] Controversies of the 1960s."
4. Christina Klein, *Cold War Cosmopolitanism: Period Style in 1950s Korean Cinema* (Oakland: University of California Press, 2020), 108–23, 170–8.
5. This prototypical tale is collected in *The Storehouse of Sundry Collectibles* (in Chinese Zabao zang jing 雜寶藏経), compiled after the second century CE in India and translated into the Chinese language by the monks Kimkarya and Tan-yao during the Northern Wei dynasty (386–534). See an English translation by Charles Wellman (Moraga, CA: BDK America, 1994).
6. Kim Yong-ui, "The Comparison of *Giro* Story between Korean and Japan [Han-il giro seolhwa eui bigyo]," *Japanese Studies* [*Ilbon yeongu*] no. 25 (2008): 315. An A-frame carrier, called *jige*, has been in use by Koreans for many centuries and has served as one of the

most essential agricultural tools. Two sturdy wooden sticks are joined to a straw mat directly covering a laborer's back, to make a shape similar to the alphabet "A," giving rise to the English term given by American soldiers around the time of the Korean War. A moderate-size A-frame carrier is said to be able to hold a weight of 50–70 kilograms.

7. Kim Yong-ui, "The Comparision of *Giro* Story,"; Choe Gi-suk, "The Fear of Becoming Old and the Imagination of Co-habitation [Nohwa ui gongpo wa gongsaeng jihyang ui sangsangryeok: Gubi seolhwa 'goryeojang' yi eopseojin yurae]," *Studies of Woman's Literature* [*Yeoseong munhak yeongu*] no. 29 (2013).

8. The possibility that the *giro* tales are at least partly based on actual practices was raised by the archeological discovery in China of a series of caves in which the remains of multiple people aged sixty and older were located. This was presumed to be for the purpose of geronticide. See Duan Xiaohong, "A Study on Chinese and Korean *Giro* Stories [Chungguk mit hanguk ui giro seupsok e gwanhan gochal: Gisayo wa goryeojang eul jungsim euro]," *Korean Gerontology* [*Hanguk nonyeonhak yeongu*] 27, no. 2 (2018).

9. Yi Yun-jong, "The Representation of *Giro* Story in North East Asia: Focusing on *Goryeojang* and *Narayama Bushiko* [Dongbuk asia giro seolhwa ui yeonghwajeok jaehyeon: *Goryeojang* kwa *Narayama bushiko* reul chungsim euro]," *Comparative Studies* [*Bigyo munhwa yeongu*] 55 (June 2019): 143–5. See also Yu Jae-yeon, "Imamura Shohei's *Narayama bushikō* [Imamura Shōhei ui *Narayama bushikō-ron*: Ubasute jeonseol ui hyeonjaejeok uimi]," *North East Asian Cultural Studies* [*Dongbugga munhwa yeongu*] 59 (2019): 340–4. The semi-historical Shinshū variant was allegedly the source of the name of the Obasute (literally "throwing away an old woman") train station in the now-defunct Japan Railway's Eastern Japan Shinonoi Line, glimpsed at the end of Kinoshita's version of *Narayama*.

10. Yu, "Imamura Shōhei," 333–8.

11. For a summary of this right-wing terror attack on Shimanaka and its subsequent negative impact on artistic free expression in Japan, see Nick Kapur, *Japan at the Crossroads: Conflict and Compromise after Anpo* (Cambridge: Harvard University Press, 2018), 255–62.

12. Ban Wang, *The Sublime Figure of History: Aesthetics and Politics in Twentieth-Century China* (Stanford: Stanford University Press, 1997), especially ch. 5, "The Sublime Subject of Practice," 155–93.

13. Yasumaru Yoshio, "Tsūzoku dōtoku-ron: haikei to denbō" (1999), in *Yasumaru Yoshio-shū*, ed. Shimazono Susumu et al., vol. 1, *Minshū shisōshi no tachiba* (Tokyo: Iwanami Shoten, 2013), 303–6. A meaningful comparison may also be made between the concept of commonsense morality and E. P. Thompson's notion of "moral economy" as applied to the early modern English peasants and the patterns of their collective action. See E. P. Thompson, "The Moral Economy of English Crowd in the Eighteenth Century" (1971), in *Customs in Common: Studies in Traditional Popular Culture* (New York: The New Press, 1993).

14. See Hikari Hori, *Promiscuous Media: Film and Visual Culture in Imperial Japan, 1926–1945* (New York: Columbia University Press, 2018), ch. 2, "Contested Motherhood and Entertainment Film."

15. Kim Yeong-jin, "Rethinking Humanity from the World of Animal: Kim Ki-young's *Goryeojang* [Dongmul ui segye eseo inganseong eul keonjeo ollida: Kim Ki-yeong ui yeonghwa segye wa Goryeojang]," Text essay supplement to *Goryeojang* Blu-ray, Korean Film Archive, 2019, 15–16. For a provocative take on Kim's usage of "rat" as a cinematic device in *The Housemaid* (1960), see Pak U-seong, "The Performativity and Position of Rat in *The Housemaid* [*Hanyeo* eseo chwi raneun jangchi ga suhaeng haneun yeokhal kwa wising]," *Film Studies* [*Yeonghwa yeongu*] no. 49 (September 2011).

16. Kim Ki-yeong, *Goryeojang*, a screenplay originally submitted to the state censor, circa 1962, reprinted as a text supplement to *Goryeojang* Blu-ray, 21.

17. Yi Yeong-il, "The Struggle of Instinct and Poverty: The Complex Nature of *Goryeojang* [Bingon gwa bonneung ui galdeung, bokhap hyeongsik euro pyohyeon doen Goryeojang]," [Film Review] *Kyunghyang sinmun* (April 5, 1963). Kim's statement quoted in this review reads, "The students lost 104 lives in cutting down an old tree during the April 19 uprising."
18. I agree with Yi Hyo-in regarding his assessment of the ambivalence of Kim Ki-young's political stance: "If the community presented in *Goryeojang* reflects reality, it remains unclear whether the object to be overcome was Park Chung Hee's military dictatorship or, on the contrary, the previous regime (society) that had retained those premodern customs that the Park regime wanted so much to eliminate." Yi Hyo-in, "Comparative Analysis of *Goryeojang* and *Ballad of Narayama* focusing on the idea of Communality and Filial Piety [*Goryeojang* kwa Narayamabusikko e natanan gongdongche mit hyo e daehan bigyo bunseok]," *Film Studies* [*Yeonghwa yeongu*] no. 37 (August 2008): 291.
19. Yu Chae-hyeong, "Conversation for Twenty-Four Years," 104–6, quoted in Yi Hyo-in, "Goryeojang," 290–1.
20. Yi, "Goryeojang," 292–5.
21. Pak U-seong, in "The Performativity and Position of Rat," argues that in *Goryeojang* "the absolute value of the anti-superstition campaign actively promoted by the Park Chung Hee regime is unhesitatingly maximized (85)." I do not find this interpretation of the film persuasive. In my view, Pak subscribes to the very tendency he criticizes in other critics, essentializing the latter's modernist traits into that of a capitulation to and identification with the state's modernization drive.
22. In a sequence in which her grandson Kakekichi confronts Orin about the latter's participation in the scheme to kill Matsu, she mutters, "When I go up to the mountain, I will meet Matsu there too" (1 hr 11 min., *Ballad of Narayama*, Imamura Shohei, dir.). It should be noted that in an earlier sequence, Tatsuhei catches Matsu stealing food from his house, threatens to kill her, but spares her life with a stern warning, "Don't do this again."
23. For an illuminating discussion of Kim Ki-young's subversion of Yi Gwang-su's deployment of the sublimity of a heroic historical subject in the novel *Soil* (1939) in his cinematic adaptation (1978), see Keum Dong-hyeon and Kim Kyeong-in, "Demystification of Sublime: Kim Ki-young's *Soil* [Sunggo ui tal shinbihwa: Kim Ki-young ui heuk biteulgi]," *Eomunhak* no. 143 (2019).

CHAPTER 3

Love Thy Enemy: Kim Ki-young's Exploration of Korean-Japanese Romance in *The Sea Knows* (1961)

Russell Edwards

Like any South Korean director working in the pre-democracy era, Kim Ki-young operated proficiently within a range of genres. Deservedly much of Kim's international reputation is based on *The Housemaid* (*Hanyeo*, 1960) and his revisitations of that film, *Woman of Fire* (*Hwanyeo*, 1971) and *Woman of Fire '82* (*Hwanyeo '82*, 1982) for their provocative representations of women and the sometimes-rickety foundations of South Korean male patriarchy. However, it is the purpose of this chapter to address *The Sea Knows* (*Hyoenhaetan eun algoitta*, 1961), a film which falls outside the portion of Kim's filmography that contributes to his "Mr Monster" appellation.[1] With its combination of colonial era melodrama, anti-war sentiment, and provocative romance, *The Sea Knows* is a showcase for Kim's versatility making it worthy of attention alongside the director's better-known films.

The Sea Knows is especially distinctive in South Korean cinema for its provision of a Japanese love interest for the Korean soldier protagonist within its colonial setting. When assuming the presidency, part of Syngman Rhee's (1875–1965) response to Japan's colonial brutality was the implementation of a suppression on Japanese popular culture that also impacted South Korean cinema and its representations of Japan.[2] This policy was periodically circumnavigated, but continued in various forms under subsequent Korean presidents, until it was lifted in 1998 by the Kim Young-sam administration in 1998.[3] Given the rarely broken, ongoing taboos around South Korean cinema's depiction of interethnic romance and the film's rarely repeated choices offered to its Korean protagonist, *The Sea Knows* continues to have both political and cinematic relevance for addressing South Korea's relationship with Japan. The surge of films concerned with the colonial era made during Park Geun-hye's presidency,[4,5] the "Boycott Japan" movement that spiked in 2019,[6] as well as ongoing controversies over Japan's culpability for the sexual enslavement of "comfort women" during wartime,[7] and the territorial disputes over the Dokdo/Takeshima islands,[8] all indicate that resentment toward Japan continues to smoulder and occasionally erupt in contemporary South Korea society. In the light of South Korean cinema's recent focus on such bilateral tensions, it is interesting to consider how twentieth-century Korean films such as *The Sea Knows* differ from recent approaches to the issue.

The Sea Knows is the story of Korean soldier Aroun as he faces obstacles both inside and outside of his tenure with the Japanese Imperial Army. Most well-known for a scene where the Korean recruit is bullied into licking feces off a commanding officer's boot, this brief précis of *The Sea Knows* debunks Yi Yeon-ho's statement that "all of [Kim's] films embody similar stories."[9] Contradicting his own argument, Yi compartmentalises Kim's films into eight different categories: (1) allure and danger of modernity; (2) tragedy of pre-modern era; (3) multiple time zones; (4) adaptations; (5) rewrite of literary films; (6) exploration of sexual energy; (7) self-deprecating low budget films of later years; and (inevitably) (8) overlaps of previous categories.[10]

Based on radio serials written by Han Un-sa, *The Sea Knows* fits Yi's description of adaptations being "melodramas with the trauma of Japanese colonial rule and the Korean War in the backdrop, but they portray the gloom of the era surrounding the fate of the protagonists in the form of mass sadism and masochism."[11] In the same Korean Film Council (KOFIC) volume, a biographical sketch of Kim by Yi Hyo-in cites the director as saying that *The Sea Knows* (as well as *Goryeojang*, 1963) was "done for the money."[12] This creates an unfavourable impression, but Yi also adds Kim's recollection that although *The Sea Knows* "did not gain box office success," the director put considerable effort into making the film.[13] According to Yi, Kim routinely reworked his adaptations, and even if a project "was based on a novel, he changed over 70 per cent of the original."[14] While the exact percentage of change is arguable, Kim's tendency to considerably rework material is also indicated by Han's protests that *The Sea Knows* had been so thoroughly renovated that it did not resemble his original radio serial.[15] Another indication of the film's significance is its inclusion on a 'Best' list compiled by Kim himself.[16] As this list of eleven 'Best' films from the director's thirty-two features is chronological rather than in order of preference, it is difficult to know what to make of this inclusion. However, auteurs rarely list films "done for the money" as a career highlight.

While *The Sea Knows* is first an adaptation, Yi also accounts for the possibility of overlaps when categorising Kim's films. The two additional categories applicable to *The Sea Knows* are: (1) "the allure and danger of modernity"; and (6) "exploration of sexual energy." If Japan is taken to be the force through which modernity was introduced to the Korean peninsula, then this film presents it in two forms. Modernity's danger manifests in the Japanese Imperial

Army and specifically through figures of the sadistic Sergeant Mori and Miyamoto,[17] the cruel army police chief. By contrast, the film's love interest Hideko embodies modernity's allure. Yi's other category, Kim's interest in sexual energy, is of course expressed by the film's central relationship between Aroun and Hideko.

"A GOOD FILM CONTAINS THE SPIRIT OF THE ERA— PLUS SOMETHING" (KIM KI-YOUNG)[18]

At the time of *The Sea Knows*' 1961 release, Japan's occupation of the Korean peninsula had been over for sixteen years. All but the youngest of the film's ticket-buyers would have had direct experience of the colonial era. Anti-Japanese protests were common in early 1960s South Korea, and opposition to the normalization of trade relations was widespread. Simultaneously, members of the government desired the economic benefits to South Korea that could result if relations with Japan were improved.[19] With the 1960 ousting of South Korea's first president, the virulently anti-Japanese Rhee, a major obstacle to that goal had been removed. Scandals such as the arresting of political opponents, the murder of protestors and the rigging of the 1960 election not only made Rhee's leadership untenable but also fanned desire in Seoul for an improved political system.[20] At the same time, the US had been attempting to reconcile South Korea and Japan as part of their New World Order and as a bulwark against the spread of communism.[21] Rhee's successor, Yun Posun, oversaw the switch to a parliamentary system that led to Chang Myon's election as prime minister and senior powerbroker. Chang was sympathetic to the idea of normalization of South Korean relations with Japan but faced opposition from both the National Assembly and, ironically, the student movement that had helped to thrust him into power.[22] The power vacuum between Rhee's deposition and Park Chung Hee's 1963 coup-driven installation as president created an environment in which debate—both peaceful and otherwise—was allowed to percolate. Such freedom of discussion did not just apply to South Korean discourse about Japan, but flowed throughout society, including the film industry. This freedom of debate not only created opportunities for Kim to make a film diverging from previous government ideology but was also partially responsible for an influx of other challenging films into South Korean theatres including *Aimless Bullet* (*Obaltan*, Yu Hyeon-mok, 1961) and, of course, Kim's *The Housemaid*. That the loosening of restrictions of censorship coincided with what Jinsoo An describes as "the era's Japanophile frenzy"[23] no doubt added to *The Sea Knows* profile.

This turbulent but often progressive environment, in which divisions about the colonial past circulated and clashed with ambitions for the economic future, was the backdrop for the production of *The Sea Knows*. As An explains, the South Korean film industry had tremendous interest in engagement with the Japanese film industry. The KFPA (Korean Film Producers Association) were eager to set up co-production networks. There was also strong interest in acquiring first-hand knowledge of Japan's higher standard of post-production facilities as well as the possibility for the distribution of South Korean films within Japan.[24]

There is no doubt that Japan was of considerable interest and a major influence on Kim and his work. Kim lived in Kyoto for three years as a young man, and during this time the director connected significantly with cinema culture including Japanese film.[25] Although anti-war sentiment was evident in the Japanese postwar films of Kurosawa Akira (*Rashomon*, 1950) and Ichikawa Kon (*Harp of Burma, Biruma no tategoto*, 1956; *Fires on the Plain, Nobi*, 1959), *The Sea Knows* particularly bears the mark of *The Human Condition: The Road to Eternity (Ningen no joken*, Kobayashi Masaki, 1959), the second part of Kobayashi's momentous anti-war trilogy.[26] In this story of Kaji, a leftist forced into military service, the Japanese soldier is repeatedly beaten just as Aroun is in *The Sea Knows*. Additionally, there are strong resemblances between the barracks sets as designed by Bak Seok-in and those provided by Ishikawa Seji. While similar experiences and locations undoubtedly account for some parallels, the depiction of *The Sea Knows'* villain Miyamoto, duplicating the action of an evil Japanese soldier polishing his sword in the Kobayashi film, takes the similarities beyond coincidence.

Being at the forefront of South Korea's interest in Japan led Kim to travel to Nagoya with cinematographer Jung Il-sung to film location-establishing transition inserts for the narrative. Although *The Sea Knows* has a diegetic Japanese setting, apart from the inserts, Kim shot his film in South Korea.[27] Kim was equally strategic in his use of actress Gong Midori, a Korean-Japanese actress, for the love interest to circumnavigate bans on using Japanese actors in South Korean films. This enabled Kim to sidestep the *waesaek* ("Japanese colour") controversy about the representations of Japan in South Korean and Hollywood films that was debated by the KFPA and the Ministry of Culture. Driven by concerns about impressionable Korean youth and nostalgic members of the colonial generation, this debate led to the censorship of appealing depictions of Tokyo in Hollywood films such as *The Bridges at Toko-Ri* (Mark Robson, 1954). Soon after *The Sea Knows* was released, further government action impeded and sometimes cancelled production of South Korean films that tried to shoot full scenes in Japan.[28]

As An points out, the depiction of a Korean-Japanese romance in *The Sea Knows* was an innovation for South Korean cinema.[29] In describing a group of colonial films with assimilationist themes that encouraged Koreans to see themselves as part of a Japanese community, Fujitani Takashi highlights a rare interethnic romance in *You and I (Neo wa na* aka *Kimi to Boku*, Heo Yeong aka

Eitaro Hinatsu, 1941) which positions a Japanese bride as a postwar reward for a Korean man's service in the Imperial Army.[30] Kim Su Yun adds that *Tuition* (*Sueomnyo*, Baek Un-haeng and Choe In-gyu, 1940), also has a Korean–Japanese romance and stresses that these films featured Japanese settlers bringing the structure of Empire to the communities of Korea.[31] Comparing these colonial films dramatizing interethnic romances to *The Sea Knows* and the films that followed in its wake such as *The Chorus of Trees* (*Garosu ui hapchang*, Kang Dae-jin, 1968) and *The Daughter of the Governor General* (*Chongdok ui ddal*, Jo Geung-ha, 1965),[32] Kim emphasises that the 1960s films omit themes of communalism. Instead, they favour a championing of "male nationalist heroes"—not for the sake of Japan's Imperial Army, but rather in alignment with Park Chung Hee's nation-building narrative active at the time of these latter films' release dates.[33]

The relationship in *The Sea Knows* is all the more surprising for the way that the romance survives—albeit battered and bruised—all obstacles placed in its path. As already established, there are very few cinematic dramatizations of romantic relationships between Japanese and Koreans. Korean/Japanese relationships that actually endure are still fewer. Kim outlines how *The Chorus of Trees* betrays a romantic ending by having politics divide the couple, whereas *The Daughter of Governor General* ends with the execution of the Korean lover of the titular Japanese heroine.[34] This tendency has continued in South Korean cinema within films that feature colonial era settings made during the recent Park Geun-hye presidency. Of these films, only the biopic *Anarchist from Colony* (*Bak Yeol*, Lee Junik, 2017) depicts consummated romances between a Korean man and a Japanese woman.[35]

"MY ONLY LOVE SPRUNG FROM MY ONLY HATE"— WILLIAM SHAKESPEARE, *ROMEO AND JULIET* (ACT I, SCENE 5)

Like many a film romance, the first meeting between Aroun and Hideko is not promising. Befriended by Nakamura, a Japanese soldier in his unit, Aroun is taken as a guest to the home of the Japanese soldier's sister. While drinking tea and admiring the contents of a bookcase in the host's home, Nakamura's niece, Hideko, unexpectedly enters the room.[36] At this moment the otherwise disinterested Nakamura informs Aroun that the books belong to his niece. While the content of the books is not divulged, Aroun is surprised that they belong to a woman. This sets up Hideko and Aroun's romance as an intellectual attraction.

The relationship immediately meets its first obstacle when during this initial encounter Hideko complains about a robbery and blames local Koreans for the missing goods. Aroun and, notably, Nakamura display dismay at Hideko's *faux pas*. Once Nakamura explains that their guest Aroun is actually Korean, Hideko uncomfortably apologises and soon excuses herself. Building on foreknowledge of the romance established by the film's poster and opening titles billing Gong Midori above debuting male actor Kim Un-ha, Kim alerts his audience about the love story's commencement by ending the scene with a reaction shot of the exiting Hideko closing the screen door. Before moving on to the next scene at Japan's military headquarters, Kim does not cut back to Aroun. This decision not to cut back to the male protagonist has the effect of granting Hideko a degree of agency in the narrative and particularly in its romance.

Kim underlines this sense of Hideko's power during the pair's second accidental meeting at a movie theatre. It is Hideko who suggests going to a teahouse and takes Aroun's arm to guide him there. This precocious initiative, which mixes Korean male sexual fantasy and Japanese authority is continually exercised by Hideko. In her discussion of *The Sea Knows*, Kate Taylor-Jones observes, "a Korean man successfully winning a Japanese woman's love and adoration would speak to a postcolonial desire to reclaim a masculinity lost in the colonial moment."[37] Hideko, from beginning to end, certainly takes care of Aroun, soothing his psychological wounds, and by the film's finish, his physical wounds too. Likewise, she is always responsible for moving the relationship forward, from their "first date" to their eventual elopement. In contrast, Aroun mostly remains a passive receptacle of Hideko's affections. This suggests that, for this Korean soldier at least, in addition to being a balm for postcolonial desire, the love of a Japanese woman is a gift bestowed, not a prize seized. This distinguishes *The Sea Knows* from later Korean–Japanese intimacy films, which as Kim Su-yun notes, along with the domestically focused Korean War films of the 1960s, accentuated masculinity as part of championing Korean heroes for the building of the South Korean nation.[38]

Additionally, Aroun's passivity in the romance accentuates Hideko's agency. This apparent timidity may be due to the fact that unlike most other Korean–Japanese romances, this soldier is stationed in the indisputably Japanese territory of Nagoya, rather than the occupied territories of Korea or Manchuria. It is also worth noting that while there is some truth in Hideko's fulfilling of a postcolonial sexual fantasy, Hideko's power is not exclusively exercised over Aroun (although always for his benefit). Thus, Hideko is openly defiant of her mother's racial prejudice, and she is similarly defiant of the Japanese military that in this film's milieu at least, frowns upon the colonial policy that "encouraged intermarriage and significantly advanced the campaign for the conjugal coupling of Japanese and Koreans during the war."[39]

A narrow view of Hideko as a postcolonial prize overlooks the film's other positive representations of Japan. Of course, it is possible to dismiss the positive representations of Japanese men in *The Sea Knows* as mere convenient plot devices. However, without Nakamura's offer of friendship to his fellow soldier, Aroun would not meet Hideko. Similarly, later in the film, the ill-fated soldier Suzuki helps Aroun to realize that their superiors in the Japanese Army are trying to frame him as a Korean traitor. I argue that, alongside the film's affectionate view of Hideko, these two Japanese males contribute to the film's overriding exploration of a peaceful coexistence with Japan. Anti-Japanese views and renewed constraints about representations of Japan in the late 1960s and later may have tarnished the film's subsequent reputation and led to the apparently mistaken belief that *The Sea Knows* was a financial failure.[40] However, its acceptance of some Japanese characters fits with the "frenzy" for Japanese popular culture at this juncture of South Korean history. Furthermore, the film's anti-war themed finale, which I will discuss later in this chapter, particularly echoes the recent wartime experiences of its contemporary audience. Together, these factors partially account for the film's popularity at the time of release.

As already observed, the film's romance crystallizes with the couple's second encounter at a movie theatre. Reprimanded by Sergeant Mori and other Japanese officers, Aroun is instructed to go to the theatre to watch a *chambara* film,[41] to see how a "real" man behaves. Repelled by the sword-wielding samurai on screen, Aroun leaves the auditorium and encounters Hideko in the lobby. In an awkward exchange where neither looks directly at the other, Aroun explains his reason for being at the theatre and Hideko asks him to join her at a café, as she takes his arm. Thus, the romance formally begins at a point where Aroun rejects both Japanese masculinity and its cultural expression. While it is unclear whether Hideko is likewise leaving the cinema or has just arrived, by approaching Aroun she not only builds on the suggested intellectual attraction implied over the couple's mutual interest in books, but is also rejecting expressions of Japanese masculinity to pursue an educated, more refined version of Korean masculinity.

This affirmation of the couple's initial bond as a meeting of "like minds" is in direct contrast to the experiences of Aroun's fellow Korean recruit Inoue, who much later in the film says to Aroun: "I hate Japanese fellows . . . Japanese girls I like!" The comment prompts the two friends to share a laugh of sexual knowingness, but it also punctuates an explanation that Inoue's involvement with Japanese women has caused him trouble during training camp. Furthermore, Inoue is unwilling to risk further engagement with Japanese women, no matter how much he likes them. Later in the film, Inoue has become Aroun's commanding officer and so is in a position to grant leave to his friend to reunite with Hideko. Inoue's accompanying winks suggest he views Aroun's affair with the same sexual exoticism that has characterized his own dalliances with Japanese women. However, from Aroun's naivety and bashfulness to the couple's mutual appreciation of books and the emotional finale, the director clearly regards the Aroun–Hideko relationship as occurring on a higher plane than Inoue's sexually eager experiences. Of course, given Aroun's tribulations it is possible that

South Korean audiences could view *The Sea Knows* as a warning about romantic involvement with Japanese people, but this would mean ignoring many other aspects of the film.

At the café where Hideko takes Aroun for their post-movie first date, the comparison between the perversity of Japanese masculinity and Aroun is reinforced as the young soldier divulges his humiliations in the Imperial Army, including his being forced to lick feces from Mori's shoe. Overcome by tears, Hideko responds by slumping forward into Aroun's arms. In the scene after their café date, as Hideko sees Aroun back to the army compound, his voiceover explains how "a woman's tears can soothe a man's pain" and that the only woman who had cried for him previously was his mother. Neither the film nor Aroun is blind to the difficulties of interethnic romance. However, just as Hideko progresses past her prejudice against Koreans, so too does Aroun come to terms with his concerns by noting that, although Hideko is a Japanese woman, "all tears are the same regardless of nationality." In a foreshadowing of difficulties to come, just as his voiceover finishes, Aroun momentarily loses his balance. Clearly the path of romance will not run smooth. However, Aroun's misstep is not disastrous. He stumbles, but does not fall.

None of this emphasis on intellectual attraction is meant to deny the erotic tension between Aroun and Hideko. As per Yi's categorizing some of Kim's films for their exploration of sexual energy, the sexual agenda of *The Sea Knows* frames the relationship before the couple even meet. Prior to Nakamura introducing Aroun to Hideko, the Japanese soldier introduces the film's sexual subtext of pleasure and masochism. Witnessing Sergeant Mori's bullying, Nakamura instructs both Aroun and Inoue to sexually fantasize about a woman removing her clothing in order to withstand the inflicted pain. This technique is intended to amuse, but it also sets up the masochistic parameters that define Aroun's and Hideko's relationship. I will further explore the couple's sexual pleasures first, before returning to how the dynamics of Aroun's pain contributes to their relationship.

In a film not generally remembered for its light-heartedness, the pleasure of the couple's relationship is most humorously characterized by the scene in which Hideko scrubs Aroun's back while he sits in a pre-dinner bath. Hideko later confides to her mother that she just wanted to see if Korean men were "different." To Aroun, however, Hideko offers the explanation that back scrubbing is a custom for welcoming honored guests. When Aroun replies that guests would not be treated in such a way in Korea, she (knowingly) asks: "Oh, you don't have baths in Korea?"

Talking after the bath episode, Hideko easily rebuts each of Aroun's objections to why Japanese and Koreans cannot become romantically involved: language ("both Japanese and Korean originate from Mongol language"); social customs ("Customs are being globalized"); and ideology ("Ideology changes with time"). When Aroun turns to ancestry as a defense against Hideko's advances and his own sexual arousal, Hideko delivers her *coup de grâce* by declaring, "We all come from monkeys. If it goes against the cosmic law, then no babies would be produced when a man and woman consummate."

In the next scene, Hideko kneels in welcome to Aroun as he enters a room decorated by a *hinakazari* doll display, patterned after a Heian wedding. Both wearing *yukata*, they drink tea, then after intimately gazing at Aroun, Hideko rises to dance while Aroun beats a drum (Figure 3.1). Thereafter she kneels again and bows to him. Aroun reciprocates by bowing back. Respect accorded to each other, they simultaneously raise their heads and their gazes lock in a suggestion of synchronized affection and love. While this interaction is quite chaste, in a similar scene shortly afterwards when Aroun visits Hideko again on his driving rounds, the sexual implications of their relationship visibly escalate. After describing his latest degradation from Mori, Aroun exclaims he hates Japan and Hideko retorts, "I'm not Japan. I'm a woman called Hideko." They kneel down once again and Kim provides a close-up of Hideko placing her hand over Aroun's hand resting on the *tatami*. In a clear suggestion of sexual contact with a phallus, Hideko's hand rises up the shaft of Aroun's forearm. Aroun reciprocates by reaching for her thigh, but it is clear that Hideko controls the relationship's sexual progress, as she returns his hand to the *tatami* mat. Further indicating the Japanese woman's control of the relationship is the later scene, when the pair are interrogated by Miyamoto. It is Hideko who speaks up and openly admits to kissing Aroun but she demurs that "anything else" is "to come in the future."

The narrative ensures that of all of the Japanese women in the film, Hideko is the most appealing. While Hideko disagrees with Aroun, she does not belittle him as Inoue's prostitute does. Nor does Hideko adhere to prejudices like

Figure 3.1 In front of a hinakazari doll display Hideko dances for Aroun while he beats a drum.

her mother. Instead, she begins from a place of prejudice and learns to accept the Korean man for who he is. Hideko's development is mirrored by Aroun's own inter-racial education. Not only is he attracted to Hideko for her intellectual interests as well as her beauty, but he learns from her that no matter what transpires he can be loved for the Korean man he is. This can be dismissed as no more than the sexual fantasy of the perfect woman as shaped by the director, but given the eccentric sexualities expressed in Kim's other films, it is unsurprising that Hideko's and Aroun's relationship has some idiosyncratic characteristics.

As previously explained, Nakamura frames the masochistic parameters of the relationship when Aroun adapts the Japanese soldier's suggestion of sexual fantasizing when being beaten. Perversely departing from the film's dominant mode of realism, this linking of sexual pleasure with pain is more in line with the tortured relationships between the various Mr Kims and their associated Myeon-jas in other, more widely acclaimed films in the director's oeuvre. At their tea salon date, when he relates his licking feces off Mori's shoe, and during his later impromptu visit to Hideko's house when he demonstrates how he was forced to bark like a dog, Aroun repeatedly reveals his degradation as a way of connecting with his Japanese girlfriend. This is equally stimulating for Hideko, and the mutuality of their humiliation-inspired arousal is underlined in the scene where the pair secretly reunite at the old house where Hideko has sought refuge from her Korean-despising mother. As the pair hide inside the house, the film cuts to a mutual POV shot which shows the tousled blankets upon Hideko's futon. When the film cuts back to the couple, they then look at each other, prompting Hideko to say: "Don't you want to tell me about your punishments?" This combination of image and dialogue specifically links their shared sexual arousal with Aroun's suffering. Aroun then relates his latest round of beatings and then reveals to Hideko how her uncle taught him to minimize pain by fantasizing about women removing their clothing. Hideko rightly deduces that Aroun thought of her as he was beaten and that the severity of the beating meant that Aroun imagined Hideko as being completely naked. As passion threatens to erupt, there is an air raid by United States bombers that sends them both diving to the floor. The framing of their embrace is distinctive. Aroun dominates the left side of the screen as he is stretched across the *tatami* floor. His and Hideko's faces meet in the middle of the frame, while her body extends to the screen's right (Figure 3.2). As Aroun nuzzles Hideko's neck, she draws him closer and a cut presents the erotic image of Hideko's crossing her legs at her ankles before cutting to Aroun's colleagues waiting in the truck outside. There is no condemnation of either Aroun or Hideko implied, and in fact the image of Hideko's legs appears to invite the audience to share her pleasure.

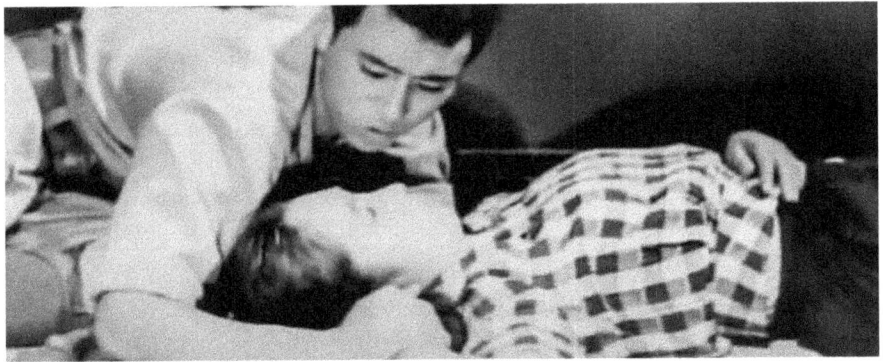

Figure 3.2 While US bombs fall, Aroun and Hideko's romance advances.

Regardless of some sexual eccentricity, when viewed as a simple love story, it is plain that *The Sea Knows* stresses the rightness of the young lovers' choice. The film holds no implied criticism of their union. That the man so adored by this Japanese woman is Korean is of course relevant. However, Korean nationality can also be seen as a substitute for any number of reasons triggering the typical melodramatic trope of parental disapproval in regard to an offspring's object of adoration.

"THE COURSE OF TRUE LOVE NEVER DID RUN SMOOTH"—WILLIAM SHAKESPEARE, *MEASURE FOR MEASURE* (ACT I, SCENE I)

Certainly, *The Sea Knows* has enough despicable Japanese characters to avoid being interpreted as an apology for Japan. Mori looms largest in the film's legacy, with Yi Ye-chun's boisterous performance being recognized as a landmark in the actor's career. As the film continues, Mori's offensive, though sometimes comical demeanor is eclipsed by the more sinister senior officer Miyamoto. Miyamoto taunts Aroun with accusations of being a Korean spy and also colludes with Hideko's mother to interfere with the central couple's romance. Later, Miyamoto not only kidnaps Hideko but threatens to sexually abuse her and kill her unborn child, before hunting Aroun through the bombed-out wreckage of the city. Given that Japanese villainy is offset by positive Japanese representations both male and female, it is clear that South Korean audiences are being asked to differentiate between the Japanese who oppressed them during the colonial era and other Japanese who accept Koreans as equals.

In addition to Hideko's embodiment of the idea that not all Japanese are the same, the film also suggests that Koreans too must be taken on a case-by-case basis. When Aroun is jailed under suspicion of funneling information to the Americans, Miyamoto instigates a plan to expose Aroun's treasonous actions. Miyamoto telephones a subordinate to let him—and the film's audience—know that Aroun will receive a female Korean visitor and he is to be allowed an overnight pass.

The arrival of Aroun's visitor, Gyeong-hui, occurs at one of two moments in the existing print of *The Sea Knows* held by the Korean Film Archive where the soundtrack is damaged.[42] Although some events are comprehensible despite the silence, matching the scenes with dialogue taken from the second volume of the Kim Ki-young shooting scripts already published by the Korean Film Archive allows for a fuller appreciation of this scene.[43]

Having known Aroun since she was a child, Gyeong-hui's mission is to expose Aroun as a Korean spy. Gyeong-hui attempts this by offering him an escape route to North Gando. Her primary narrative function, however, is to distract Aroun from Hideko, therefore proving to the Japanese heroine that he, and other Korean men, are untrustworthy. The script therefore splits the loyalties of the South Korean audience and challenges their expectations as it asks them to compare the Japanese woman to a Korean woman. Given that the South Korean audience would typically expect a Korean hero to marry a Korean woman, the narrative's placement of Gyeong-hui confounds expectations by revealing her to be deceitful and therefore unworthy of Aroun's attention. That Gyeong-hui is to be compared to Hideko is evidenced by the way Aroun takes her to the same teahouse that he visited with Hideko after the cinema. The comparison is further forced by Aroun's naive decision to take Gyeong-hui to Hideko's house. This visit creates a rift between himself and his Japanese girlfriend. This rift is visually demonstrated by the fact that, while Hideko's mother and Aroun cheerfully host Gyeong-hui in the lightness of the living room area, the disgruntled Hideko is confined to the darkened kitchen. While Hideko misconstrues the nature of Aroun's relationship with Gyeong-hui, the misunderstanding is not hers alone. With some relief, Hideko's mother also assumes that Aroun has a romantic history with Gyeong-hui and that the "natural order" has been restored, making her Japanese daughter, and therefore Japan, safe from miscegenation. That relief is short lived as Aroun leaves the house to sleep alone in a hotel rather than taking Gyeong-hui with him.

A final comparison is made after Aroun has departed. Gyeong-hui warns Hideko about marrying Aroun because they are from different nations. In reply, Hideko proudly states that their child would transcend such divisions. Confident that her love is purer than her rival's, Hideko pushes the conversation further as she theorizes that Aroun must be lonely at the inn by himself. Rather primly, Gyeong-hui declares that following a man to an inn is not something an educated lady would do. Hideko replies that "education always requires sacrifice" and announces her departure.

In the pages of the shooting script, the descriptive text at the end of the scene says: "Hideko leaves the room." Notably, in the available print, this scene cuts directly from the two rivals sitting on the bed to the image of four American planes under attack with the sound of Japanese artillery fire. Accordingly, the described action of Hideko leaving the room is omitted. Due to the lack of sound, it cannot be confirmed whether or not Kim filmed the discussion between Hideko and Gyeong-hui exactly as it is written. However, as this published shooting script is the best existing record of Kim's intention for this scene, it can be concluded that Hideko does join Aroun at the inn after this scene, even though her departure is not portrayed. Furthermore, unsuccessful in her mission to be a wedge between the film's central couple and thus defeated in both love and war, Gyeong-hui then disappears from the narrative completely. The next section of the film concerns another attempt by Miyamoto to frame Aroun as a Korean spy. This sub-plot means that Hideko also disappears for approximately twenty minutes—her longest absence on the screen after her initial introduction sixteen minutes into the film. Hideko's return moves the narrative into its final act. Aroun, via his fellow soldier, Suzuki, receives word that Hideko is pregnant. I deduce that the sexual consummation of the couple's relationship takes place when Hideko leaves Gyeong-hui behind to join Aroun at the inn, and the unspecified diegetic period that has elapsed is sufficient to suggest that Hideko's pregnancy has had time to develop.[44]

For contemporary viewers, the timing of Aroun's notification of Hideko's pregnancy is indeed fortuitous, as it is immediately after this announcement that damage to the original print again causes the soundtrack to cease operating. Again, consultation with the published shooting script reveals valuable information. As can be deduced from viewing the soundless footage, Hideko's mother places the news of an expected grandchild above her prejudices against Koreans and finally blesses Aroun and Hideko's union. This is confirmed by the mother's dialogue in the shooting script: "Better to live as a coward than die. Run. Follow your husband, to the end of the world. Let the world know that a Japanese girl never betrays her husband." This sudden switch in view by Hideko's mother is an odd, albeit convenient, twist for the narrative that is nevertheless consistent with Japanese patriarchy. However, as the film clearly supports the interracial romance, the mother's patriarchal outpouring is presumably also intended to be compatible with the beliefs of the film's South Korean audience. Secondly, and what cannot be deduced from the images alone, is that while both Aroun and Hideko agree that Japan will lose the war, it is Hideko who insists that running away from Japanese authorities will be their best action. By contrast, Aroun, if only for Hideko's approval, remains loyal to the military, saying: "I still want to be a great Japanese soldier for Hideko-san." This exchange places a 1960s South Korean audience—as well as contemporary audiences—in a bind, as it sympathetically depicts a Korean declaring loyalty to the Japanese Army. Furthermore, any audience desire to see the relationship continue happily also places them in alignment with the opinions of the film's Japanese women. This is later reinforced after the pair—with some assistance from Inoue—manage to hide from the Japanese Army and particularly from the cruel Miyamoto. Outraged by Hideko's pregnancy and determined to kill Aroun, Miyamoto represents the argument against co-operation between Japan and (South) Korea.

If the film is regarded as having either entertainment or dramatic value, let alone political value, Aroun's relationship with Hideko, stemming from shared intellectual passions and ripening through the gradual progression of their sexual union, suggests that the people of the two nations have more in common than those who oppose co-operation. This differs from the Greater East Asian Co-Prosperity Sphere propagated by Imperialist Japan in that Hideko and Aroun are proposed to be "equal" partners, rather than a hierarchy with Japan placed at the crest. South Korean discomfort with bilateral co-operation is suggested by other films which examine Korean–Japanese intimacy that block the couple's happiness. In contrast, *The Sea Knows*' emphasis on commonality (albeit unresolved) between the Korean and Japanese, suggests the universality of all people's experiences, and is an important aspect of the film's unforgettable final sequence.

The equanimity with which the film treats Hideko and Japanese culture generally suggests that the director regards the benefits of co-operating with Japan as transcending any threat from Japan. Nevertheless, the film does not romanticize the former colonizers. Once Hideko's mother (implausibly) accepts Aroun and Hideko's union, the remaining obstacles to the relationship always take masculine, notably military form. Even with the elimination of Miyamoto, Aroun still faces a threat in the form of a Japanese soldier who attempts to strangle him as they both seek shelter from American bombs. This desperate attempt by the Japanese soldier leaves audiences without any doubt as to the pervasiveness of Japanese villainy, but the climax that follows speaks more eloquently to a wider anti-war sentiment.

In the film's final sequence, bodies, including Aroun, are loaded onto trucks for eventual cremation. Hideko is amongst the crowd of mostly women looking to reclaim the bodies of relatives, many of whom appear to be soldiers. Emphasizing government security, Japanese military authorities prevent the mourners from accessing the corpses and implore them to keep the deaths secret to protect national morale. Thus, once again, the obstacle to Hideko and Aroun's union is male, uniformed, and zealously militarized.

That the lovers are ultimately reunited, after Aroun arises out the crematory pile of bodies, could reinforce Taylor-Jones's reading of the film's romance as a reclaiming of "a masculinity lost in the colonial moment."[45] However, the emotional impact of the film's ending, with its equal emphasis on Hideko, suggests that Kim's intentions go beyond this. Yecies and Shim write that South Korean film audiences of the early 1960s were predominantly women, often dismissed by theatre owners as the "rubber shoe brigade (*gomusin gwangaek*)" due to the footwear left behind after screenings.[46] In addition, if the anecdotes of female audiences yelling out "Kill the bitch" during the screenings of *The Housemaid* are anything to go by, these women were not passive consumers of the films they watched.[47] Different audiences overlap, and this encourages multiple readings. Thus, I prefer to embrace *The Sea Knows*' romance, and based on the previously described elements of the film, presume that the director anticipated a sympathetic reception to the love story on the part of his audience.

While diegetically all of the film's action takes place in Japan, the then-recent Korean national experience is a valuable prism to assess this final sequence. Klein writes of a "culture of despair" as evidenced by *Aimless Bullet* and other South Korean films of the era.[48] Such despair was fueled by the strong and recent memory of the Korean War and disillusionment with the Rhee government who had welcomed the ideologically driven conflict and subsequently also saw reclaiming the peninsula's North as the only way forward to circumnavigate engagement with Japan. This was not helped by the fact that once the Korean War was over, many of the freedoms that Rhee had promised failed to materialize. With police and government at Rhee's command and a weak, disorganized opposition, until the student protests occurred, "the cloak of democracy obscured the reality of autocracy", as sociologist John Lie puts it."[49] While South Koreans were still wary of Japan, many of Seoul's urban audiences also held no illusions about the postcolonial period, as overseen by Rhee.

The final sequence of *The Sea Knows* dramatizes the collapse of Japanese authority, but echoes of the recent breakdown of the corrupt Rhee government would have also been clear to contemporary audiences. Just as Koreans experienced substantial censorship under Japanese rule, the Rhee era continued to constrain South Korean life. The most obvious of these restrictions in terms of this discussion of *The Sea Knows* was the suppression of Japanese representation in South Korean cinema. However, the understanding of these government restrictions can be extended from Rhee's heavy-handed use of police forces to frame all threats as "Communist," to the fraudulent result of the 1960 election. In addition, although *The Sea Knows* focuses on the Pacific War, this final sequence also encouraged a moment of reflection on the considerable death toll of the more recent war experienced by Koreans. Furthermore, while Korean soldiers were sent to the Manchurian front and other Japanese battlefields such as the Philippines, Korea itself as an occupied colony, was not a part of World War II's theatre of war. Given this, I argue that the film's climax, with its piles of corpses, anguished Japanese women, and its accompanying anti-war sentiment would have resonance for the era's audiences, particularly female audiences, in terms of their more recent wartime experiences, rather than as a reflection of Japanese Occupation. Moreover, by this stage of the narrative the South Korean audience's identification with the couple, including Hideko, is complete and consideration of the heroine's Japanese-ness will have dropped away. Thus the scene echoes South Koreans' more recent experience of the dead and wounded of the Korean War. Hideko's recognition of Aroun as rising from the dead amplifies the hope amongst the other (Japanese) women that their family members may have also survived. While the South Korean public's support for anti-war sentiment did not flourish until disillusionment with Park's militarist project arose in the early 1970s,[50] I argue that the parallels between the climax of *The Sea Knows* and South Korea's experience of civil war are too important to ignore.

That Kim also saw hope in the alliance between South Korea and Japan is evident by the way the romance's final moments play out in the film's visually powerful ending. The images of corpses being burned while women and children scream as they helplessly observe would be a fitting representation of postwar trauma and the despairing times to which Klein alludes. However, the extraordinary moment where Aroun, having been revived by the splashing of gasoline, rises from the pile of corpses refutes such despair. Although Aroun is like the living dead, his resurrection energizes not just Hideko, but the women, men, and children around her to push over a barbwire barricade. Running with the crowd, Hideko reaches and then passionately embraces the barely alive Aroun, before the film cuts to a wide shot as the crowd swarms around the pyre of burning corpses. The reunited couple take up a small portion of the screen dominated by trauma (Figure 3.3). Of all the pictured, only Aroun supported by Hideko has survived. Although not a joyous ending, their reunion offers a thin sliver of hope.

Figure 3.3 Aroun and Hideko (far left) leave the horror of (Japanese) war behind them.

On a surface level, Japan is destroyed and the military is a shambles, but symbolically, Korea, like Aroun, will rise from the ashes of war. As survivors of the Korean War, contemporary audiences would be prompted to wish for or recall similar reunions with loved ones separated from them by the peninsula's internal conflict and subsequent division. With the memory of the Korean War so fresh in the minds of the South Korean populace, Hideko and Aroun's reunion is also a call for Koreans to rise against the trauma of the more immediate past. The film's audience are left to conclude that such scenes must not be allowed to happen again, whether caused by Japanese or Koreans. Thus Hideko's earlier statement, "I'm not Japan," comes back with a greater significance. The identification with the former enemy is a powerful moment in a national cinema. However, it is an experience that the South Korean film industry and its audiences have been reluctant to revisit. The film's astonishing finale deserves to be recalled as an example of Kim's remarkable ability to create an atmosphere but also has resonance beyond mere drama. *The Sea Knows* speaks to South Korea's still unresolved conflict with Japan. For now, Kim's film still remains on the wrong side of history, but if Japan and South Korea are ever able to come to equal terms over the "comfort women" issue and the Dokdo/Takeshima territorial issues, then *The Sea Knows* may eventually be redeemed in the eyes of South Korean audiences.

NOTES

1. Chris Berry, "Introducing 'Mr. Monster': Kim Ki-young and the Critical Economy of the Globalized Art-House Cinema" in Korean Film Festival Committee ed., *Post-Colonial Classics of Korean Cinema* (Irvine: Korean Film Festival Committee at the University of California, 1998), 39–47.
2. Jinsoo An, *Parameters of Disavowal: Colonial Representation in South Korean Cinema* (Oakland: University of California Press, 2018), 36.
3. Jinhee Choi, *The South Korean Film Renaissance: Local Hitmakers/Global Provocateurs* (Middletown: Wesleyan University Press, 2010), 64–5.
4. Yi Hee-seung Irene, "Remembering to Reset: Representations of the Colonial Era in Recent Korean Films," in *Popular Culture and the Transformation of Japan-Korea Relations*, ed. Stephen Epstein and Rumi Sakamoto (London: Taylor & Francis, 2020), 63–77.
5. Russell Edwards, "The Dictator's Daughter and the Rising Sun: Scars of Colonialism in South Korean Cinema During the Park Geun Hye Era," in *The Two Koreas and their Global Engagement*, ed. Andrew Jackson (London: Palgrave MacMillan, 2022).
6. Timothy Martin and Kim Na-young, "Snapshot of a South Korean Boycott: 'This Mart Doesn't Sell Japanese Products!'" *Wall Street Journal* (July 18, 2019). https://www.wsj.com/articles/boycott-of-everything-japanese-mushrooms-across-south-korea-11563461208.
7. Frances Gateward, "Waiting to Exhale: The Colonial Experience and the Trouble with My Own Breathing," in *Seoul Searching: Culture and Identity in Contemporary Korean Cinema*, ed. Frances Gateward (New York: State University of New York Press, 2007), 207–8.

8. Krista E. Wiegand, "The South Korean-Japanese Security Relationship and the Dokdo/Takeshima Islets Dispute," *Pacific Review* 28, no. 3 (2015): 347–66. https://www.tandfonline.com/doi/abs/10.1080/09512748.2015.1011209.
9. Yi Yeon-ho, "Introduction," in *Kim Ki-young*, ed. Hong-joon Kim (Seoul: Korean Film Council, 2006), 6.
10. Ibid., 6.
11. Ibid., 7.
12. Yi Hyo-in, "Biography," in *Kim Ki-young*, ed. Kim, 102.
13. Ibid., 101. On this topic see also: Kim Su Yun, "Transwar Continuities of Colonial Intimacy: Korean-Japanese Relationships in Korean Cinema, 1940s–1960s," *Asian Studies Review* 40, no. 1 (2020): 400–19. She cites ticket sales for *The Sea Knows* as reaching 100,000 in the first month of screening in Seoul, with the total number of tickets sold nationwide calculated to be somewhere between 250,000 and 300,000. As ticket sales last century usually remained uncounted outside of Seoul, this is at best an educated guess.
14. Yi, "Introduction," 21.
15. Yi, "Biography," 101.
16. Kim Ki-young, "Eleven Best Films," in *Kim Ki-young*, ed. Kim.
17. While he is not referred to by name in the film, Kim's shooting script refers to this soldier as Miyamoto. To prevent confusion this is the name I will use to refer to this character.
18. Yi, "Introduction," 18.
19. Van Jackson, "Getting Past the Past: Korea's Transcendence of the Anti-Japan Policy Frontier," *Asian Security* 7, no. 3 (2011): 252.
20. John Lie, "Aid Dependence and the Structure of Corruption: The Case of Post-Korean War South Korea," *International Journal of Sociology and Social Policy* 17, no. 11/12 (1997): 48–89.
21. Jackson, "Getting Past the Past," 238–59.
22. Ibid., 252–3.
23. An, "Parameters of Disavowal," 36.
24. Ibid., 42.
25. Yi, "Biography," 96.
26. Catherine Russell, *Classical Japanese Cinema Revisited* (New York: Continuum, 2011), 133–48.
27. An, "Parameters of Disavowal," 42, 150.
28. Ibid., 36–9, 42–3.
29. Ibid., 163.
30. Takashi Fujitani, *Race for Empire: Koreans as Japanese and Japanese as Americans During World War II* (Berkeley: University of California Press, 2011), 356–62.
31. Kim, "Transwar," 403–6.
32. Ibid., 402, 413.
33. Ibid., 402, 410–12.
34. Ibid., 411–12.
35. Other recent films suggesting Korean-Japanese romance include: *Asako in Ruby Shoes* (*Sunaebo*, E. J. Yong, 2000), which depicts a Korean council worker's online obsession with a Japanese sex worker he discovers on a website; *Dongju: Portrait of a Poet* (*Dongju*, Yi Junik, 2016), which hints at an unfulfilled romance between Yun Dong-ju and his fellow student Gumi; *Spirits' Homecoming* (*Gwihayng*, Cho Jeongnae, 2017) atypically suggests a romance between a Korean woman and a Japanese male when a "comfort woman" is scolded by one of her colleagues for being "sweet on" a Japanese soldier who guards them. Additionally, *Anarchist from Colony* not only portrays the central romance between Korean poet Bak Yeol and his Japanese lover, Kaneko Fumiko, but their anarchist circle

also includes another interethnic couple. It is a negative example as the Japanese woman, Hasuyo, is mentally disturbed, untrustworthy, and is arguably responsibly for Bak and Kaneko's arrest by Japanese authorities.

36. Non-Korean speakers will be confused by the Korean Film Archive subtitles that indicate that Hideko's mother is Nakamura's aunt. An alternate translation of their introduction has Nakamura suggesting that Aroun can consider the woman as "his" aunt. She is actually Nakamura's sister. I thank Song Won-jeong for her translation and clarifications of familial Korean terminology.
37. Kate Taylor-Jones, *Divine Work, Japanese Colonial Cinema and its Legacy* (New York: Bloomsbury Academic, 2017), 140.
38. Kim, "Transwar," 413.
39. Fujitani, "Race for Empire," 337.
40. Yi, "Biography," 101.
41. The Korean Film Archive's Youtube video is too dark to easily discern the film's actions or its origins. The film appears too authentic to be a facsimile of a Japanese film that Kim shot himself. However, even in the freedom of the post-Rhee era, the inclusion of footage from an actual Japanese film is a daring skirting of established restrictions. Whatever the origins of this "film within a film," this scene is an early expression of South Korean cinemania. *The Sea Knows*, YouTube video, 1:48:37. Posted by Korean Classic Film Channel, May 1, 2012. https://www.youtube.com/watch?v=esLWhJhrHP0.
42. The sound drops out for around four minutes at the one-hour mark. The soundtrack drops away again at the eighty-three-minute mark and the film remains silent for a further six minutes.
43. Kim Ki-young, *Kim Ki-young Screenplay Collection II [Kim Ki-young Sinario Seonjib]* (Seoul: Korean Film Archive, 2008). English versions of this shooting script dialogue appears in the Appendix. I thank Song Won-jeong for her translations.
44. The other possibility for Hideko's impregnation is the earlier meeting that is punctuated by the erotic image of Hideko's legs crossing at the ankles. The subsequent cut to Aroun's fellow soldiers waiting outside in the truck could represent a temporal lapse. However, given the continuity of sound overlapping the cut, and a return cut inside which reveals Hideko and Aroun have not changed position, this is unlikely.
45. Taylor-Jones, "Divine," 140.
46. Brian Yecies and Aegyung Shim, *The Changing Face of Korean Cinema: 1960 to 2015* (New York: Routledge, 2016), 143.
47. Kim Soyoung, "Questions of Woman's Film: The Maid, Madame Freedom and Women," in *South Korean Golden Age Melodrama: Gender, Genre, and National Cinema*, ed. Kathleen McHugh and Nancy Abelmann (Detroit: Wayne State University Press, 2005), 185–200, 191.
48. Christina Klein, *Cold War Cosmopolitanism* (California: University of California Press, 2020), 81.
49. Lie, "Aid Dependence and the Structure of Corruption," 71.
50. Kim Dong Choon, "The Great Upsurge of South Korea's Social Movements in the 1960s," *Inter-Asia Cultural Studies* 7 no. 4 (2006): 619–33. https://www.tandfonline.com/doi/abs/10.1080/14649370600983071.

PART 2

Beyond the Norm: Psychology, Biopolitics and Sexuality

CHAPTER 4

Refiguring *The Housemaid*'s Singularity: From Dualism to Triadism Based on the Lacanian Perspective

Kim Sohyoun

INTRODUCTION: AN AUTEURIST MASTERPIECE AND ITS DISCONTENT

No one would deny that *The Housemaid* (*Hanyeo*, 1960) is Kim Ki-young's most celebrated film. It was the first film in the Housemaid series, and its story concerned a happy family whose life was shattered following the adultery between the husband and a newly hired housemaid, and the subsequent revenge of the housemaid.[1] When released, it was a box-office hit. Nonetheless, a few critics were cynical about its artistic value: the lack of sophistication,[2] the over-grotesqueness, and its theatrical style[3] were all indicated as problematic elements. When *The Housemaid* was shortlisted as one of five Korean films for potential inclusion in the 8th Asian Film Festival, the jurors were reluctant to include it. The reason that it was finally chosen was that the other four films shortlisted didn't depict modern urban life, and that *The Housemaid*'s unique cinematography was recognized.[4]

The underestimation of *The Housemaid* was connected to the inclination of Korean film criticism since the colonial era, which had sought to establish a genealogy of "Korean nationalist and realist cinema"[5] and disparage commercial genre movies. It is well known that Yi Yeong-il, the most influential film critic as well as a film historian in the 1960s and 1970s, categorized *The Housemaid* as a "psychological thriller"[6] and excluded it from his list of "post-April Revolution masterpieces."[7] However, unexpectedly, *The Housemaid* attracted great attention and praise from the Asian cinephiles at the Asian Film Festival (1961).[8] Probably because of this international attention, Kim could win two domestic awards for best director, afterwards.

It was in the early 1990s that *The Housemaid* was rediscovered as a cult masterpiece. The new generation in the Korean film industry around the late 1980s was influenced by the spirit of the Gwangju Democratization Movement in 1980 and the student-led democratizing movement in 1987 against the military dictatorship. The obsession with a realist and anti-Hollywood orientation was very intense for the first generation of newcomers, including Park Kwang-su and Jang Sun-Woo, who were committed to the independent cinema movement against the military dictatorship. However, the second new generation, including Park Chan-wook and Bong Joon Ho, were different from the earlier newcomers. They did not hesitate to use genre conventions in their films to embrace the social and political issues in South Korea. They have stated that they were deeply inspired by Kim Ki-young's films, especially by *The Housemaid*.[9]

The Housemaid was introduced into the pantheon of Korean film history as an outstanding expressionist film, not a realist film, and Kim Ki-young was almost the only Korean filmmaker referred to in terms of cinematic expressionism until the 1990s. However, in an interview with Yi Hyo-in, Kim Ki-young said that "it would be more appropriate to categorize it as 'psychologicalist (*simnijuui*)' rather than expressionist."[10] He confessed that he was enthralled by Freud when making *The Housemaid*. That might be why he dared to coin the new term "psychologicalism." Presumably, he wanted to be remembered not as an expressionist stylist, but as an artist dealing with the profound inner world of the human psyche. In this sense, unlike other auteurs of his period, a focus on illicit love affairs was a common subject matter in his Housemaid series. Nonetheless, he also emphasized that *The Housemaid* reflected the reality of the period.[11] The script was inspired by the *Geumcheon* case involving a murder committed by a housemaid. At that time there were lots of young women coming to Seoul who ended up working as prostitutes, housemaids, or bus attendants since there were not enough jobs for uneducated young women.

Today, *The Housemaid* is admired as an allegorical text that reveals the complicated desire and antagonism that existed in Korean society as it took its path toward modernization, or westernization, after the Korean War (1950–3). The complex dynamics between the characters have been read as epitomizing various reactions to modernization. Most criticisms have been propped up by the logic of binary opposition between the male protagonist's happy family pursuing the virtues of modernity and the housemaid as a femme fatal undermining the family's promising future. The housemaid, an incarnation of monstrous impulse and dangerous pleasure, has been interpreted as an implicit threat of Korean premodernity, or "the residual"[12] of such, to the masculine order of modernity.[13] In that sense, *The Housemaid* seemed to offer an arena of competition between modernity and premodernity, the masculine and the feminine, employers and employees, and love and lust.

However, the binary approach to this arena misses something intuitive and original in *The Housemaid*. Here I will use the logic of triad to analyze the film in terms of the topological states within, drawing upon Jacques Lacan's theory of psychoanalysis and his three orders of ontology: the imaginary, the symbolic, and the real. The symbolic, whose effect structures the imaginary, is always already undermined by the ambiguity of the real, which cannot be integrated into the symbolic. To apply Lacan's triad, *The Housemaid* can be read as an arena of the struggle between premodernity, modernity, and X. In short, it is not premodernity but an unknown and undefinable X in modernity that drags modernity toward the ultimate crisis.

The film is full of tripartite relationships. I will first analyze the narrative structure by focusing on the difference between reality and dream. Then I will investigate how the gaze works relative to the topological relationship between the rats, the housemaid, the family members, and the other characters around the family. In addition, I will scrutinize many objects and details such as trains, cigarettes, fabric patterns, and walls, along with the protagonist's house itself, from a triadic viewpoint. From this starting point, I will explore how *The Housemaid* acutely detects notions of masculine desire and anxiety, especially in the post-April Revolution period in South Korea.

THE TRIPLE LAYERS OF NARRATIVE CONNECTING FICTION AND REALITY

In *The Housemaid*, a direct trace of Freud appears in the wife's nightmare after moving to a new house. To interpret this ominous scene, it is necessary to recall the previous day. On that day Gyeong-hui, a factory worker and a student of Dong-sik, the husband, first brings the housemaid-to-be to Dong-sik, when the family is eating curried rice on western-style plates. The menu, the fact that the husband cooks for the family, and the western dinner service would have all been considered as exceptional in the 1960s. After the housemaid beats a rat to death in the kitchen, Dong-sik asks her to poison them from now on. Then, the maid makes a trap with "the yellow rice" sprayed with rat poison. At the end of the fuss, Gyeong-hui goes upstairs to take her piano lesson from Dong-sik, a music teacher for the female workers in a textile factory, and the maid starts spying on them, savoring the smell of cigarette smoke left behind by Dong-sik. Suddenly, with music abruptly breaking the atmosphere, a shot of two rats dead and overturned on the plate follows. Is the plate the same one that the housemaid set in the kitchen? The next shot shows the wife in bed; she screams and sits up. Dong-sik wakes up to this sound and hears that she had a "bad dream" about these poisoned rats having human faces.

This scene connecting reality and dream leads us to think of the narrative structure of the whole film. In short, *The Housemaid* consists of three layers of fiction, or fictional reality. The first layer is the wife's dream as described above. The second is the main part of the story about adultery, and the third is the epilogue, which reveals that the main body of the story was simply an outpouring of the husband's wild imagination after reading a newspaper article about a *crime passionel*. In fact, spectators are not informed that the first scene in the piano room is the same situation as the last scene until the last scene ends. There is a temporal interval between the first scene where Dong-sik's family first appears and the second scene at the textile factory. Perhaps here, Kim Ki-young might have wanted to resolve the existing story already filmed and edited to make it imaginary. As a result, the entire narrative is structured like an onion, in such a way that the first layer is wrapped by the second and the second by the third. As the layers are unpacked from the first to the last, the intimacy and severity of the adultery story becomes more and more diluted until there is nothing. Such a narrative structure is called a frame narrative. However, as the film has three layers of story frame, it is more complicated to distinguish between what is reality and what is fantasy. Following plain common sense, only the third situation is reality, whereas the second is an embedded fantasy in the frame of the third as reality, and the first is an embedded fantasy in the frame of the second as fantasy. This structure of frames results in the binary opposition of reality and fantasy.

However, let me twist the argument a little with Lacan, who divides the real from reality. In Lacan's terms, reality is the symbolic, that is, the symbolic order or the symbolic function, and the symbolization (socialization) of human beings is structured with language and dominated by law. However, the symbolic always accompanies its lack or excess, which Lacan conceptualized as the real, "undifferentiated," "outside language," and beyond the symbolic.[14] The relationship between the real and reality is antinomic because the real is at the level of unconsciousness and reality is at the level of consciousness. Nonetheless, the symbolic and the real are not only separated but also continuous, like a Moebius strip. Just as one cannot dream while conscious, the real, the kernel amid reality, must be masked for reality to work. In other words, what is considered as reality is not an objective world but a subjective and imagined fantasy because reality can be constructed only by masking, or suturing, the real. Thus, reality is not the locus of truth, but the real is what leads us to the unconscious truth. In that sense, Lacan explains that "the fictitious is precisely what I call the symbolic."[15] Here, the fictitiousness refers to the topological character of reality, which is defined as the imaginary. Lacan's triad of the symbolic, the real, and the imaginary is related as such.

The real exists only as the failure of reality. When the fissure of reality is open, the real intrudes into reality. The antagonism between classes, genders, nations, or ethnic groups, in short, anything foreclosed and repressed in society, could be exposed by accidental events, namely the social noise. As is well-known, Freud has already made a similar argument that jokes, dreams, parapraxis, and symptoms generated by the intervention of repressed unconscious ideas can disturb seemingly natural psychic processes and reveal the existence of unconscious truth. Lacan, while elaborating the ideas of Freud, claims that "just as it is from Speech that Truth receives the mark that instates it in a fictional structure."[16] It is noteworthy that truth is structured like fiction. When Lacan explains that it is when *Choangtsu* was the butterfly that he apprehended his identity and *Choangtsu* is *Choangtsu* because of this,[17] he means that the essence of existence lies in the dream, that is, at the level of the real. From this point of view, like dreams, films could be one of the most effective media to stage the real in the guise of a fiction far more excessive, far beyond realistic probability, or verisimilitude.

This Lacanian perspective makes the relationship between reality and fantasy in *The Housemaid* more intertwined. The narrative of this film is not, as is often said, a structure in which the prologue and epilogue as reality cover the imagined middle part, but rather a structure in which the prologue and epilogue as fictitious reality conceal the middle part as the real. Besides, the middle part itself is divided again into the wife's dream and the reality outside her dream. Therefore, applying the Lacanian theory of topology, the narrative structure of the film seems quite complex. From the perspective of the middle part about the affair, the wife's dream touches the level of the real which leaks the truth concealed in her unconsciousness, while from the perspective of the prologue and epilogue, the middle part shows the real, that is, Dong-sik's unconscious desire, within the whole story. Without the wife's dream scene, one may say that the prologue and epilogue become the surface of a Moebius strip, and the middle part becomes the back of it. However, the middle part must be doubled: one as the reality containing the wife's dream and the other as the real masked by the epilogue where Dong-sik's jokes and laughter rather confirm that the middle part is the stage for the real of his desire.

Furthermore, the entire film itself as a fictional world on the screen is at the level of the real addressing the unconscious desire of the spectators, when thinking in connection with the audience's reality. Ultimately, what penetrates the whole structure of the layered dreams, or fantasies, is the spectators' intimate desire which oscillates between the law and enjoyment. Insofar as the intimacy of their desire is out there fully revealed on the screen, it is the extimate (*extimité*) desire, as Lacan puts it.[18] In that sense, *The Housemaid* is an extimate desire of the audience, and the imagined adultery story is an extimate desire of the husband, and the wife's dream is her extimate desire. The pleasure and displeasure of seeing *The Housemaid* all springs up from this extimacy. Then, what about turning the direction outwards? One may dare to make a wild guess that *The Housemaid* could be entirely an extimate desire of the rats, on condition that they could think and imagine with language. However, rats do not speak; therefore, they are not split between the enunciated and enunciation or consciousness and unconsciousness. After all, one can say that there is only a void at the innermost kernel of the three-layered fictional structure.

THE ONTOLOGY OF RATS AS THE SUBJECT OF GAZE

In *The Housemaid*, rats are not simply the means for a surprising effect. They are essential to constitute the narrative in a triadic logic. Before explaining the metaphorical meaning of domestic rats, it is necessary to consider that there are three kinds of rats in the film: living ones, dead ones, and the squirrel that Dong-sik bought for his children. In Korean, rats are *jwi* and squirrels *daramjwi*, which means that squirrels are treated as a kind of rat, no matter how cute and adorable. Earlier I argued that the rats' topological property is at the level of the real. To be more precise, rats at the level of the real are only living rats whose location, numbers, and whereabouts are unknowable and untraceable. Once they are captured and killed, in other words, their existence is signified in the symbolic, their topological position connected to the real is symbolized.

What is desired in the family's fantasy is the squirrel in contrast to rats. But paradoxically, the squirrel is locked up in the cage. No matter how hard the squirrel spins the treadmill in the cage, its activity is from zero to zero. Compared to the rats dead on a plate, the only thing the squirrel enjoys is at least being alive. This metaphor reflects a pessimistic view on modern life. After all, the film carries out a double critique through the metaphor of a triad of rats. There is nowhere to go for the people imprisoned in modern society, and the seemingly sturdy society-like-prison is always already threatened by something against which people's fantasies ultimately fail. That something in *The Housemaid* is rats that ruin the fantasy of a sweet home in a new western style two-story house.

Here, one needs to address the wife's dream scene. The ending image in the dream creates an immediate question: when it comes to the human faces of the rats, whose faces do they stand for? Incomprehensibly, the wife's curiosity does not go further. She dismisses her nightmare as a silly dream and Dong-sik also does not care about such details. Instead, Dong-sik recalls the old and poor days of his family in rented houses. After watching the movie to the end, the viewer may be able to guess what her nightmare connotes. Could the two rats be Gyeong-hui and the housemaid? Throughout the film, the wife hardly goes out of the house, while Gyeong-hui and the housemaid come from somewhere outside. The two women should have been taken as a threat to the wife who has managed her household by carrying on her sewing work to earn money, even to the extent of wishing for them to die. Or maybe the two rats could be the housemaid and Dong-sik. The wife may have thought that both of them deserved to die if they were having an affair. However, the wife's anxiety subsides as she has a conversation with Dong-sik about their hopeful plan of "having one more son and getting all the children to go to college." How naive is her new dream?

The ontological status of rats is well expressed in the economy of eye-line matches. Throughout the film, the character who takes the lead in the economy of exchanging glances is the housemaid. She is the master of voyeurism: the "eyes" shown in close-up in this film are always the housemaid's, and everyone in the house is the target of her peeping. In terms of the power hierarchy, she is at the bottom. She must run errands, even for the children. However, in terms of the power of vision, she is at the top. She dominates the space in the house, wandering upstairs and downstairs as the omnipresent master of looks. Before starting her sexual relationship with Dong-sik, she spies on Gyeong-hui and Dong-sik having a piano lesson. Then, after she has had sexual relations with Dong-sik, she bursts open the main room and disturbs the intimate moments of the married couple, casting her jealous eyes over the pair. This is how Kim Ki-young denounces the blindness of a bourgeois family. The married couple and their children cannot see the otherness of the housemaid. Only the housemaid, free from the oppression of desire, can open her eyes and see all the scenes in the house.

However, the housemaid is not the only one afforded a voyeur's perspective. Ultimately, it is rats that watch everything going on in this house. The camera is placed inside the kitchen cupboard to show the wife or the housemaid opening the cupboard door. The shots showing their faces looking inside the cupboard are assumed to be objective shots at first glance. Of course, such a direction of filming is possible because it is filmed on a set. Even so, the direction from the inside of the cupboard looking outward gives an awkward impression. If it were a real house, no one could look out from the narrow cupboard. Then, when a rat suddenly jumps out of the cupboard, spectators finally realize that the strange direction of the previous shot is designed as a subjective shot from the rat's point of view.

Still, it is hard to know exactly where the rats are from and what the rats look at. In other words, the rat's watching is not at the level of a conscious look that can be attributed to a specific viewpoint, but at the level of unconscious gaze that cannot be captured from any viewpoint, following Lacan's theory of the look and the gaze.[19] Imagine that rats, being in an asymmetric relationship with humans, are watching everything and everyone in the western-style two-story house, anytime and anywhere. Does it feel uncanny to see the house? In that sense, what brings the profound anxiety and fear is not the presence of the housemaid but of the rats, because the housemaid can finally be controlled and repressed, while the rats remain always unwelcome, and still ultimately appear to torment all the human inhabitants of the space, including the housemaid.

Kim Ki-young said that he paid attention to the motif of rats because they are animals with a strong "reproductive instinct" and always live near people's residences.[20] What makes rats essentially a collective object of human fear is their fertility and vitality. They cannot be eradicated. No matter how many are repressed and killed, they still appear and intrude into reality to reveal the unconscious truth. In the narrative of *The Housemaid*, rats are an unknowable X beyond symbolization or the Thing in the register of the real. The housemaid's and rats' peeking create an antinomic structure of conscious look and unconscious gaze together like a Mobius strip. Nonetheless, the dynamic for sublimating *The Housemaid* into a grotesque thriller comes ultimately from the narrative premise that rats are watching from somewhere and their perspective cannot be traced.

In terms of infiltrating the new house, the status of rats is projected onto the housemaid. Kim Ho-yeong argues that rats and the housemaid have something in common in the sense that they share the same space in the house, the kitchen, and they are terrifying beings who make (physical or psychological) holes in the modern house.[21] Pak U-seong also supports this view by analyzing the film's mise-en-scène and asserts that the entrance into a frame of the rats and the housemaid as a "rat woman" is similarly directed to trigger a fear reaction from spectators.[22] From that viewpoint, the film could be understood as a dichotomy between the married couple and the housemaid and rats. The former leads an institutionalized life through marriage or profession, whereas the latter lives outside the systems of economy, education (piano lesson), or marriage. The housemaid, who is not qualified to be a factory laborer,[23] is hired for a family without any legal contract. Like rats sneaking into the kitchen, she is an alien to the family. However, this distinction does not explain why the housemaid antagonizes the rats. To elucidate this, we need to take account of the ontological status of the housemaid and rats. It is time to break away from dualism and to adopt triadism.

Let us think about the three groups: the married couple, the housemaid, and the rats. Since the housemaid is out of the family and economic system, she contrasts with the married couple. She fights for what the married couple has and enjoys, but she fails. The film seems to celebrate the victory of modernity. Just as Dong-sik's family succeeds in suppressing their intimate and clandestine desire while continuing an imagined happy life, so will a nation state, South Korea, prosper. However, the victory can be desecrated, just as rats can contaminate the modern kitchen at any time. To put this in Lacan's terms, the couple's way of life meets the housemaid's standards of the imaginary, but rats are disgusting enough to be foreclosed as the real. Meanwhile, from the couple's position, the upper-middle class way of life they pursue satisfies the imaginary criteria of their future life, but the housemaid and rats are to be distanced because of their uncanniness as the real.

Lacan's theory of sexuation explains the difference between the masculine subject and the feminine subject depending on the relationship with the phallic function. The former, whose formulae are "for all x, the phallic function is valid ($\exists x\, \Phi\underline{x}$)" and "there is at least one x which is not submitted to the phallic function ($\forall x\, \Phi x$),"[24] believes the possibility of "the one-less of the exception"[25] subtracted from the set of all. The set is a closed universe where the universality and the exception complete the totality. The latter, whose formulae are "there is not one x which is not submitted to the phallic function ($\underline{\exists x}\, \Phi\underline{x}$)" and "for not all x, the phallic function is valid ($\underline{\forall x}\, \Phi x$)," believes the possibility of "the immanence of the exception"[26] turning "all" into "not-all." The set is an open universe with its infinite splitting.

Both the couple and the maid seem to be on the masculine side because they believe that they can be out of the universal position of experiencing the inescapable antagonism but in the exceptional position of taking the enjoyment of what they have dreamed. Thus, the housemaid and the family are compelled to compete with each other in order to occupy an exceptional position, like the father in the *Totem and Taboo* who monopolized every woman in the tribe.[27] Their confrontation has nothing to do with the real, which introduces something new and unknown to jeopardize the existent symbolic. In this film, the dangerous role is given to rats. Without the existence of rats, the allegorical world of *The Housemaid* would become totalized and contained. Again, the achievement of *The Housemaid* is to show that the human symbolic reality the couple and the housemaid dreamed of is always already dug out by the rats.

UNRAVELING THE RELATIONSHIP OF CHARACTERS WITH TRIPARTITE SCHEME

Apart from the triadic relationship between Dong-sik's family, the housemaid, and the rats, there are many other triads in *The Housemaid*. There are four children in the house: Dong-sik's daughter Ae-sun, his son Chang-sun, the newborn son, and the housemaid's aborted fetus. There are two kinds of oppositions among them: Chang-sun versus Ae-sun and the three siblings versus the aborted baby. Considering the feudal tradition of the first-born son's succession of the family register, Chang-sun's position is very important. When he teases his elder sister, he seems to know his masculine superiority, which is supplemented by the existence of his younger brother. Ae-sun is very withdrawn and vulnerable probably because of her disabled legs. Their cooperation against the housemaid, who ends up being pregnant with their stepsibling, obscures the gender competition and reinforces the fantasy of them as siblings "stuck in the same boat." However, the rivalry between Chang-sun and Ae-sun is just an opposition between the universal and the exceptional in the symbolic order. Both are still protected by the patriarchal system, unlike the housemaid's baby, who could not even be born.

However, the difference between the couple's children and the aborted baby is critical. The unnamed baby is not accepted by anyone, including its mother. Particularly compared to the newborn son, being cared for by his parents, this genderless aborted baby is ghost-like. Slavoj Žižek argues that spectral apparitions can be conceived as the guise for the real which exposes the failure of the symbolic: "the spectre gives body to that which escapes (the symbolically structured) reality," or to "the irrepresentable X on whose 'repression' reality itself is founded."[28] In that sense, one can say that the aborted baby is at the topological level of the real.

There are four female characters in *The Housemaid*: Dong-sik's wife, Seon-yeong, who was fired by the factory because of her love letter to Dong-sik, Gyeong-hui, and the housemaid. Whereas the status of the wife is fully legitimized by the institution of marriage, the three seducers are forbidden to Dong-sik, a married man. Then, why does Dong-sik so easily succumb to the temptation of the housemaid despite the fact that he was determined to reject Seon-yeong and Gyeong-hui's seduction? The most important difference is that the housemaid works at Dong-sik's private home unlike Seon-yeong and Gyeong-hui, who work at the same company as Dong-sik. In contrast to his wife, who is in charge of the family's economic situation, and the factory workers, who can get him fired from his job due to the affair, the housemaid cannot threaten Dong-sik's social status in any way. Since she is his employee, a power hierarchy between them is evident. When she approaches him in a sexual manner, he does not keep the same distance as he did with Seon-yeong and Gyeong-hui. It is presumably because her existence satisfies his narcissistic desire for power, considering that he lives under the influence of his wife's financial stability. From Dong-sik's viewpoint, the wife occupies the exceptional part in the symbolic, Seon-yeong and Gyeong-hui the universal part. The housemaid is related to the dimension of the real. She intrudes on Dong-sik's reality by provoking his concealed sexual desire, which has already been exposed when Dong-sik seemed to enjoy physical contact with Gyeong-hui during piano lessons.

Another topological triad can be traced in terms of Dong-sik's whereabouts: the first and second floors of his house and the spaces outside his house. The second floor with his piano room and the housemaid's room is where Dong-sik's *jouissance* about music and sexual lust is realized, whereas the first floor, with the wife's sewing room and the main bedroom, is where Dong-sik's repression of sexuality is required. The outside world, such as the music room for the choir at the factory, the bar, and the city streets, is also where Dong-sik makes attempts to be moral, decent, and discreet. Following Freud, these three spaces could be allocated to the three agencies of psyche: id, ego, and superego. The second floor is where the intrusion of the real takes place, and the other spaces are dominated by the symbolic order. Still, there is a big difference between the first floor and the outside world. Dong-sik is freer at home but more intimidated and discouraged in the public spaces. The imaginary community called "sweet home" works well on the first floor, but the outside world, where mutual surveillance, condemnation, and immorality are prevalent, is not at all communal. Therefore, in terms of the domination of modernity, the outside is the universal space, and the first floor is the exceptional space in the symbolic reality. The second floor is related to the level of the real.

However, the above analysis is limited to Dong-sik's viewpoint. *The Housemaid* is far more balanced in representing women's sexuality. The superficial impression about them from the masculine perspective fails to explain their characters. All the female characters are straightforward about their sexual desires. Even the wife was bold enough to visit Dong-sik's boarding house, confessing that "I want to give my all to you" even before their marriage. Seon-yeong dares to send a love letter to Dong-sik, and Gyeong-hui also throws herself into Dong-sik's arms, ripping her clothes. And we all know how reckless and unprincipled the housemaid is to win Dong-sik's love.

The housemaid is portrayed as the most uncivilized and erotic of the four with her wet hair, exposed breasts, and bare feet. The image of her bare feet on Dong-sik's dress shoes while she clings to him relies on the conservative notion of primitive femininity and cultural masculinity. The fact that she is one of the two smokers in the film (the other one is Dong-sik) means that she has no control over her desire, which results in the catastrophic ending. Smoke is the signifier of allure in this film because the permeating smoke makes a scene obscure and vague. In that context, the first shot showing a clenched fist that opens to reveal five outstretched fingers in the hazy smoke is quite connotative. Since the next shot shows Dong-sik's family, four members at first glance but in fact, five members including the fetus, the shot of a single fist turning into five fingers could be interpreted as a sign of the family dissolution. The mise-en-scène where her cigarette smoke is wrapped around Dong-sik's head after he first offered her a cigarette also suggests the future murky events that will transpire between them.

However, these four women also want to gentrify, or symbolize, their sensual pleasure. The wife already achieved it through the marriage system, and Gyeong-hui succeeded in repressing it, which can be presumed when she blamed the housemaid for smoking and defended Dong-sik in front of the angry choir. The housemaid also wanted to settle down in the family as a concubine. In addition, all of them have—or want to have—a close relationship with modern technology.

The wife is good at the sewing machine job, and Seon-yeong and Gyeong-hui at the weaving machine job. The housemaid is also at least learning how to work on a sewing machine from the wife. Even the new television set shows female singers dancing on the screen. These machines are a kind of social prosthetic device for women, and even Dong-sik's daughter Ae-sun uses crutches. In short, women in *The Housemaid* are not primitive and savage but rather harness cutting-edge modern machines which allow their women users financial independence. In contrast, the musical instrument, a piano, signifies the dangerous but unavoidable enjoyment, which swallows up Dong-sik, Gyeong-hui, and the housemaid while one of each teaches, learns, or wants to learn to play the piano.

From the analysis so far, the characters in *The Housemaid* are not stereotyped in such a way that good and evil are assigned by dividing those who enjoy and those who do not. More precisely, they are split and bifurcated in their desire. Since *The Housemaid* is a film that weaves complicated triadic relationships, the main characters, far from being flattened and simplified, are also created to show the psychic mechanism under the tripartite scheme. For example, the wife, who wants to realize the dream of a sweet home under the patriarchal order of the symbolic, makes attempts to fill the cracks in her home caused by the intrusion of the real, that is, the housemaid's provocation. Meanwhile, the housemaid also wants to make a family even as a concubine, an illegal position in the symbolic, although she ends up facing the impossibility, that is, the real that breaks her dream. In short, *The Housemaid* serves to reveal that the smooth surface of orderly everyday life is just an alibi for the twisted and distorted desire underneath.

SPACES, OBJECTS AND VISUAL DETAILS IN TRIADISM

Then, what makes these characters divided and destroyed? Things start with the wife's desire to buy a new house. Their western style two-story house was very rare in those days in Seoul. It is more than enough for Dong-sik's family considering his and his wife's humble jobs. In this regard, the house is a metaphor for the modern way of living that Koreans dreamed of. However, modernity was not necessarily the object of admiration and envy for Koreans because they had to go through the colonial period due to the late introduction of modernity. In the same context, Elaine H. Kim and Chungmoo Choi have asserted that "the fundamental sociopolitical problems in postcolonial Korea after 'liberation' has been the tenacity of colonialism."[29] Since the change to a modern society was forced from the world outside Korea, the expectations for development in modernity have been entangled with anxiety and caution about loss of identity. After all, didn't the fatal and disastrous events take place in the newly built modern house the Dong-sik family moved into?

This wariness of modernity was reflected in the costume code of female characters in Korean films until the 1970s. A female character wearing a *hanbok* used to be a figure in the system that supports traditional and premodern values, while a character wearing a western costume was provocative and dangerous to the system. A change in a character's position or mindset is first expressed with a change in clothing. Kim also adopted this typical convention. In *The Housemaid*, only the wife wears *hanbok*, whereas the other characters wear western clothes.

Kim's delicate touch is added to this distinction: not only the wife's *hanbok* but also the other women's western dresses have striped or checkered patterns. The patterns with straight lines metaphorize the linearity of modernity.[30] These patterns appear on Seon-yeong's skirt, Gyeong-hui's one-piece dress, the wife's *jeogori* (top), Dong-sik's shirt, and the children's clothes. Even the housemaid wears a striped nightdress after she gets pregnant. It signifies that everybody in this film is under the influence of modernity. Therefore, the widespread categorization of the housemaid as being premodern is too simple and naive. When she wears the straight-lined clothes, she exposes her expectation that she will become a part of the modernized family, at least as a concubine. The straight lines, including vertical and geometrical lines, are also applied to architectural structures and props: the wooden walls of the room for the choir, the window grates in Dong-sik's house, the piano keyboard, and the bar where Dong-sik meets his friend. A roundish shape should be also noted: the plates, bus and taxi ceilings, tunnels, the pattern of the walls in Dong-sik's house, and the patterns on the fabric of *hanbok*. While the straight line is a signifier of modernity, progress, and teleology, the roundish shape implies the dysfunction, postponement, and failure of modernity.

In that context, a cigarette is an interesting object because it combines a straight line and a round shape, and the smoke from it blurs the surroundings: again, a triadic composition. A cigarette might connote that modernity contains the force to interfere with modernity within itself. There are only two smokers in the film: Dong-sik and the housemaid. Back then, it was taboo for women to smoke, so she had to keep her guilty pleasure of smoking a secret. When the housemaid tries to seduce him for the first time, she steals Dong-sik's cigarette box and runs away to drag him into her room. Her provocation is an act of defiance against the male-dominated order and patriarchy. In the last scene, where the male protagonist comments about the newspaper article while smoking, and the housemaid sniffs the cigarette stealthily, it becomes clear that her disobedience to the existent order is suppressed. Put simply, the threat to modernity signified by women's smoking is completely repressed by the conclusion that smoking is only permitted for men.

It is often said that elongated objects like cigarettes represent the phallus. Trains are another example. Obviously, the train is the "most" modern invention or at least the invention that made modernity possible. Its speed annihilated human's physical control over time and space, and dramatically accelerated the pace of life. As a result, the train becomes a signifier of attraction as well as fear. In this film, trains appear six times: when Seon-yeong goes back to her hometown; when Gyeong-hui first comes to Dong-sik's house; when Dong-sik and Gyeong-hui go to Seon-yeong's funeral; when Dong-sik comes back home to confess to his wife about the affair with the housemaid; when the wife finds the poison to kill the housemaid; and right after the housemaid falls dead upside down on the stairs. Every shot with running trains with their unique sound appears when the characters cannot take control of their situation and are swayed in their overwhelming fate. Kim Ki-young's way of disposing of phallic straight lines and slender objects in the narrative, far from praising the speed and capability of the phallic, is to present such devices as a signal of ominousness and anxiety. The phallic images do not imply domination and power, but rather the lack and failure of such domination and power. Looking carefully, those straight lines within the mise-en-scène and even on the clothes partition the characters and the spaces much like bars of a prison or a door of jail, which constrain the freedoms of people living in modern society.

Kim's critique of modernity does not end with bringing phallic objects into the negative context but goes further to make the phallic signification itself nullified by overlaying other materials. For example, the cigarette smoke makes a part of the mise-en-scène hazy, and the rainwater flowing over the window obscures what is going on inside. It is impossible to see the entirety of any train included in the film because of the obstruction of short shot duration, glimmering light, or oblique angles. This is the way Kim Ki-young hinders and criticizes modernity where the phallic function works. What he achieves is to neutralize the existing boundaries in the symbolic order to create a completely different path, not the opposite path in the symbolic, but the path toward the real; that is, the void without which the symbolic cannot be constructed.

After all, the displayed mise-en-scène of sexuality is bracketed. Cowardly Dong-sik, who blames everything on the women around him, including his wife, turns away from the real of his desire and eventually flees into death. He seeks forgiveness from his wife and expects to carry on his immortal life through the heir of his genes: the newborn son. On the other hand, for the housemaid in a black dress juxtaposed against the wife's white *hanbok*, the moment of dying with Dong-sik is an opportunity for "short-term happiness." She believes that a suicide pact is the negative perfection of a romantic love which can be finally realized in heaven. They choose to die to protect their fantasy of love and immortality. To some degree, it seems successful.

Then, is it a happy ending or not? The effect of warning about the uncontrollable eruption of desire and its fatal consequences seems very stoic. Is it the position of *The Housemaid*? Does the film inscribe sexuality as only anti-communal? Is this the method of illumination in *The Housemaid*? In the eyes of a drunken Dong-sik, frustrated that there is no ethical role model he can rely on, everything at night looks shaky. The only alternative that comes to his mind is to simply "escape from the earth." Dong-sik is not alone in this crisis of masculinity. Throughout the 1960s, Korean films showed us a lot of powerless male protagonists agonized by their inability to act.

CONCLUSION: BETWEEN DECADENCE AND ENLIGHTENMENT AFTER THE APRIL REVOLUTION

One may ask why triadism is so critical to interpreting *The Housemaid*. Here, it is necessary to think about the historical context when this film was produced. *The Housemaid* was released on November 3, 1960, after the April Revolution, a mass protest led by students from universities and high schools because the first president Syngman Rhee tried to amend the constitution to prolong his presidential term and rig the election. The economy was also in crisis due to the rapid reduction of economic aid from the US from $382,893,000 in 1957 to $222,204,000 in 1959.[31] Before the economic crisis, life in Seoul after the Korean War (1950–3) was full of superficial affluence, pleasure in consumption, and sexual pleasure, as *Madame Freedom* (1956) shows well. Then, in the end, Rhee, the tyrant dictator who claimed to be the forefather of the nation, stepped down from power.

Let us go back to the ending of the film, when Dong-sik changes his suicidal action into an action that "never happened." The surprising effect of this ending was not the filmmaker's intention.[32] However, Kim decided to film one more scene in the piano room for the first and last scene since the local investors complained a lot about the tragic ending after the preview. The original ending and the changed ending seem to be the surface and the back of a Moebius strip. The former stages Dong-sik's desire on the level of the real (he should be punished for his unconscious enjoyment), while the latter stages his desire on the level of the symbolic and the imaginary (he is a decent and faithful husband).

The two versions of the ending both reflect the social atmosphere in post-revolutionary Korea. During the era of revolution, everything repressed is bound to explode and implode at once. The April Revolution worked like a gateway for the public to enjoy the political, economic, and cultural decadence only the upper-class had enjoyed up until then. Therefore, the intellectuals' communities were warning against the spread of liberal trends including erotic films, pornographic magazines, exclusive saloon bars with *gisaeng*,[33] etc. Meanwhile, the revolution was also expected to be the moment when the nation moved forward to being a modern country defined by the spirit of enlightenment. For example, at this moment, the Korean film industry sought to organize a civilian institution for censorship free from the government authorities.[34]

In this context, *The Housemaid*'s conclusive repression of sexuality in the changed ending is entirely understandable. In fact, it was not the only film which emphasized the self-disciplined and suppressed life: *Seong Chun-hyang* (1961), *A Coachman, Aimless Bullet, Mother and A House Guest* (*Sarangbang sonnim gwa eomeoni*, Shin Sang-ok, 1961), and *Evergreen Tree* (*Sangnoksu*, Shin Sang-ok, 1961), other remarkable films released also in 1961, maintained a similar attitude. Chun-hyang endured torture to keep chaste; the coachman devoted his life to his family; the first son endured toothache; the widow tried to keep distance from her new affection; the teachers wanted to be dedicated. Therefore, one may claim that what *The Housemaid* killed was the force of decadence, and what it saved was a marriage system for the hardworking middle-class patriarch. Then, why should the saved be a middle-class man living in Seoul? The answer could be that the film succeeded in exposing the class, gender, and locality of the group that eventually appropriated the victory of the April Revolution.

However, it is also required to note that what makes *The Housemaid* unique and original is not that it ends up delivering the victor's narrative of enlightenment dramatically, but that it unveils the hidden energy of decadence to hinder the boundary between unyielding enlightenment and uncontrollable decadence through its elaborate weaving of triads. Even the changed end scene finishes with a shot of the housemaid sniffing the smoke from Dong-sik's cigarette. The seemingly decent and faithful husband is already masked a little by the cigarette smoke which stimulates the housemaid. Thus, I would say that the *Zeitgeist* of the revolutionary period that captivated Kim Ki-young was the dimension of the real, of decadence, and the danger inherent in modernity, as his original ending revealed. For Lacan, singularity is a force of difference itself that introduces something new by threatening the way of distinguishing the exceptional from the universal. From this perspective, *The Housemaid* is clearly a singular film amid revolution.

NOTES

1. The series consists of *The Housemaid* (1960), *Woman of Fire* (*Hwanyeo*, 1971), *Insect Woman* (*Chungnyeo*, 1972), *Woman of Fire '82* (*Hwanyeo 82*, 1982), and *Carnivorous Animals* (*Yuksik dongmul*, 1984).
2. O Gap-hwan, "What Kind of Movies Do the Students Prefer? [Haksaengdeul eun eotteon yeonghwa reul joahana?]," *Hankook ilbo* (July 12, 1959).
3. Myeong, "A Tragedy in a Family [Han gajeong ui chamgeuk]," *Hankook ilbo* (November 4, 1960).
4. Baek Cheol, "A Report on the Jury's Review on the Korean Entry Films for the Asian Film Festival [asea yeonghwaje chulpumjak simsa gyeongwi], *Kyunghyang shinmun* (February 13, 1961).
5. On the discursive history of Korean realist film criticism, see Kim Sohyoun, "What 'Realism' Means in the Postwar Korean Film Criticism: a Meta-critical Approach to *Piagol*

[Jeonhu hangug ui yeonghwa damnon eseo 'rieollijeum' ui uimi e gwanhayeo]," in *The Age of Attraction and Chaos: Korean Cinema in the 1950s* [*Maehok gwa hondon ui sidae: osimnyeondae ui hanguk yeonghwa*] (Seoul: Sodo, 2003), 17–60; Kim Sohyoun, "Immortal 'Realism' in Modern History of Korean Film Criticism," *Korean and Korean American Studies Bulletin*, East Rock Institute 15 (January/February 2005): 4–20; Kim Sohyoun, "How Does *Aimless Bullet* Become 'the Best Korean Realist Film'? [Obaltan eun eotteoke 'hanguk choego ui rieollijeum yeonghwa ga doeeonna?]," in *Map of Fantasy: Korean Cinema Asking the Way against the Grain* [*Hwansang ui jido: Hanguk yeonghwa, geu gyeol eul geoseuleo gil eul mutta*] (Seoul: Ulyeok, 2008), 63–100.
6. Yi Yeong-il, *The Complete History of Korean Cinema* [*Hanguk yeonghwa jeonsa*] (Seoul: Sodo, 2004), 282.
7. Yi Yeong-il's list includes *Aimless Bullet* (*Obaltan*, Yu Hyeon-mok, 1960), *A Petty Middle Manager* (*Samdeung gwajang*, Yi Bong-rae, 1960), and *A Coachman* (*Mabu*, Kang Dae-jin, 1960), ibid., 288.
8. O Yeong-jin. "What the Asian Film Festival Tells about Korean Cinema [Asea yeonghwaje ga malhaejuneun uri yeonghwa]," *Seoul shinmun* (March 15, 1961).
9. When *Sight & Sound* asked 358 filmmakers to select their 'Best 10' films in 2012, Bong Joon Ho included *The Housemaid* as the only Korean film. https://www.wikitree.co.kr/articles/199512
10. Yi Hyo-in, *Thirteen Filmmaker in South Korea* [*Hanguk ui yeonghwa gamdok sipsamin*] (Seoul: Yeolinchakdeul, 1994), 360.
11. Korean Film Archive, "The Filmmaker Kim Ki-young." https://artsandculture.google.com/exhibit/%ED%95%9C%EA%B5%AD%EC%98%81%ED%99%94%EC%9D%98-%EA%B4%B4%EB%AC%BC-%EA%B0%90%EB%8F%85-%EA%B9%80%EA%B8%B0%EC%98%81/wQzZ6tgQ.
12. Raymond Williams, *Marxism and Literature* (London: Oxford University Press, 1977), 121–7.
13. It was Kim Soyoung who led this interpretation. Kim Soyoung, *Phantom of Modernity* [*Geundaeseong ui yuryeongdeul*] (Seoul: Ssiaseul ppurineun saram, 2000), 92–6; Kim Soyoung, *Primitive Landscape of Modernity* [*Geundae ui Weonchogyeong*] (Seoul: Hyeonsilmunhwa, 2010), 101–28.
14. Dylan Evans, *An Introductory Dictionary of Lacanian Psychoanalysis* (London: Routledge, 1996), 159.
15. Jacques Lacan, *Seminar VII: The Ethics of Psychoanalysis 1959–1960*, trans. Dennis Porter (New York: W. W. Norton & Co., 1992), 12.
16. Jacques Lacan, *Ecrits*, trans. Bruce Fink (New York: W. W. Norton & Co., 2006), 684.
17. Jacques Lacan, *The Fundamental Concepts of Psychoanalysis*, ed. Jacques-Alain Miller, trans. Alan Sheridan (London: Penguin Books, 1977), 76.
18. Lacan coins *extimité* by mixing the prefix ex with intimacy (*intimité*). This term shows how psychoanalysis deals with the interior psychic system, and how the unconscious is not only inside but also outside, as the topological structure of a Moebius strip demonstrates.
19. See Jacques Lacan, *The Four Fundamental Concepts of Psychoanalysis*, ed. Jacques-Alain Miller, trans. Alan Sheridan (London: Penguin Books, 1979), 67–78.
20. Yu Ji-hyeong, *Conversation for Twenty-Four Years* [*Isipsanyeongan ui daehwa: Kim Ki-young gamdok inteobyujip*] (Seoul: Sun, 2006), 89.
21. Kim Ho-yeong, "The Pre-modernity in the Modernity: A Study of Space in Kim Ki-young's Movies [Kim Ki-young yeonghwa ui gong'gan gujo e natananeun geundae wa jeongeundae ui galdeung yangsang]," *Semiotic Inquiry* [*Gihohak yeongu*] no. 20 (November 2006): 205.

22. Pak U-seong, "The Performativity and Position of a Rat in *The Housemaid* [Hanyeo eseo jwi raneun jangchi ga suhaenghaneun yeokhal gwa wisang]," *Film Studies* [*Yeonghwa yeongu*] no. 49 (September, 2011): 69–76.
23. The housemaid first appears in the first shot at the factory as a janitor showing her back while mopping. But she seems not formally hired by the factory because she is not a member of the choir for workers.
24. For the diagram of sexuation with the formulae, see Jacques Lacan, *Seminar XX: On Feminine Sexuality*, trans. Bruce Fink (London: W. W. Norton & Co., 1998), 78. For the interpretation of the formulae, see Dylan Evans, *An Introductory Dictionary of Lacanian Psychoanalysis* (London: Routledge, 1996), 180.
25. Alenka Zupacic, "The Case of the Perforated Sheet," in *Jacques Lacan: Critical Evaluations in Cultural Theory Vol. IV* (London: Routledge, 2013), 69.
26. Ibid., 74.
27. Sigmund Freud, "Totem and Taboo," in *The Standard Edition of the Complete Psychological Works of Sigmund Freud*, trans. James Strachey, vol. XIII, (London: Hogarth Press, 1953), 1–161.
28. Slavoj Žižek, "The Spectre of Ideology," in *The Zizek Reader*, ed. Elizabeth Wright and Edmond Wright (Oxford: Blackwell Publishers Ltd., 1999), 74.
29. Chungmoo Choi, eds, *Dangerous Women: Gender and Korean Nationalism* (New York: Routledge, 1998), 3.
30. Hong Jin-hyeok, "The Expressionist Mise-en-scène and Modernism in *The Housemaid*: Focusing on Style with Vertical Lines [*Hanyeo* ui pyohyeonjuui mijangsen gwa modeonijeum: sujikseon eul jungsim euro han seutail bunseok]," *Korean Journal of Arts Studies* [*Hangukyesul yeongu*] no. 16 (June 2017): 239–64. For an analysis of greed in *The Housemaid*, see also Yi Dae-beom and Jeong Su-wan, "The Symbol of Compressed Modernization in *the Housemaid* Trilogies [Hanyeo yeonjak e natanan apchukjeok geundae ui damjiche roseo woebuin]," *Cine Forum* no. 28 (December 2017): 37–73.
31. https://en.wikipedia.org/wiki/April_Revolution.
32. The backstory about the changing of the ending was offered by Kim Ki-young's son. https://m.blog.naver.com/PostView.naver?isHttpsRedirect=true&blogId=rohani1747&logNo=220543034193.
33. A traditional prostitute or courtesan, trained to play musical instruments, sing, write, and draw.
34. Ham Chung-beom, *Korean Cinema and the April Revolution* [*Hanguk yeonghwa wa sailgu*] (Seoul: Korean Film Archive, 2009), 22.

CHAPTER 5

Men, Women and the Electric Household: Kim Ki-young's Housemaid Films[1]

Steve Choe

I

A series of interpretative difficulties concerning the politics of representation seems insurmountable in Kim Ki-young films, even after multiple viewings. In its audacity and shameless presumptuousness, his cinema portrays notions of masculinity and femininity in perplexing ways, associating male and female characters with non-human or animalistic traits, such as insects and rats, while also degrading them, making them unsympathetic, and reducing their function in the story to their sexuality or obsessiveness. Men and women repeatedly exploit and are exploited by each other, often violently, and one begins to wonder if Kim's depiction of character and plot are intentionally exaggerated. Such representations are typically problematic for the contemporary viewer. They pose questions about how the films are to be read and the extent to which they reflect the ideologies circulating around gender in Korean society or perhaps views that the filmmaker himself may have held. Men and women in Kim's cinema routinely assert seemingly self-evident truths about the nature of the masculine and feminine condition, truths that are nevertheless chauvinistic and often contradictory. "When a woman has a baby, she thinks she's going to die," Jeong-suk says as she looks at her own newborn child in *Woman of Fire* (*Hwanyeo*, 1971). "Most of the patients here," a man in a mental hospital comments in *Insect Woman*, "are poor men who became impotent because of their wives' nagging." Men and women are engaged in a perpetual battle of the sexes in Kim's films. "A man who can't have one affair in life has nothing to brag about," boasts the patriarch Dong-sik in *Woman of Fire '82* (*Hwanyeo 82*, 1982). "A woman in her twenties is like an angel, thirties a cat, forties a wolf, and fifties a wicked witch," the madam of a bar remarks in

Carnivorous Animals (*Yuksik dongmul*, 1984). Hearing this, the husband protagonist quickly concludes, "My wife is a wicked witch then. Right, women in their fifties are all wicked witches." Taken out of context, these and other lines from Kim's films defy the principle in good screenwriting to show and not tell, as his characters bluntly declare their internal emotions and states of mind, as if to refuse the opportunity for the film viewer to interpret and deduce. (In the case of *Carnivorous Animals*, Kim's stated intention with this declarative dialogue was humorous, after his own film company had gone bankrupt and he was "in a mood of self-mockery."²) Characters make public private thoughts and intentions, at times directly addressing the audience sitting in the theater and not just the characters in the diegesis. This is made most explicit in the famous ending to *The Housemaid* (*Hanyeo*, 1960), when Dong-sik turns to the camera and announces, "Ladies and gentlemen, as men get older, they spend more time thinking about young women. That's how they get drawn into women, which could lead to their destruction. This is true for all men!" In these and other films by Kim, a pattern of representation quickly emerges: dogmatic and weak-willed men who are unable to control their raging desires while wallowing in self-pity and needy and ambitious women whose value is consolidated through class position and motherhood.

In this essay I would like to work with Kim Ki-young's approach to issues of gender through the 'Housemaid' series of films in order to shed light on a major theme in his cinema more generally: the ideological problem of sexual difference within the Korean context. While films including *Goryeojang* (1963), *Promise of the Flesh* (*Yukche ui yaksok*, 1975), and *Ieo Island* (*Ieodo*, 1977) also construct gender and sexuality in Kim's unique style, I want to show that the Housemaid series shows us that the nature of masculinity and femininity is constituted through the notion of reproduction, or repetition, whereby each iteration revives pre-existing schemas of gender. *The Housemaid*, *Woman of Fire*, and *Woman of Fire '82* series, in addition to the "spin-off" works, *Insect Woman* (*Chungnyeo*, 1972) and *Carnivorous Animals*, explore this reproduction of gender as each remakes the Housemaid story and each relates to the others through the dialectic of difference and repetition. In varying ways, each of these films work critically with notions of "appropriate Koreanness," notions that for Won Kim are constituted by a national ideology of revitalization that is linked to the biopolitics of Park Chung Hee's regime in the late 1960s and 1970s.³ Appropriate Koreanness names that idealized Korean national subject who exemplifies the characteristics of fertility, discipline, docility, propriety, collectivism, and capitalist productivity, among other normative Korean virtues. In lieu of the hierarchies that govern relations between the original and a derivative remake, I would like to show how the Housemaid films reveal the continuous production of difference that animates each film in their form and aesthetics. My argument revolves around the construction of the household, which includes the human and non-human beings that occupy it, that is bestowed a kind of electric life, not only through the animative power of the moving image, but also through the inappropriate use of household objects and the depiction of inappropriate Koreanness.

In their insightful and generative essay on Kim Ki-young's Housemaid remakes, Nikki J. Y. Lee and Julian Stringer propose that the four follow-up films of the director's well-known work from 1960 should be thought in terms of the concept of "revival." Comparing these subsequent iterations to the production of a play from an original theater script, Lee and Stringer write that, "In both cases, the same material is creatively worked over and over again. Moreover, each individual theatrical performance or production differs inexorably from the next."[4] Each iteration of the Housemaid story imbues the original film with contemporary relevance in that the repetition of plot elements, characters, and settings reflect the continuing significance of its melodramatic plot, while their differences from one film to the next reflect the contingencies of history. "Film always contains the circumstances of the times as a 'plus something,'" Kim Ki-young remarked in interview, thus corroborating this dialectic of repetition and difference, "a film can be considered good only when it contains that."[5] By thinking of each film of the Housemaid series as a revival, Lee and Stringer write that "the act of remaking a prior text involves making the past film alive," and deploy the language of death and the afterlife to rethink traditional theories of the remake.[6] Moreover, this way of framing the films that follow *The Housemaid* as revivals serves to implicitly critique the kinds of judgments that deem the sequels to be debased copies of a unique film. *Woman of Fire*, *Woman of Fire '82*, *Insect Woman*, and *Carnivorous Animals* are not mere copies of a Platonic ideal that is embodied by *The Housemaid*; rather, each constitutes a stand-alone iteration whose meanings cannot be discursively delimited by those of the original film on which it is ostensibly based. The notion of the revival moves us away from thinking of the Housemaid series as comprising a singular, originating film and subsequent copies, but allows us to think of them in series, in terms of theme and variations perhaps, or even something more radical, as I will suggest below.

II

Many of us are aware of the basic plot to the Housemaid films, which revolves around a nuclear family that takes in a female housemaid who is of a lower economic and social class. Following the first film in 1960, Kim wrote and directed the revivals *Woman of Fire* in 1971 and *Woman of Fire '82* in 1982. Two "spin-off" films, *Insect Woman* in 1972 and *Carnivorous Animals* in 1984, also work with the plot of *The Housemaid* while differing in a number of their narrative details.

The name of the family patriarch and housemaid herself, when their names are explicitly invoked, is the same in all the films, Dong-sik and Myeong-ja, respectively. The housemaid in the 1960 version is not named. In addition to Dong-sik and his wife (who is not given a name), the family includes their two children, a son and daughter, who are both defiant and cruel. Over the course of the story the wife and Myeong-ja may become pregnant and may successfully give birth to two infants. The drama unfolds mostly in a two-level home that was purchased by the hard-working wife who is at odds with the housemaid. Dong-sik works as a piano teacher or is a failed businessman and, while he works with their piano, an object that signifies the family's bourgeois aspirations, he nevertheless earns less than his spouse. Dong-sik's wife is the family breadwinner in all the Housemaid films, working as a seamstress (in *The Housemaid*), running a chicken farm (in both *Woman of Fire* films), or leading as a CEO (of a construction company in *Insect Woman* and a real estate company in *Carnivorous Animals*).

"I've ruined my business but my wife was different," the physically impotent Dong-sik observes in *Insect Woman*, "she's a true hero." This emasculated position is underscored after he sleeps with Myeong-ja, she becomes his mistress, and is confronted by his domineering wife. The women fight over Dong-sik and because his wife refuses to let herself be humiliated by his adulterous behavior, they agree to "share" him between them. Myeong-ja possesses her own sense of feminine pride and refuses to be used after losing her virginity to Dong-sik. Expressing her predicament, in *Woman of Fire* she remarks that, "my body is not pure anymore, I'm not going to be able to get married." Myeong-ja becomes pregnant and the baby, either born or unborn depending on the film, becomes an object that further provokes the grievances between the warring protagonists. When Myeong-ja's child is killed to protect the integrity of Dong-sik's family, she demands that his wife's newly born infant is killed as compensation. "All children are equal. My baby is dead, yours should die too," she declares in *The Housemaid*, reiterating the old law of moral equivalence that demands an eye for an eye and a tooth for a tooth. The culmination of this story is typically death for Dong-sik and Myeong-ja, either by murder or suicide, again depending on the film.

All of the films of the Housemaid series feature men and women who may be characterized as grotesque in their manifestations, depictions that border on the absurd and, particularly in the subsequent revivals, are rendered through surreal and hallucinatory imagery. The representations of the Myeong-ja character may also be placed within the ideological legacy of the femme fatale as this trope has been understood within the context of the film noir, but Kim's iterations are wilder and more exaggerated. Reflecting on her capacity to bring disaster to the men she attracts, we could deploy psychoanalytic categories and observe how Myeong-ja embodies an ambivalence between threat and fetish that revolves around male castration as she exploits her sexuality to gain power over Dong-sik. And, as this psychosexual dynamic is repeated throughout the films, we may be compelled to show how they reflect the continuity of patriarchal desire within the postwar Korean cultural context from 1960 to 1985. At the outset, it may be argued that Kim's men and women reflect patriarchal notions of gender that circulated during these years of authoritarian rule and rapid economic development. In his essay on the dream of home ownership during the 1970s, Han Sang Kim links this dream with that of the ideologies surrounding the proper nuclear family and notions of individual freedom.[7] Men and women are to sacrifice themselves to the nation by adopting these ideals, working outside and inside the household respectively, and in so doing are to negotiate contradictions between collective and individual pursuits that often result in frustration, according to Kim. Notably, he writes that in some fiction and cinema in the 1970s—and he mentions *Carnivorous Animals* in passing—we can see how the household becomes "hystericized" through the depiction of the family in crisis. My elucidation of the poetics of Kim Ki-young's cinema will continue in this spirit.

Dong-sik's narrative trajectory emphasizes the destructive force of male desire, particularly when it is pursued outside the confines of the bourgeois Korean family. He is not the hardened, productive warrior-citizen celebrated by the ideological injunctions of Park's government but is weak-willed, unable or unwilling to protect the integrity of his family. In *Insect Woman* and *Carnivorous Animals* he encourages his son to "become a man" by paying a woman to sleep with him or simply by being less of a "mama's boy," while he himself is incapable of standing up to both his wife and Myeong-ja. In all the Housemaid films, male virility is constantly at issue and especially so in the case of *Carnivorous Animals*, where Dong-sik observes that men with a domineering wife become impotent and that blood is sacrificed each time men experience orgasm with a woman. When Myeong-ja tells Dong-sik about a magazine article about feeling young, she explains that, citing Freud, men have an unconscious desire to become a baby again. While this character aims to realize an idealized concept of masculinity, he is merely an infantile creature ostensibly caught within the Oedipal drama and remains eternally obsequious to the women in his life.

Dong-sik's wife may also be read to illustrate ideological constructions of gender in her vigilant upkeep of her roles as mother and wife. In all the Housemaid films, she is determined to stand by her husband. In both the original and *Woman of Fire*, she states that adultery is a more serious offence than that of theft or murder. What is particularly unacceptable to her is the notion that he sleeps with another woman and gets this other woman pregnant. As with the housemaid character, her depiction is hyperbolic and frenzied at times, manifest through a kind of obsessive focus on ideal motherhood. Lee and Stringer write that in her case, a "set of three variously interrelated impulses—for social reputation, material affluence, and economic stability—are merged into a desperate need for survival of the family."[8] She is adamant that no one know that Dong-sik is sleeping with their housemaid in *Woman of Fire*, as this knowledge will result in their children becoming shamed outcasts. When a character is murdered within the house, whether Myeong-ja's unborn child or her own young son, she also insists that the authorities not be notified so that the façade of their being a normal family may be maintained. This pursuit of family at all costs turns hysterical when she engages Myeong-ja in a war for Dong-sik's time and sexual attention.

Ultimately, the pursuits of both women revolve around the protection and purity of their feminine integrity. For Myeong-ja this is embodied in her chastity and for Dong-sik's wife in the boundaries of the family that delineate members from non-members. Once Myeong-ja's virginal chastity is corrupted, she insists that she become Dong-sik new young wife as she believes that no man will want her as her virtue has been tainted forever. Meanwhile, the question of how she is to be integrated into the household, and of how she will be referred to by others (*hoching*)—as housemaid (either the older term, *hanyeo*, or the more modern *singmo*), older sister, a second mother, in any event as someone who lives with but is not related to the family: these questions embody the ethical problematic for Dong-sik's wife. Dong-sik is alarmed when Myeong-ja calls him "*yeobo*" for the first time, which induces the married man to begin thinking of her as an intimate partner who will perhaps join his family somehow. In all the Housemaid films she moves quickly from stranger to housemaid to mistress, progressively infiltrating Dong-sik's home. That her character is repeatedly associated with signifiers of otherness—rats, dogs, her smell, cigarettes, insects, poison—underscores her presence in the Housemaid films as a contaminating force. "Our blood is mixed together now? How could you sleep with me with that filthy body? I can smell the filth on my body," Dong-sik's wife cries out, following the admission of his infidelity in *Woman of Fire '82*.

For both women, at stake is the question of whether it is possible to allow for changing conceptions of sexuality and family, particularly as these may have been understood in postwar South Korea. The films raise questions about the ethical issues that underpin the meaning of premarital sex, hospitality, the politics of blood relations, who is worthy of sympathy, of familial inclusion, and the meaning of these problematic dynamics within the context of upward mobility. Both women exploit the damage to their sexual and familial integrity as means to justify their hysterical outrage, efforts to blackmail, and retaliatory violence. Kim's Housemaid series plays out the anxieties revolving around otherness and the ethics of the other that are inseparable from the ideological changes wrought by the experience of compressed modernization in Korea. The narrative problems surrounding Dong-sik's wife and Myeong-ja can be linked to the tensions produced between tradition and modernity, the familiar and foreign, masculinity and femininity, superstition and science, and other ideological binaries in order to interrogate the social and ethical consequences of Korea's modernization process. In her consideration of how Kim's Housemaid films figure the feminine as associated with the premodern and even the primordial, Kim Soyoung notes that the character of Myeong-ja expresses women's dependence

> on their supposedly dangerous instinct for reproduction, evidently as a means to move up in society. Yet, in a manner at once eerie and perfectly appropriate, the menace of these remnants only emerges in contemporary settings, as if the force of the premodern could only be configured and conceptualized within the framework of modernity.[9]

Women in these films, including Dong-sik's wife, are essentialized and fetishized, characterized through their difference in relation to bourgeois Korean modernity.

These hyperbolic constructions of gender through the Housemaid films invite viewers to see whether the nature of Korean femininity and masculinity may be read from them. These constructions acquire an almost mythical status in that they are instigated through the encounters between the three protagonists, each inciting the others toward frenetic, exaggerated representations of the mistress, wife, and emasculated husband.

With each iteration of the Housemaid plot, new elements are introduced into the story, differences that carry narrative significance by filling out details while explaining the seemingly irrational behavior of the characters in the previous films. In the sequels, Myeong-ja agrees to serve as the housemaid without pay and asks only that Dong-sik's wife find a suitable husband for her. The beginning of *Woman of Fire* includes some commentary, spoken by a detective to a news reporter, on the responsibility of the media in contemporary society and its incitement toward violence. "News outlets just report the truth," the reporter retorts, "It's like the twenty-five-year Cold War. We're all victims. It's not a shock that minors have become more violent." Each remake provides additional backstory to the characters. In *Insect Woman*, Dong-sik expresses concern about his duty to continue his family blood line. As he does so, his wife hands him a drink that has been mixed with a tranquilizer. She then takes her unconscious spouse to the hospital so that he can receive a vasectomy, a procedure that is undertaken without his consent. In the 1972 version of the Housemaid plot, Myeong-ja does not give birth to her baby, but is found in the basement of her home among the rats. The infant, associated in the film with blood-thirsty vampires, finds its way somehow into the refrigerator. In *Woman of Fire '82* the housemaid demands that Dong-sik wear red socks, which signify that he is now her husband. In *Carnivorous Animals* a truce between Myeong-ja and Dong-sik's wife is manifest in a legal contract, which helps to explain how they agree to share their time with him (each woman gets half a day). Perhaps most significant in the changes throughout the Housemaid series is the wife's occupation, which affects how she dominates her husband and her perceived standing outside the house. (In the films where she runs a chicken farm, a feed machine provides the technical means for grinding rat and human flesh.) There is also the presence of loudly ticking clocks, notable for their signifying of the passing of time, filling a wall in Dong-sik's music room in both of the *Woman of Fire* films. Meanwhile, rats constantly make an appearance throughout the entire Housemaid series, symbolizing filth, contagion, and the intrusion of the non-human into the space of the bourgeois household. The rats also invite interpretation along other lines perhaps as presented in Freud's case history of the "Rat Man," where the psychoanalyst links the distressing rodents not only to disease but also to money and the male genitalia.

While the main drama takes place indoors, exterior shots showcase the development of Seoul throughout the years depicted in the Housemaid films. Images of concrete road structures, increasingly dense traffic jams, tall office buildings, and high-rise apartment complexes attest to the meteoric economic rise of the city. Myeong-ja and her friend, who both come from the countryside, aspire to live on the highest floor of the Samil Building in *Woman of Fire*, which was then the tallest building in Korea, completed in 1970. The music in each film is contemporary to the period—*trot* music about lost love is featured in the earlier films while a folk-rock song that includes the lyrics "I don't know anything," is repeated in *Woman of Fire '82*. Other than the wife in the first Housemaid film, all the characters wear modern, western-style clothes. Containers of food with labels in English, white glass bowls, a fish broiler and other modern kitchen appliances also mark the time and place of the settings.

III

As we consider the five films of the Housemaid series and focus on their representations of gender by comparing and contrasting narrative details, we inevitably reiterate logics of difference and repetition. This is the case as we reflect on the entire series in tandem or when we allow our analytical attention to shift from one film to another. A signifier from one scene, and the possible meaning surrounding it, is taken as a model and in the next moment another signifier from another film is brought into relation with the first that is deemed similar or dissimilar. Differences and repetitions may then be treated as indexes toward cultural and historical meanings outside the text, and as allegories of modern Korean history. Yet in identifying and drawing out similarities and differences, we would also do well to consider the metaphysical schematic that underpins this very process, the epistemological assumptions that make possible the very operations of comparison and contrast, and that which ranks the text either as exemplary or derivative within these operations. Lee and Stringer, in their rethinking of the remake in terms of the notion of revival, nevertheless seem to reassert this need for an *a priori* exemplar that places the remade film within a Platonic hierarchy, as derived *a posteriori* from a model text ("the act of remaking a prior text involves making the past film alive").[10] From Form or Idea, to physical reality, to its imitation in art: one can think of this hierarchical sequence in terms of art's mimetic relationship to reality but also in relation to the biases of cinematic critique as it evaluates the remake in relation to an idealized original film. Correspondingly, as one attempts to consider Kim's Housemaid films as consisting of a series of remakes or even revivals, one presupposes an original, inert text that is to be resurrected. *The Housemaid* begets undead offspring, like the vampiric baby in the *Woman of Fire* films, so that its cinematic progeny may be made relevant for more contemporary contexts and open to new meanings. Identifying differences and repetitions reunites this hierarchy while subjecting Kim's exuberant singularities to metaphors that delineate one work from another.

I would like to radicalize the concept of the filmic revival by considering how the vitality implied by it not only inspires each instantiation of the Housemaid series but surges in the aesthetics of each work while also bringing forth the animistic vitality that is inherent to the moving image itself. My aim is to critique the metaphysics of representational thinking with regard to the cinema so that we can begin to consider how this modernist reading of vivacity informs Kim's cinema more generally. In his early philosophical work, *Difference and Repetition*, Deleuze aims precisely to launch such a critique of this metaphysics. He begins his analysis by asserting that "repetition is not generality" and through this assertion sets out to separate the concept of repetition from that of mere repeatability.[11] Repetition as Deleuze understands it is unrelated to the generalizability of an instantiated trait, for it refuses the everyday notion of repetition as defined through a series of reciprocally determined elements that nevertheless disappear when ostensibly universal, timeless concepts are applied to them. Kim's Housemaid films progressively defy established genre categories but other meaningful concepts, such as narrative, character, history, the nature of Korean masculinity and femininity, and so on, may be traced consistently through them. Deleuze's repetition does not generalize a series of singular elements as these singularities are always in the process of continually becoming and thus exceed the Idea whose objective is to domesticate them. From the standpoint of metaphysics, the concept of repetition presupposes a universal notion of identity as its determining principle, a "third" term that grounds the generality against which two representative instantiations may be compared. The general model ensures that these two traits (or singular elements) may be compared at all. Repeating this notion of identity to reproduce a dissimilarity, the Idea of difference is typically understood to develop through an equal and opposite process, whereby one instantiation is set over-against another in negative relation. This schematic process enables the subjection of singularities to the laws of exchangeability, translatability, and even moral determinability. In the cases of both similarity and dissimilarity, the underlying generalizability of the concept, that which grounds and legitimates the very notions of difference and repetition, is left unchanged.

As Deleuze explains, to effectuate such notions is to cover over thinking and domesticate the continuous invention of difference by what he calls the "image of thought."[12] To contain this endless outpouring by translating it into representation therefore fundamentally distorts its excessive vitality. Traditional theories of the film remake impose this image of thought as they reiterate dichotomies between a celebrated original over-against a debased copy, a before and after that implicitly privileges the primary firstness of the former over against the derived secondariness of the latter. The aim of these operations is to reify and reinstate the image of thought, and to reiterate the "correctness" that is legitimated by this metaphysics.

Underneath this schema of representation is the continuous generation of difference in itself and the production of non-exchangeable and non-totalizable living movement. For Deleuze, the work of art and its production of simulacra is key for representing this non-representable vital force. "It is a question," he writes, "of producing within the work a movement capable of affecting the mind outside of all representation; it is a question of making movement itself a work, without interposition; of inventing vibrations, rotations, whirlings, gravitations, dances or leaps which thereby touch the mind."[13] Unmediated and without telos, these movements underlie but also surreptitiously inspire the very apparatus of representation while constituting its submerged interior. Not negation, not generality, but singular and without end, this phantasmatic form of repetition is shot through with radical difference and not simply opposed to it. It is the art of the theater that for Deleuze "extracts real movement from all the arts it employs," not by rendering sensuousness as the means for mimetically representing the real but by presenting it as simulacra, like an image that has been relieved of its promise to mimetically represent reality.[14] Affirming its status as a copy without an original, Deleuze aligns this primordial movement with performativity and the production of "real movement." In the theater of repetition, he writes, "we experience pure forces, dynamic lines in space which act without intermediary upon the spirit, and link it directly with nature and history, with a language which speaks before words, with gestures which develop before organized bodies, with masks before faces, with spectres and phantoms before characters."[15] These forces are integral to the very means available to the moving image and the production that is inherent to its reproducibility.

With this in mind, it is significant that Kim began his directing career in the theater. After Liberation, while he enrolled as medical student at Seoul National University, Kim became the head of the National University Theater on campus. In his youth, he was interested in all the arts—including literature, fine art, and music—but his interests would eventually culminate in his decision to become a cinema director. His first film, *I Am a Truck* (*Na neun teureogida*, 1953), is a cultural film that depicts a military vehicle from dawn until late at night. Featuring voice-over that speaks and narrates the visuals from the perspective of the truck, it is a work that figures the vehicle as an inorganic form of life as it is imbued with a wry personality. Kim's depiction here underscores the alignment of the moving image with this uncanny vitality. In interview, the director was asked what the movies have meant to him as he reflected on his career. He responded that they are "a vital way of life I can't abandon even on the day I die."[16] Taking this statement seriously, we ought to consider how this vital life, a kind of life lived ecstatically, suffuses the content and form of his films, each of them expressing a vitality that evades straightforward representation precisely in the manner Deleuze describes above.

Perhaps one of the most striking characteristics of his Housemaid films is that most of them (except for *Carnivorous Animals*) include a frame story that lends the main story a provisional status, aligning it with memory, dream, or simulacra. The flashbacks in both *Woman of Fire* films, the narration of a mental patient in *Insect Woman* that initiates a cut into the main story, and the famous admonition to the male audience at the end of *The Housemaid*: all these framing narratives function like the proscenium arch to a theater play, marking the outside of the main story's diegetic world while also figuring the events depicted in it a liminal status between illusion and realism. Kim implements the framings, not to create narrative drama in the movement between past and present, or the real and unreal, but in order to affirm the prospective "as if" potential of the Housemaid story. In doing so, Kim gives the cinema permission to diverge from the expectation that it represents historical reality while also affirming its surreal, hallucinatory potential. *The Housemaid* films do not simply represent and reproduce the worlds of Korea between 1960 and 1985, they also produce these worlds, revealing how we might think of historical reality during this time as mere simulacra.

This creative force is manifest explicitly through Kim's focus on the non-human forms of life throughout his cinema. Animals are presented to underscore the bestial nature of human beings. Critics and scholars of Kim's cinema have noted the seemingly constant presence of rats throughout all the Housemaid films—as metaphors, in the dreams of the characters, appearing in strange cinematic delusions, and of course directly on screen. Dong-sik's wife in *The Housemaid* distressingly reports having dreamt of rat heads attached to human bodies. When the young son bites Myeong-ja's arm, after she tells him the water he just drank was poisoned, his attack is almost rat-like in his manner of biting. In *Woman of Fire*, Dong-sik and Myeong-ja drink rat poison together to commit suicide. He remarks that it does not taste so bad and that he has now become a rat. She responds with a bit of defiance and says, "Now we can be whatever we want—the earth, water, wind, sun [. . .]." Myeong-ja dreams of a swarm of rats invading her body in *Insect Woman* and of losing her middle finger and toes from the rodents chewing them off; upon waking she says a "dream of rats predicts pregnancy." The sex scene in *Woman of Fire '82* features the sound of a mass of rats squeaking and hissing, equating the act of intercourse with the noisy interactions between the rodent animals. In *Carnivorous Animals*, Myeong-ja sets up a tray of poisoned food in the basement that is meant to kill the rats which she believes have harmed her baby. Instead, a stranger, who turns out to be the brother of her neighbor, somehow enters the house, eats the food, and dies. The crime of accidental manslaughter is a supplemental narrative in the Housemaid films and this stranger's body, in the *Woman of Fire* films, is ground up in the chicken feed machine. Replicating a cyclical pattern, this 'feed' is then consumed by the chickens that then produce eggs and meat for the human characters to consume.

In Kim's cinema, distinctions between human characters and other, non-human beings aim toward dissolution, whereby one is subsumed into the other. Like a fundamental element ("earth, water, wind, sun . . ."), the fire that is embodied by the women put the non-representational, *élan vital* of Kim's cinema into motion, dissolving analytical categories in film analysis that focus only on character and narrative. "The idea of fire," writes Deleuze, "subsumes fire in the form of a single continuous mass capable of increase. The Idea of silver subsumes its object in the worm of a liquid continuity of fine metal."[17] Further references to animals and non-human forms of life, other than rats, make their way throughout the films. Dong-sik advises his daughter in *The Housemaid* to exercise like the caged squirrel so that her disabled legs can become stronger (her disablement is not replicated in the subsequent films). When he has sex with Myeong-ja in *Insect Woman*, the chaotic buzz of an insect swarm fills the soundtrack. Appearing later, the baby drinks blood and is even referred to as a kind of vampire. In this film, as well as in *Carnivorous Animals*, Dong-sik's son refuses to eat anything that was once alive, in a seemingly defiant gesture to negate the carnivorous lifestyle adopted by his family. He vows to eat only honey instead. All of these references to non-human life and animality visualize the dynamic forces that circulate in and around Kim's films, between human and animal life and back again. They recall what Akira Mizuta Lippit calls the "animetaphor," bringing to the fore the alliance of cinema with animal life, each feeding the other through the passage from animation to animal.[18] We are also in the realm here of Epstein's "*photogénie*," which is particular to the animistic cinema in its manner of attributing "a semblance of life to the objects it defines."[19]

Inanimate objects in Kim's cinema can take a kind of uncanny life as well, enabled by the vital movements brought about by the animating look of the camera. The appearance of objects like cigarettes, a plate of curry rice, a glass of water, a chandelier with colorful glass orbs, stained glass, hard candies, and the infamous stairs that are often interpreted as a status symbol, when they come into contact with human bodies, induce social relations and potentialities while reiterating habituated Korean ethics. The director has stated that he attempted to reveal "everything that lay hidden," including perhaps the material and affective relations between bodies in the world, and that he "tried to show the facts and the truth anatomically."[20] These items may or may not be used appropriately, as a glass of water or a plate of food fulfill the basic need for sustenance and bring human characters together while also carrying the potential as instruments of murder. The higher one climbs on the stairs, the closer one reaches the safety of the second floor while the danger of death by falling rises. "The stairway is a very good prop in creating a hazardous atmosphere," he remarked in interview.[21] The stairs and other signifiers are associated with modern, typically non-Korean forms of life, forms that clash with the affective relations inspired by the objects of indigenous Korean domesticity. As such, a palpable ambivalence surrounding their use and integration into everyday life persists throughout the films. The viewer may find him or herself feeling dread at who or what will be cruelly victimized next as objects are used in inappropriate, but creative new ways by the films' characters. The uncertainty and anxiety felt by the viewer cannot be separated from the syncretic worlds depicted in all the Housemaid films and the phenomenological look at these worlds inspired by Kim's camera. The foreign is always already inside the home, the rats were there before the families moved in, the stairs already a means for terminating a pregnancy—Kim's cinema simply realizes these distressing potentialities, manifesting the virtual violence intrinsic to these inert signs through their actualization on screen. The efforts undertaken by the characters to eliminate these signs of uncanny foreignness, in order to protect the integrity of their chastity or the boundaries of the family, will thus be futile as they attempt to expunge that which is already integral to themselves. The life of the human characters springs from the same source as that of the non-human and inorganic beings—the animetaphor that is the cinema. In this sense, the ruining force that destroys the traditional family did not originate with the foreign housemaid, outside the family home, but was always already internal to the cinematic representation of the modern Korean family. The cinema technology makes evident this insight possible through the story of this household, summoning the beings and objects that occupy it to electric life.

That the characters in Kim's films act out irrationally or in exaggerated ways reflects a wild vitality, an accelerated movement toward survival above all, and the force of life amplified without exhaustion. His films tend toward fast cutting, soliciting the glance and not a prolonged gaze from the viewer, that constructs narratives through a series of spectacles and outrageous plot turns rather than the accumulation of narrative tension through careful continuity editing. Myeong-ja's incendiary behavior and Dong-sik's submissive demeanor confound the melodrama surrounding the space of innocence that may be located in the Korean family. These are not the ideal national subjects portrayed in national policy films disseminated by Park Chung Hee's Yushin regime. Moral and legal norms are repeatedly disregarded and transgressed throughout the Housemaid films. But these incendiary representations of male and female function as accelerated depictions of the force of pure difference that animates them while pushing them to their breaking point of manic productivity. The rapid cuts in Kim's cinema heightens this accelerated production of expressive difference and exacerbates its hyperactivity.

IV

During Park Chung Hee's presidency, state apparatuses were tied closely to industry and society, pushing the economy toward aggressive, nationalist market expansion and hypergrowth. In the private realm, the Korean family was also expected to participate in the project of nation building and industrialization through an adherence to traditional hierarchies and morality. Men were supposed to be providers for the family through their industrial and military mobilization, while women were responsible for managing the household and its finances in a rational manner.[22] Contextualized within the authoritarian regimes of the 1970s and the 80s led by the presidencies of Park and Chun Doo-hwan, the period during which the films after *The Housemaid* were produced, the repetitions of Kim's cinema depict these ideologies around gender in their most obsessive manifestation and in doing so also reveal their hysterical scope. On the one hand, we can think here of the mass production of textiles, chickens, and eggs, and then the commodification of land and property that track Korea's meteoric economic rise and the nation's mobilization of technology and labor. On the other, as the use of the chicken farm in the *Woman of Fire* films makes explicit, the living labor that produces these commodities aims only to reproduce this labor, as chickens and eggs become feed for humans and in turn the human bodies become feed for the chickens. This circulation between humans and animals, a kind of circle of life, turns on the militarized ideology of Korean modernization in the 1970s and 80s and its insistence on the virtues of productivity. Moreover, in all the Housemaid films the reproduction of human labor and of babies are repeatedly at stake, the production of more bodies that will continue to maintain economic growth for the nation. But like the caged squirrel in *The Housemaid*, living things are not allowed to roam free in Kim's films and must labor endlessly as if on a running wheel. Here is a life pushed toward hyperproduction, where the primary aim of men and women in families is to become affluent by producing an appropriate number of offspring. Moments from *Carnivorous Animals* are particularly humorous as quantified bites of knowledge about fertility are cited: "A city of ten million. Two hundred trucks of rice and one thousand cows are consumed in a day. Every day, men impregnate women for five thousand offspring"; "Yes, I have three thousand eggs in my body, waiting to come to life," "Half of our bodily functions is all about the instinct to have offspring." This depiction of biopolitical knowledge around the fertility of Korean men and women plainly reflects the ideology of human reproduction while rendering it absurd in its brute facticity on screen. Kim's films not only simulate this national ideology and its insistence on appropriate Koreanness, they also critique it through the depiction of family life as domestic warfare, of life under capitalism overflowing with the desperate pursuit of survival, however paranoid and surreal its means toward doing so.

At the beginning of *Insect Woman*, a teacher enters a classroom and, after asserting that the school should be a protected space, even for students who steal, he goes ahead to ask his students about the meaning of "youth" ("*cheong-chun*"). One by one, the students in this all-women's school stand up and declare: "Youthfulness," "Courage," "Being active," "Amateurism." The last response comes from a student wearing glasses: "Fever. Nietzsche said youth was a fever just like the flu or malaria." From this the teacher then summarizes the notion of youth as the "pure, amateurish courage to challenge the established." The youthful students then clap, expressing their assent, ironically perhaps, to the figure of authority. On the one hand, this moment may be read as a reflection on youth culture in Korea in 1971 and the spirit of rebelliousness expressed through outward signs and fashion – short skirts, long hair, blue jeans, and American music. On the other, this concept of youth may be associated with a Nietzschean will toward life that inspires a revolutionary revaluation of old values. Throughout Kim's Housemaid films, this will aims to overturn conventions and upend the established expectations of the worlds depicted in the films, but also their aesthetics as well. They take the animistic that is at the heart of *photogénie* to its aesthetic and discursive limits, revealing the myriad ways in which hyperactivity motivates the characterizations, plot, mise-en-scène, montage, and their sound and image design. Indeed, this electric animism seems to inform Kim's production practice more generally, his remaking and reviving of previous films while re-rendering their stories in his own feverish manner. Like an affliction such as influenza or malaria, this productive will toward life seeks death, one that is appropriate to its own manner of being, and which is made explicit in the depiction of the double suicide of Dong-sik and Myeong-ja at the conclusion of the Housemaid story. Postwar Korean subjectivity demands that life exhaust itself through continuous labor. However, this death is no loss and does not evoke despair in the simulacra of the cinema, for Kim's animist aesthetics will be manifest in his next production, alive and life-affirming once more.

NOTES

1. I am grateful to Mayumo Inoue for his expertise on key ideas that appear in this essay and to Jinsoo An for further discussion of these ideas, particularly in relation to Kim Ki-young's cinema.
2. Hong-joon Kim, ed., *Kim Ki-young* (Seoul: Seoul Selection, 2006), 74.
3. See Won Kim, "The Race to Appropriate 'Koreanness': National Restoration, Internal Development, and Traces of Popular Culture," in *Cultures of Yusin: South Korea in the 1970s*, ed. Youngju Ryu (Ann Arbor: University of Michigan Press, 2018), 21–57.
4. Nikki J. Y. Lee and Julian Stringer, "Remake, Repeat, Revive: Kim Ki-young's Housemaid Trilogies," in *Film Trilogies: New Critical Approaches*, ed. C. Perkins and C. Verevis (New York: Palgrave Macmillan: 2012), 150.
5. Kim, *Kim Ki-young*, 73.
6. Lee and Stringer, "Remake, Repeat, Revive," 150.
7. Kim, "'My' Sweet Home in the Next Decade: The Popular Imagination of Private Homeownership during the Yusin Period," in Ryu, *Cultures of Yusin*, 119–40.
8. Lee and Stringer, "Remake, Repeat, Revive," 156.
9. Soyoung Kim, "Modernity in Suspense: The Logic of Fetishism in Korean Cinema," in Kim, *Kim Ki-young*, 31.
10. Lee and Stringer, "Remake, Repeat, Revive," 150.
11. Gilles Deleuze, *Difference and Repetition*, trans. Paul Patton (New York: Columbia University Press, 1994), 1.
12. See Chapter 3 of Deleuze, *Difference and Repetition*.
13. Deleuze, *Difference and Repetition*, 8.
14. Ibid., 10.
15. Ibid., 10.
16. Kim, *Kim Ki-young*, 86.
17. Deleuze, *Difference and Repetition*, 171.
18. See Akira Mizuta Lippit, *Electric Animal: Toward a Rhetoric of Wildlife* (Minneapolis: University of Minnesota Press, 2000), 192–7.
19. Jean Epstein, "On Certain Characteristics of *Photogénie*," in *Jean Epstein: Critical Essays and New Translations*, ed. Sarah Keller and Jason N. Paul (Amsterdam: Amsterdam University Press, 2012), 295.
20. Kim, *Kim Ki-young*, 83.
21. Ibid., 73.
22. See Part 1 of Seungsook Moon, *Militarized Modernity and Gendered Citizenship in South Korea* (Durham: Duke University Press, 2005).

CHAPTER 6

To Speak and To Be Spoken For: Deafness, Stuttering and the Women in the Films of Kim Ki-young

Ariel Schudson

As hundreds of thousands of people watched the 93rd Academy Awards ceremony from their homes (including most of the nominees themselves due to continuing COVID-19 restrictions) elegant actress Youn Yuh-jung walked confidently up to the microphone to accept her Best Supporting Actress Award for her role in Lee Isaac Chung's hit film *Minari* (2020). Looking at the audience and raising the golden statuette upwards, she said "I'd like to dedicate this award [to] my first director Kim Ki-young, who was [a] genius director. I made a movie together with him, [my] first movie. I think he would be very happy if he was still alive." This aspect of her speech went mostly unnoticed. However, when the glitter and glamour were swept from that Oscar stage, one burning question remained: who was this Kim Ki-young?

While the door to discuss Kim Ki-young's film work has never been closed, it was rare that anyone knocked, let alone opened it wide for international audiences and critical consumption. Overall, the usual inquiries have centered on his most famous film: *The Housemaid* (*Hanyeo*, 1960), or the other two works included in what is known as the Housemaid Trilogy: *Woman of Fire* (*Hwanyeo*, 1971) and *Woman of Fire '82* (*Hwanyeo '82*, 1982). But now, with Youn's explicit reference and the extended discourse after the awards show, who knows? The oeuvre of Kim Ki-young may be on its way to greater cinematic appreciation and exploration.

Youn's speech was a crucial moment in the life of this director's work and in the study of his women characters. This now globally recognized actress used her voice to direct attention to one of the most important filmmakers in South Korea. This 'woman's voice' brought him to the Western entertainment industry's attention, deftly pulling his memory onto the Oscar stage and demanding that the world remember and give respect to this filmmaker.

Where women and the films of Kim Ki-young are concerned, I do not use the term "voice" or its associated vocabulary—speak, enunciate, articulate—lightly. I abide by the definition that Christine Ashby uses in her intricate study on disabled individuals that considers typing as a means of communication. As she states, "voice is the right and the ability to make oneself heard and to have one's experiences and perspectives available to others; to participate in the construction of the self and to decide how to represent that self to others."[1] Working on this basis, it is clear that invoking one's voice/vocalization/speaking need not adhere to traditional means of talking. Taking this open path of communication one step further, we must also recognize that the way voice is "heard" can be diverse and plentiful. Taking these as precepts, we can approach Kim Ki-young's films and the women in them with a greater level of openness and understanding.

In this chapter, I will explore and focus on the voices of women in Kim Ki-young's films. His filmic vision examined the female experience in ways that were brutally original, radically creative, and almost always at odds with the very definition of "normative." His career was full of ups and downs. Critical opinion, censorship issues, and politics played havoc with his ability to do everything he wanted to do. But Kim's influence as a filmmaker continues to this day. He was an artist ahead of his time.

Kim Ki-young was an unusual director. His films centered complex discussions of psychology, power struggles, and gender dynamics. His oeuvre delved deep into ideas of sexuality, desire, and class. His characters and their individual arcs reflected all these things. The bulk of his main characters were women. His explorations of eroticism, lust, and desire are deeply connected with femaleness, something well at odds with social mores of the time. This has created a special, even unique space for these films to occupy. Kim's work stands alone in what it does; his films play a critical role in political and social histories, gender representation in cinema, and examinations of sexuality and women's agency. Modern films may have investigated these topics, going so far as to remake Kim's own 1960 masterpiece, *The Housemaid*,[2] but no one has managed to build the kinds of characters or evoke the tones and challenging visions that Kim did. A landmark director with a defiantly independent focus, his work was rarely like his peers. Kim certainly tried to make a few films "just for the money" although he never truly saw much reward. He also began his career relatively traditionally, making documentary shorts and propaganda reels for the US Information Service (USIS) like his peers. But it didn't take him long to become recognized as the singular director he would remain for the rest of his life.

My focus will be on two of Kim Ki-young's lesser-known works: *Water Lady* (*Sunyeo*, 1979) and *Neumi* (1980). I will consider these films and the way women's speaking voices are represented, the way social identities are "othered," and how women's stories are negotiated within. Both films position disabled women as protagonists and explicitly study issues of communication engagement through ableist perspectives and conceptions of bodily normativity. I will further this examination into character-specific situations of motherhood and sexuality, opening rich discussions of Korean history, agency, disability discourse, and power dynamics. Drawing from definitive and respected texts in the fields of feminist and critical disability studies, film theory, and Korean historiography, I will consider how constructed normalcy, fragile or shattered masculine identities, and the "normative gaze" can have a profound effect on how disabled women and their voices are interpreted. By discussing these films and the intimate lives of the women in them, we will see how Kim was able to advance subversive concepts for women, their bodily autonomy, and the disabled in general.

A DISABLED FOR A DISABLED: *WATER LADY*, DISABILITY HIERARCHIES AND SEX

Water Lady explores concepts of gender performativity, motherhood, and sexuality all through the lens of disability. While *Neumi*'s coupling presents two people from opposite sides of the tracks whose differences eventually drive them apart, *Water Lady* presents a couple whose shared disabled identification is ruptured by the constructed nature of normalcy, gender troubles, and compulsory able-bodiedness. This film explores their relationship and the way they experience trauma, gender roles, and sexuality while starting a new family.

Jin-seok is a Korean Vietnam veteran returning home after the war with a debilitating leg injury. He grudgingly accepts an arranged marriage with Su-ok, a woman with a severe stutter, in exchange for farmland. When he is unsuccessful in working the land, Su-ok introduces her husband to the bamboo basket-making craft that has been in her family for generations, and she begins to financially support both of them through basket sales. Jin-seok sees this as an opportunity, sells their land and creates a business out of selling the bamboo baskets, demanding that Su-ok produce more and more merchandise in order to compete with rival businesses. Su-ok's pregnancy announcement comes at a very inconvenient time for Jin-seok, and while he hires women from the village as employees, his business sense is less than ideal. As their son, Yong-il, matures, he begins to stutter and Su-ok's father and Jin-seok insist he is sent away to a specialized school in Seoul while the business continues to expand. This action prompts an ultimatum from Su-ok to her husband—if you reject my son, I will reject you. She stops sleeping with him and tells him that she will bear no more children by him. Jin-seok's solution? He seeks solace in Chu-wol, a beautiful, scheming femme fatale. Yong-il returns from school, without any speaking issues and, after exploring her own desires and needs, Su-ok breaks free from her previous self, becoming free and independent.

Before meeting Jin-seok, Su-ok's stutter had made her unmarriageable, forcing her into a life of (mostly) shamed silence. In a study done by Michael Petrunik and Clifford D. Shearing, they discuss the coping mechanisms used by stutterers, listing them as concealment, openness, and disavowal. They note that "avoiding stuttering has many costs. Some tactics exclude the stutterer from fully participating in life as a 'normal person' infringing on the very status the stutterer wishes to preserve."[3] We first meet Su-ok in the house she lives in with her father. Pak Am, the town head, has brought Jin-seok to see what he would be getting as a wife in this arranged marriage. He manages to convince the Vietnam War veteran that this woman's disability would be to his advantage. He tells him that his own wife's talking is irritating and that a mostly silent wife is good. His exact words, "Women are the workforce, not the sound of the radio," go a long way in telling us how women's voices (whether able or disabled) are seen by men in this world.

During this meeting, Su-ok refuses to speak. Jin-seok, frustrated after having to show his future father-in-law that he can walk and is not the "cripple" that everyone thinks he is, almost throws up his hands and leaves at her silence. "At least she should be able to sing the national anthem!" he says, ready to walk out. At this point, Su-ok grabs his legs and begins to sing, making her way, however haltingly, through the Korean national anthem. The obvious analogy here is Su-ok and Jin-seok are two pieces of a shattered postwar Korea, broken and disabled but thrown together in the hope that they can somehow make it work. In this regard, while *Water Lady* is a work that discusses nationalism, post-colonial devastation, and the masculine search for identity in a messy postwar existence, a glib analogy such as the one mentioned above does the depth of this film a disservice. As we will see below, the parts that masculinity, disability, and Korean history play in this film are much more sophisticated.

The speaking "test" that the town head administers to Su-ok for Jin-seok to better assess her speaking (dis)ability is the entrance to the film as much as Jin-seok's own walking test. Aside from being an example of inhumane treatment at the hands of the able-bodied, this scene identifies the kind of "looked-at-ness" that disabled women face. It is an experience that exceeds the kind of sexual objectification from the male gaze that Laura Mulvey has written about in her work. It moves promptly forward to seeing disabled women as spectacle. Rosemary Garland-Thomson has aptly identified this as "the stare" and posits that vocabulary such as "leering" or "gawking" would be the appropriate terms attending this kind of viewing of the disabled form.[4] In the case of *Water Lady*, we must adjust. It is not the stare but "the listen." It does remain an identical mode of separating the normative body from "the freak" or performed/seen/heard physical deviancy. From the very start of the film, Su-ok's voice and disabled-ness in her voice are front and center.

Lennard J. Davis's discourse on understanding disabled bodies in the context of enforced and performed normalcy is vital to the consideration of *Water Lady*. We cannot look at disability without studying how "normalcy" is constructed; it is central to discerning the way that abled people think of disability as an illness or a problem. In Davis's seminal work, "Constructing Normalcy: The Bell Curve, The Novel, and the Invention of the Disabled Body in the Nineteenth Century," he discusses the field of eugenics and its relationship to the disabled body. He details the connection between statistics and eugenics, recounting that "almost all early statisticians had one thing in common: they were eugenicists." Using this research, he examines ideas of physical normativity from the viewpoint of nineteenth-century scientists. Davis's conclusion? Through their studies, these men can be held at least partially responsible for establishing the social concept of a "normal body." Their work rejected disability and the disabled body, establishing it as non-normative and an outlier to the standard to which all else should be held. Davis explores the way these nineteenth-century ideas of an "ideal body" relative to the general population were developed, and then concludes:

> First, the application of the idea of a norm to the human body creates the idea of deviance or a "deviant" body. Second, the idea of a norm pushes the normal variation of the body through a stricter template guiding the way the body "should" be . . . This statistical ideal is unlike the classical ideal which contains no imperative to be the ideal. The new ideal of ranked order is powered by the imperative of the norm, and then is supplemented by the notion of progress, human perfectibility, and the elimination of deviance, to create a dominating, hegemonic vision of what the human body should be.[5]

Disabled people are not the problem. The issues that arise in and around disability lie with the historically centered theories of normalcy based on eugenics. We create these terms to identify/signify difference and, more times than not, do it based upon systems of oppression and privilege. This construction is directly applicable to disability and terms such as "normal," "regular," "typical," "average." As follows, disability or illness are the deviant positions, identifiably a problem. Normal is the status quo. But going back to Davis's discourse, this also means that "normal" is solidly privileged, constructed, and oppressive, intentionally created in order to suggest that anything that would stray from that identity would be somehow in the "wrong" category.

The construction of normalcy is why both Jin-seok and Su-ok have to "perform" for other people and each other before they are allowed to marry. The construction of normalcy is why Jin-seok, himself disabled, is incredibly disappointed at having to marry a woman who stutters but figures that it is the "best he could get." This false notion may claim to have a basis on ideas of social acceptability within Korean culture,[6] but it has a much stronger foundation in privilege and structural oppression. Furthermore, Jin-seok may have to prove his physical viability for Su-ok's father/family but Su-ok? She must speak in front of Jin-seok, the town head, and her father. She must prove her worth and value as a woman in front of multiple representations of masculinity: familial (father), matrimonial (future husband), and governmental/political (town head). This is the way of the world for women and Kim Ki-young meticulously constructs each of these scenes in a way that expresses the pain and the outrage of that experience.

Soon after the birth of their son, Su-ok refuses to help Jin-seok with the business. This is not the first time she has done this. Ever since he sold their farmland in favor of starting their bamboo basket business, he has been making up excuses as to why Su-ok should be making all the baskets. She keeps telling him that he should learn the skill and that he should be able to do it too. She tells him that her mother told her that a woman with good skills will never be happy because she will have a lazy husband. Jin-seok ignores her, satisfied with her doing the hard work and him running the company. As Carol Thomas observes:

> The experience of disability is always gendered, that disablism is interwoven with sexism (and racism, and homophobia, and so on). This is not to say that disabled men and women have no common ground, no shared experiences of disablism, but that the forms of disablism are always refracted in some way through the prisms of gendered locations and gender relations.[7]

Jin-seok places himself higher than Su-ok on what is commonly recognized as the "disability hierarchy" because his disability was acquired during war. He was not always disabled; he was disabled in service of the nation! He was born healthy/able. He did not always limp. Jin-seok sees himself as having given up his ableness and in so doing his masculinity in service to his country. Korea's involvement in Vietnam was complicated and Jin-seok's own relationship to his military past is complicated as well, perhaps deserving of its own study. But when it comes to the way that this formerly able but now disabled man relates to his own body, Jin-seok's connection to his physical form and abilities has become complex and he makes Su-ok suffer as a result.

When their marriage is being brokered by Pak Am, Jin-seok mutters to himself, "a disabled for a disabled," with a disgusted look on his face. He does not see himself as disabled. He sees himself as an able man having sacrificed something for his country. He has lost something, never to be gotten back. And now this disabled woman is being foisted on him, after all he has worked for? For some land? He is resentful, angry, bitter. Doesn't he deserve better? Su-ok's stutter was congenitally received, not received through sacrifice and therefore, in Jin-seok's purview, his leg injury is somehow superior to her stutter. Jin-seok doesn't listen to Su-ok when she speaks and feels fine about ignoring her. Not only does he not like hearing her voice because it reminds him of her disability (and, in turn, his own), but he also does not feel that he must since he is the "man of the house," whether he is making the baskets or not.

Walking into the room where Su-ok is feeding Yong-il, Jin-seok sits next to his wife, and asks her to do several work-related tasks. Su-ok stops feeding the child, stands up, and tells her husband no. She says that it is time that he stopped asking for help. Even if he makes mistakes, it's time to do things himself. Now he has no other choice but to listen. He protests, saying that he feels insecure when she doesn't lead the way. Su-ok reiterates, saying that it is time that he "walked for himself" and "stopped breast-feeding." She gives an example of how she taught Yong-il that it was time to stop breast-feeding (she drew a goblin on her breast and slapped him). She then makes a face like a goblin at Jin-seok and says, "I'm going to hit you now," and slaps him. Jin-seok seems shocked at Su-ok's actions, but he wouldn't be if he had been listening. She has told him the same thing several times: do it yourself, figure it out on your own, try to do it independently. While her words and phrases infantilize him, she is not doing it to ridicule or embarrass him. She just wants him to gain some independence.

Released in 1979, *Water Lady* comes just at the height of the period where the Korean government felt that it was right and just to mark disabled women for, among other horrific practices, involuntary sterilization. Eunjung Kim's work on motherhood and disability is of critical use here. Her discussions on colonialism and the history of disability in Korea play out to eerie perfection within the narrative confines of Kim Ki-young's *Water Lady*. Discussing the ideas of disability and "curative intervention," she details how the theories and practices of eugenics (a Western invention) were adopted in post-war Korea. Kim writes:

> [The] process by which eugenics was codified into Korean law in the 1970s—specifically targeting disabled women—is directly connected to the eugenics movements of the 1920s and 30s, but this time with a pronounced emphasis on strengthening the sovereign nation-state . . . The first legislation, the National Eugenics Bill, came in 1964 and proposed legal abortions for disabled women and permanent sterilization. This bill did not pass but the one that originated from it, the Mother and Child Health Act of 1973, did. This law was less obviously anti-disabled women given its more palatable name, but still violated disabled people's reproductive rights that the Mother and Child Health Act made legal . . . the

language of eugenics reveal[ed] an extremely problematic conception of maternal health. It automatically disqualifi[ed] disabled women from reproducing at all.[8]

Disabled women becoming mothers is still a difficult concept for the able-bodied world to grasp.[9] The article in the Mother and Child Act that allowed doctors to sterilize patients if they are found to have an "illness" that could be handed down genetically was not removed until 1999. As Kim states, while officials may have insisted that sterilization never actually happened, the law definitely "promoted involuntary sterilization as the duty of medical professionals under state authorization."[10] In the eyes and minds of most able-bodied people, a disabled woman's maternal ability and actualization pushes the boundaries of what is "appropriate" or "socially acceptable."

When Su-ok's father discovers that Yong-il has developed a stutter similar to the one that Su-ok has, this has a major impact on Su-ok. While she sees no problem with her son, no deviancy, Jin-seok and her father see the child as disabled and needing to be "fixed." After the speech lessons she was giving their son failed to prevent him from developing a stutter, her father visits and suggests a special school in Seoul. Su-ok refuses to let Yong-il go. Jin-seok asks his father-in-law if he thinks the school will help him. The man shrugs and replies, almost sadly, that the child needs to have teachers that speak well; Yong-il is just copying the way that Su-ok talks. Su-ok watches this conversation, a look of horror and devastation coming over her face. Jin-seok's extreme desire to remove their child from the family home and "cure" him of the stutter that the boy shares with his mother screams of the kind of gender-centric and culturally focused curative violence Eunjung Kim writes about. She states:

> In Korean culture, placing responsibility on mothers not to reproduce disabled children has a history of eugenic campaigns and postcolonial nation-building and of cultural representations of heredity drama. [C]ure thus represents the denial of different bodies not only in the form of prevention but also in the form of the elimination of disability.[11]

The removal (even temporarily) of Yong-il also represents Jin-seok's rejection of Su-ok and her disability. From where she is coming from, if you want to oust the challenging child, why would you want to keep the equally challenging adult, especially since Su-ok can't be 'easily fixed' like Yong-il apparently can?

When her husband makes the decision to eliminate the undesirable voice from their family, Su-ok makes a powerful decision to reject Jin-seok from her bed, future procreation, and communication with her. She tells him, in no uncertain terms, that she will no longer have sex with him, no longer bear his

Figure 6.1 Scene from *Water Lady*.

children, and no longer speak to him. "I will be quiet forever," she says. In this pivotal moment of the film, we watch as Jin-seok uses his male power to take away their son due to what he sees as a problem: disability. Returning to Davis, Jin-seok is part of the process that constructs normalcy, making disability "deviant"; it is something that needs to be cured. It seems impossible for him to see the disabled body, even his own, as diverse, plentiful, human. For him, there is only normative existence and the imagined landscape of physical perfection; he wants his progeny to conform to a classification that does not exist.

Su-ok is a disabled woman, placing her at the center of the matrixes of oppression suffered by multiple disenfranchised groups (disabled, women, mothers, economically disadvantaged) that have had to struggle under the weight of constructed labels such as "normal," "polite," or "well-behaved." When Jin-seok non-consensually removes her child, something inside Su-ok shatters. While she has (literally) voiced her opinions to him before in regard to his laziness and his need to get on his own two feet with the business, this is the final straw. She becomes proudly transgressive. She claims her own space, liberating her sexuality and her voice concurrently. She no longer allows Jin-seok in her bed, ordering their company to begin producing body-sized, phallic-shaped bed companions called bamboo wives. As one of the men walking by the women weaving the wives wryly notes (almost with a wink and a nod), they were "Egyptian creations, made for the summertime for the queen in bed." Clearly, these objects are not just to help keep the bed "cooler during the summertime."

The film, capitalizing on Kim Deok-jin's excellent cinematography, gives us two exquisite scenes with Su-ok in bed with her bamboo wife, experiencing significant sexual satisfaction. These scenes stand out from the rest of the film as do Jin-seok's responses to seeing the bamboo wife in the bed where he thinks

Figure 6.2 Scene from *Water Lady*.

he should be. She has told him that she no longer wants him there but the presence of something else there angers him. He sees that his fragile masculinity, his easily fracturable sexual pride, has been replaced by a manufactured item. To make it worse, it is a woman-made item, from the business that he (incorrectly) thinks is his and that he started. Su-ok asked the women to make it. His wife's sexuality is threatening to him but so is the idea that she asked the team of women to help her create this erotic object that (as we later learn) is selling quite well. His wife would rather have a body-shaped bamboo basket than him in her bed. He thought her bed would remain empty since she was disabled and helpless in his purview.

Su-ok may have a stutter but separating her from her child has given her the power to develop strong sexual agency and a voice all her own. These intimate scenes between Su-ok and her bamboo wife shift how her sexuality and desire have been seen by the viewer. Although this is not the first time we have seen her experience sexuality on-screen, it is the first time she experiences personal pleasure. Previously, she sought to soothe Jin-seok's wounds when they were first married which evolved into a beautifully shot erotic encounter between the couple. But this was localized in a desire to want to be a good, obedient, helpful wife. When Su-ok puts her arms around the long-woven bamboo body-shaped object, she is alone in bed. The apparatus is empty on the inside. As the music and lighting rises and falls around her, showing her face as she rolls around on her sleeping mat, she has never enjoyed her own body so much.

For a woman whose life has been full of people telling her that her body is not "normal" and she is broken, less than, un-able, this scene is critical. Through her own sexual pleasure, she discovers that she is not broken. Su-ok works just fine. Her body is beautiful, wonderful, gives her joy, and is of value.

As the film draws to a close, Su-ok backslides a little bit in terms of how she engages with Jin-seok and how she treats herself as a woman, a wife, and a disabled person. But there can be no question that her finale allows her to declare strength and identity. In a striking final sequence, Su-ok takes a stand. She asserts her independence and her voice, stating (without a stutter), "I'm going to say what I have to say and live." She announces to the entire community that Jin-seok has treated her poorly and she will no longer tolerate it. Hugging her young son who has just recited an emotionally charged rendition of the Children's Charter, she walks off, leaving Jin-seok alone on the beach.

Water Lady is honest about its portrayal of human beings. Jin-seok and Su-ok have a deep and intimate relationship. While they may understand and care for each other on several levels, it is an indisputably toxic relationship; Su-ok's ability to challenge this, through her disability, her voice, makes her character all the more meaningful.

FORCED PERSPECTIVES: *NEUMI* AND AUDIENCE INTERACTIVITY

Neumi tells the story of Jun-tae, a recent college graduate who has become obsessed with Neumi, a married deaf brick factory worker. When her husband is murdered by the factory's truck driver, Jun-tae forces Neumi to accept him into her life, taking her from what he sees as a pitiable existence into a relationship with him (which he feels will be much better). Ultimately, Jun-tae's efforts to "rescue" Neumi lead her, ironically, into asserting her independence. She leaves him and he meets a solidly more tragic end.

Before we venture into the text, I want to clarify some of the terms and explain their use. Within Deaf culture, deafness is not seen as a disability. In fact, as one source rightly suggests, "in a room full of Deaf people it is the hearing person who cannot sign who is disabled."[12] While not all deaf individuals identify with Deaf culture or this line of thinking, I want to make space for those that do. I will discuss concepts of disability and able-bodied-ness within this section but only to underscore larger issues of ableism and ableist stereotypes that exist. I want to suggest that while this film may portray how the world sees deafness as a disability, it does not view Neumi as a disabled woman, which is significant and says something very important for Deaf culture.

As the film begins, we see Jun-tae watching Neumi from the window of his house. She is drawing water from a pump, putting it in buckets. She is engaging in her daily labor, quite unaware she is being watched as well as being visually documented. While she goes about her business, not only is Jun-tae evaluating her physical presence, aesthetic, and actions, he is taking photos of her. Trying to possess and control her through the visual image. In this one act, Jun-tae shatters any privacy she had, exploiting it for his own use; in this secret invasion, Jun-tae announces his intention to invade her life, which he eventually does.

In the earlier discussion of *Water Lady*, we engaged Rosemary Garland-Thomson's work on disabled women and sexual objectification, specifically in and around the concepts of "looked-at-ness" and disabled women as spectacle. It is in *Neumi* that Kim Ki-young plays with ideas that are directly analogous with Garland-Thomson's vocabulary and further concepts introduced by Laura Mulvey in "Visual Pleasure and Narrative Cinema." The relationship that Kim creates between Jun-tae and Neumi is all at once about leering/gawking (Garland-Thomson) and ownership, attraction, power, and the male gaze (Mulvey). *Neumi* is a film that engages ideas about deafness and motherhood; it is also a critique on how men view and treat women. Concepts of power, ownership, and entitlement loom large.

Mulvey writes, "man can live out his phantasies and obsessions through linguistic command by imposing them on the silent image of woman still tied to her place as bearer of meaning, not maker of meaning."[13] *Neumi* is a film about a deaf woman and her relationship with a man who is obsessed with her. This is a critical area to examine. What does Jun-tae want with her? Jun-tae's obsession and stalking of Neumi does him no favors, but her eventual assumption of a life with him doesn't seem to ring approvingly of feminist independence either. So how do we determine meaning in a film where meaning and language is the very crux of the story? It is here that we look at who is the bearer of meaning, and who the maker of meaning, and how the audience might distinguish between the two, identifying each voice.

Neumi's deafness renders her non-verbal, but her voice is represented through physical expressions and actions. When she does choose to verbalize/put words to her communications, it is always through writing on Jun-tae's hands who in turn reads the phrases out loud so that the audience can be involved. This performative triangle must be examined carefully. I would like to bring in some definitions from Johnson Cheu as they have direct bearing on the relationship between the audience and Neumi's articulations. In Cheu's incisive work on the blind female gaze in American cinema, he takes the time to define important concepts regarding the able and disabled body. Cheu states:

> The terms "disabled/able-bodied people" historically allude to the idea of impairment. The terms "disabled/non-disabled people" are gaining parlance in disability studies to signify cultural identity. By

utilizing the term "able-bodied," I am attempting to serve the dual purpose of referencing the historical use of the "disabled/abled" paradigm—that is, impairment—while simultaneously recognizing the reclamation of naming as part of the process of claiming a disability identity. I use the term "Able-bodied gaze" as the polar opposite of the "Disabled gaze" . . . when I intend to reference literally physically embodied difference. In this way I examine a doubly marginalized, "othered" group, namely, characters who are both female and blind. Since both these groups are subject to dominant ways of looking, the term "normative" better encompasses the dominant power structure in play.[14]

As the audience listens to Neumi through Jun-tae, we do so through the dominant power structure: an able-bodied/man. Cheu's discussion is on blind women, and how they are othered twice as much by the cinematic gaze due to their woman-ness and disabled-ness. Neumi most certainly is also part of that community. Here is the crux: Neumi is the protagonist of the film and the character that we are designed to align ourselves with. This is an awkward and challenging situation to put viewers in. The audience is a group that looks through what Cheu has noted as the "dominant lens" and could certainly be considered to be "normative" in this context. Thus, the viewer is positioned as able-bodied, hearing, and, in a certain sense, male or at least male-facilitated; essentially serving as a consumer but participating as part of the dominant system of power.

By titling the film and making clear who you are supposed to be identifying with, Kim Ki-young flips this concept with *Neumi*. He is challenging the audience to try harder, dig deeper into what now might be a very uncomfortable viewing experience. Throughout the film, Kim reminds us that Neumi is the character that we are supposed to be supporting and yet, with Jun-tae, he has provided an example of everything that Neumi is not. The able-bodied, educated, middle-high class man versus the disabled, deaf, uneducated, working-class woman. This film certainly gives the "normative gaze" a run for its money. It is easier and more comfortable to follow Jun-tae than Neumi. I would argue that it is precisely in this viewer disorientation where the audience is able to discover the most meaning. In this respect, while it is difficult trying to meaningfully identify and have empathy for a character that is intentionally being singled out as "different from you, the Able-bodied viewer," Kim Ki-young has always aimed for the most cinematically satisfying, not the most simplistic approaches to his craft.

Historically (and in the context of the film) it would have been likely that Neumi knew KSL (Korean Sign Language). According to Susan Fischer and Qunhu Gong, "Sign language has been in use in Korea since 1889, thus

Figure 6.3 Scene from *Neumi*.

predating the Japanese occupation; KSL has been used in Korean schools since 1908."[15] But since Jun-tae was not trained in this capacity, Neumi must communicate with him using fingerspelling (dactylology). Fingerspelling can be done in two ways: visually (in the air) or tactually (on someone's hand) and simulates the shapes of a given language (in this case, *hangul*). When Neumi speaks to Jun-tae, she adjusts her voice and speech for a non-deaf audience. She translates what she has to say from her own language and methods of communication to one that he can understand. Each time she takes his hand and traces something on it, she is making an extra effort so that her voice may be heard. But her undertaking—this extra effort at "translation"—is not appreciated by Jun-tae.

Neumi's voice, when heard by the audience, is controlled by Jun-tae. His vocal cords say her words, his visage reads and reacts to the characters she writes on his palm. By verbalizing the messages written on his hand, Jun-tae becomes part of a deeply performative communication act, giving the audience access to what Neumi must "literally" say. Without this exposition, viewers would have a hard time figuring out what Jun-tae and Neumi were saying to each other. The choice to have Jun-tae serve as "interpreter" was at least partially made for diegetic simplicity. The audience needs to know what is going on, the film needs to be able to keep moving. However, having Jun-tae speak for Neumi also underscores major character and power issues. There is not one point from the start to the finish of the film where Jun-tae does not want to have control of or own Neumi. The power dynamic here is real.

Examining this triangulated relationship that Kim Ki-young sets up between the audience, Neumi, and those trying to speak to/with Neumi is highly valuable in trying to evaluate Neumi's methods of communication. While many scenes throughout the film show Neumi in conversation with Jun-tae, how often do we, as an audience, question if she is "hearing" what he is saying? The film itself becomes a commentary about listening/hearing, respect for others, and ultimately, a deaf woman's choice whether to engage with the ignorant hearing people around her who, most of the time, are simply talking to hear themselves speak.

One of the strongest examples of the audience—Neumi—conversant relationship can be seen at the beginning of the film. Neumi's husband has been killed and she is in mourning. Jun-tae goes to check on her when a neighbor tells him she is considering revenge on the man who killed her husband, a driver called Gwak. When Jun-tae enters Neumi's home, she is sitting on the floor holding her baby, staring vacantly ahead of her. Jun-tae disregards her feelings about her husband's death by saying that she shouldn't consider revenge or think that her husband's death was anything but accidental. He goes so far as to say that she's delusional, and that he himself was the one who was able to prove the death was simply manslaughter. Jun-tae continues to disparage her feelings and experiences, saying that no one would actually cause an accident just because they were interested in someone else's wife. This is, of course, completely foolish because he had seen Gwak sexually harassing Neumi while she worked. He had also witnessed Neumi's husband get severely angry about Gwak's behavior. Jun-tae doesn't seem to care about the reality of what has happened, just about his own truth and how he will benefit the most.

He continues walking around the room, chattering on and on about how Neumi needs to eat to stay healthy and keep milk flowing for the baby. As Jun-tae walks, talks, and paces around the living space, telling Neumi exactly what she should/shouldn't be doing, Neumi's face and body stay in the same position, sitting on the floor, eyes focused in front of her.

There is something desperately wrong with this picture. Neumi is deaf. She. Reads. Lips. Even when Jun-tae makes food and sits down with her, she still doesn't move her head or respond. She just looks straight ahead. And Jun-tae? He's still chattering on. He thinks he's being charming and has simply made a social faux pas. He glosses over it lightly as though it were nothing, saying that he "forgot! Only married couples eat together!" and laughs, saying he will go wash the diapers. He leaves the room. The minute Jun-tae is out of the camera frame, Neumi tears into the chicken he has made, hungrily. The camera cuts to a grinning Jun-tae, washing diapers in the kitchen, a room positioned at the back of the house. Neumi continues eating in the front room, and he looks in, again watching Neumi without her knowledge. He cheerily shouts a kind of "I told you so" about how eating food is good for her and the baby and asks her if she would like more chicken soup. If there was a moment in the film that best demonstrated Jun-tae's ignorance of the situation, this would be it. If Neumi didn't respond to him talking to her when he was walking around next to her or sitting across from her, did he really think she would be able to hear him from the other room? On the issue of communication the National Deaf Center on Postsecondary Outcomes notes:

> There is no "one-size-fits-all" approach to communication, nor is there a "typical" deaf person. Each individual is unique and brings their own set of communication needs and preferences, based on the setting and the purpose of the interaction. Determining how to communicate effectively is a joint effort shared by both the deaf individual and the hearing individual. Trial and error until a solution is achieved is often the rule rather than the exception. Flexibility and creativity are key.[16]

While this is undoubtedly the case, they also underscore the necessity for certain visual cues for the deaf person and point out helpful tips such as "Look directly at the individual while speaking," "Do not cover your mouth or look around while speaking," and "Get the attention of the deaf individual before speaking. If the individual does not respond to the spoken name, a tap on the shoulder or another visual signal is appropriate." Jun-tae's attitude towards Neumi's deafness is indicative of how he views her: as an object, a thing, something to be owned. She is not a person, someone to be listened to, nor someone who needed to listen to him. This attitude towards Neumi as an individual and a woman continues throughout the film until he, too late, learns his lesson.

In these scenes, the audience witnesses direct exchanges between a deaf woman and a hearing man. Returning to Cheu's discussion on the normative gaze and a character who is a member of not one but two marginalized groups, it is only fair to ask: how are these conversations consumed by the audience? Due to the high likelihood that the viewer will assume the hearing/able-bodied position, Neumi's perspective will not be recognized. No one will see anything awkward about Jun-tae prancing around the house, donning the hat of domesticity, happily making food for Neumi to eat, and chatting to her as though she can respond. This is part of Kim Ki-young's challenge to the audience: will you evaluate who is speaking within this film and how? Will you look to see how characters express the act of listening? If Jun-tae continues to speak to Neumi without acknowledging that she can only hear him when she can see him, what does that say about the speeches he makes to/for/about her when she has her back turned to him and is not facing him?

In his text, "Distending Straight-Masculine Time: A Phenomenology of the Disabled Speaking Body," Joshua St. Pierre calls upon the work of Nick Crossley and Kevin Paterson to discuss ideas of communication in conversation with choreography and the disabled speaking body. He notes:

> The choreography taken for granted by able-bodied speakers is not simply a neutral script guiding human communication, but consists of normalized rules played *against* disabled bodies who cannot hit the right cues, or speak quickly or fluidly enough. For Paterson, disabled speakers are accordingly objectified because they belong to a different communicative culture.[17]

As the film presses on, the communication choreography between the couple demonstrates St. Pierre's assertion. Jun-tae's discourse takes place over the silences that Neumi's disability produces. He is allowed to speak, discuss, perform things that are happening in his world or his consciousness. He speaks *over* her. She must speak "through" him. He never thinks about whether she hears him, shown by the numerous times he continues to speak when he is not facing her and/or his lips are not visible to her eyes. And so Neumi's objectification continues, initially done through the lens of the camera (in reference to Jun-tae's perspective), it is now undertaken via Jun-tae 's control of their communications.

Jun-tae quickly moves into Neumi's home, buying her expensive clothes, promising her marriage and wanting to sleep with her, all of which she responds to with hesitancy and even flat-out rejection. When Jun-tae goes to work one day, her neighbors destroy their home. This newly widowed woman with fancy clothes and a man in her house? Not in our neighborhood! They think that Neumi is living immorally, as an "easy" or "dirty" woman, but they fail to realize that she did not have a say in Jun-tae's actions. The disjointedness of the power dynamic between Jun-tae and Neumi therefore remains at the forefront in terms of how she is treated by others around her in the narrative. As Brenda Brueggeman has written, "[w]hen the woman is deaf, in a culture in which the woman is still seen as typically more 'dependent' in a male–female relationship, her further dependence on a hearing partner can dangerously diminish her autonomy."[18]

Their lives together continue to fall apart. Jun-tae is reduced to being just another member of the lumpen, disadvantaged working class, something he is not very good at. In fact, he is miserable at it. Neumi has been treated poorly by everyone she encounters as a result of her association with Jun-tae, and she makes a deadly decision. She attempts a murder–suicide by placing a burning briquette in their bedroom as Jun-tae and her child are sleeping. As Eunjung Kim writes:

Revenge and suicide practiced as a form of private justice defy distanced anger and depoliticized compassion toward the images of victimized disabled individuals [. . .] As a *pharmakon*, the violence against oneself and others becomes a conceptual and practical response to violence committed in the name of cure.[19]

Although Jun-tae never set out to "cure" Neumi of her disability, he certainly sought to "fix" her life, which arguably amounts to a "cure" mentality. Here, her murder–suicide attempt has as much anger behind it as it does compassion. By lovingly placing the pillow over Jun-tae's face, she shows equal measures of consideration and desperation. Neumi is tired of this situation that Jun-tae has created for the two of them. None of her exigent circumstances are due to things she has created: her class status, single motherhood, living circumstances. Yet Jun-tae has continually placed her in situations where people are punishing her for all these things, and he takes no accountability.

After a troublesome finale where Neumi tries to punish herself by reconnecting with the driver Gwak, she finally leaves Jun-tae but not without having her final say. Neumi is selling her things while Jun-tae looks on, devastated. When the makeshift garage sale ends, he puts out his hand for her to say/write something. She looks directly at him and shakes her head. She is done talking "his way." While she has come to care for Jun-tae, she has become quite aware that their relationship is toxic and must end. She has no words left for him. She severs their communication and conversation pathway forever and takes leave of that space. Saying nothing and physically leaving is a way of directly making her voice heard and physically felt.

VOICES CARRY: THE IMPACT OF *WATER LADY* AND *NEUMI*

Kim Ki-young championed ideas of disability representation and women's agency in *Water Lady* and *Neumi*, developing forceful stories and dynamic characters. These films engage in incisive inquiries into normativity and call attention to the notion that being "normal" is a performative or constructed act, something Kim returns to again and again in his films. Neumi and Su-ok's voices are revealed with care and honesty; they are given personhood in a cinematic environment where many other films featuring disabled and deaf women regard those attributes with pity. Each woman has the space required to communicate to the audience who she is as a person, her pain, her desires, and her story, above and beyond what her disability might be.

Neumi and *Water Lady* gain even more import as we head further into the world of critical disability theory, feminist disability theory, and Korean classic film history studies. While these fields are still mostly new, these media texts are in serious conversation with the academic work that has already been produced by luminaries such as Lennard J. Davis, Rosemary Garland-Thomson, and Eunjung Kim. For newer scholars, these films provide a panoply of topics to discuss and work with, allowing them to expand and engage these areas of study in new and dynamic ways. *Water Lady* and *Neumi* and the characters within offer a space for rich discussions centered on disability, gender, sexuality, class, culture, and their intersections, as these are critical aspects of both the films' narratives and the world at large. Crucially, these are Korean films featuring Korean women with disabilities and they cannot for one moment be taken out of that sociopolitical and sociocultural landscape. Their value (and indeed Kim Ki-young's value) to Korean film history and Korean history itself is inestimable and only grows with time as these films are reconsidered through these various lenses. What I have discussed within this chapter is only a small portion of what could be potentially examined from these films relative to Korea as a post-colonial, postwar nation with a deep and complicated context of social inequality in particular relation to gender and disability. We are just at the beginning of the process of unpacking Kim Ki-young's contribution to cinematic culture and the relevance of his films to the larger academic environment.

NOTES

1. Christine E. Ashby, "Whose 'Voice' is it Anyway?: Giving Voice and Qualitative Research Involving Individuals that Type to Communicate," *Disability Studies Quarterly* 31 (2011).
2. Director Im Sang-soo remade *The Housemaid* in 2010, while award-winning South Korean filmmakers Bong Joon Ho and Park Chan-wook have repeatedly made mention of the fact that that Kim Ki-young is a major influence on their work.
3. Michael Petrunik and Clifford D. Shearing, "Fragile Facades: Stuttering and the Strategic Manipulation of Awareness," *Social Problems* 31, no. 2 (1983): 125–38.
4. Rosemary Garland-Thomson, "*Re-shaping, Re-thinking, Re-Defining: Feminist Disability Studies,*" Barbara Waxman Fiduccia Papers on Women and Girls with Disabilities (Washington, DC: Center for Women Policy Studies, 2011), 9.
5. Lennard J. Davis, "Constructing Normalcy: The Bell Curve, the Novel, and the Invention of the Disabled Body in the Nineteenth Century," in *The Disability Studies Reader*, ed. Lennard J. Davis (New York: Routledge, 2006), 3–16.
6. Eunjung Kim details the immense pressure put on Korean women not to produce disabled offspring. This extended itself to an overall feeling that a disability (or disabled person) should simply not exist. It is, as she states, "the mobilization of biopolitics based on the presumed desire for disability's absence." Eunjung Kim, *Curative Violence: Rehabilitating Disability, Gender, and Sexuality in Modern Korea* (New York: Duke University Press, 2017), 79.
7. Carol Thomas, *Female Forms: Experiencing and Understanding Disability* (Buckingham: Open University Press, 1999), 28.
8. Kim, *Curative Violence*, 61.

9. These applications of eugenics and laws that enforced sterilization of and abortions for disabled women only reinforce the way the world buys into what Lennard J. Davis has framed as the normative body discourse. Julia Daniels writes, "This normalcy positions disabled women as asexual, lacking, and, especially regarding the case of reproductive rights, non-maternal and somehow 'sick.' This system of thinking fixes disabled women in a position where they are somehow inferior to able-bodied women and it becomes prescriptive, seeing disabled women as not deserving of motherhood or the maternal experience due to their inability to 'measure up.'" Julia Daniels, "Disabled Mothering? Outlawed, Overlooked and Severely Prohibited: Interrogating Ableism in Motherhood," *People with Disabilities: The Overlooked Consumers* 7, no. 1 (2019); https://doi.org/10.17645/si.v7i1.1551.
10. Ibid., 65.
11. Ibid., 79.
12. "Deaf Culture," Aussie Deaf Kids, last updated October 27, 2021, accessed December 30, 2021, https://www.aussiedeafkids.org.au/deaf-culture.html.
13. Laura Mulvey, "Visual Pleasure and Narrative Cinema," in *Feminism and Film Theory*, ed. Constance Penley (New York: Routledge, 1988), 57–60.
14. Johnson Cheu, "Seeing Blindness On-Screen: The Blind, Female Gaze," in *The Problem Body: Projecting Disability on Film*, ed. Sally Chivers and Nicole Markotic (Columbus: Ohio State University, 2010), 67–81.
15. Susan Fischer and Qunhu Gong, "Marked Hand Configurations in Asian Sign Languages," in *Formational Units in Sign Languages*, ed. Rachel Channon and Harry van der Hulst (Berlin, Boston: De Gruyter Mouton, 2011), 19–42.
16. "Communicating With Deaf Individuals," *National Deaf Center on Postsecondary Outcomes*, accessed December 31, 2021, https://www.nationaldeafcenter.org/resource/communicating-deaf-individuals.
17. Joshua St. Pierre, "Distending Straight-Masculine Time: A Phenomenology of the Disabled Speaking Body," *Hypatia* 30, no. 1 (2015): 49–65. Accessed September 12, 2021, http://www.jstor.org/stable/24542058.
18. Brenda Jo Brueggemann, "On (Almost) Passing," *College English* 59, no. 6 (1997): 647–60. Accessed September 12, 2021, doi:10.2307/378278.
19. Kim, *Curative Violence*, 165.

PART 3

Becoming an (Global) Auteur

CHAPTER 7

The Intersection of Authorship and Film Regulation During the Period of Military Rule: An Analysis of Kim Ki-young's National Policy Films, *Soil* (1978) and *Water Lady* (1979)

Molly Kim

1. INTRODUCTION

Kim Ki-young produced a total of thirty-two feature films from his first, *Boxes of Death* (*Jugeom ui sangja*, 1955), to his last, *An Experience to Die For* (*Jugeodo joeun gyeongheom*, 1990). More than half (eighteen to be precise) of Kim's works were created in the 1960s and the 1970s, when the South Korean film industry was most severely regulated by Park Chung Hee's military regime. Through the enactment of the Yushin System (1972) laws were established to oppress the growing public opposition towards Park's prolonged dictatorship,[1] and the state maximized its direct control over filmmaking, studios, and personnel. It would be a mistake to assume that Kim Ki-young's constant productivity during this period was because his films somehow escaped government interference. As the director himself mentioned in interview, "I wouldn't be exaggerating if I said all my films have been impaired by film censorship in some way or another."[2] Indeed, his script for *Ban Geum-ryeon* (1974/1981); the title changed from *Geum Byeong-mae*) for instance, had immense trouble with state censorship and was charged with containing "obscenity" and "violence" even at the pre-production stage,[3] an issue that resulted in a delay of seven years before its theatrical release following the completion of filming in 1973.[4]

Nevertheless, compared to his contemporaries (including Yu Hyeon-mok, Ha Gil-jong and Yi Man-hui), many of whose films were severely cut and sometimes completely banned from public exhibition,[5] most of Kim works have remained relatively intact. This despite his challenging representation of illicit sex, necrophilia, and various other taboos that not many Korean films of the time dared to deal with. Perhaps this leniency was possible because Kim's films seemed to focus on surreal, fantastic themes and visual images as opposed to a realist depiction of society, class, or politics, more concrete concerns which often caused trouble with state censorship. Ha Gil-jong's biggest commercial hit, *The March of Fools* (*Babodeul ui haengjin*, 1975), for example, was reviewed by state censors multiple times, and a total of 30 minutes (including four entire sequences) was ultimately cut from the final approved version due to being "unacceptably anti-regime."[6] Yi Man-hee's *Holiday* (*Hyuil*, 1968) suffered even more brutal censorship, after government reviewers reported that the film's treatment of working class poverty was "too depressing" and would be a negative influence on young people.[7] The director and the producer did not comply with the censors' revision request and eventually gave up on obtaining a theatrical release.

Park Chung Hee's regulation of the film sector was not limited to the censorship of films and scripts. Most notoriously, the regime facilitated a regulatory system that effectively functioned to holistically control the film industry. Directly before his promulgation of Korea's first systematized Motion Picture Law in 1962, Park founded the National Film Production Center (NFPC) in 1961 as a foundational part of this regulative system.[8] According to Brian Yecies and Shim Ae-gyoung, the NFPC distributed specific political messages through commercial cinemas and community screening services. Simultaneously, the Park regime forcibly consolidated the number of feature film production companies from seventy-six to sixteen, based on its impracticable requirements of company registration (a.k.a. "the producer registration system"), imposing the ownership of: 1 × 35mm camera, 50 KW lighting kits, and contracts with one engineer and at least two professional actors per company.[9]

From the critical perspective offered here, the Park regime's stifling regulation and censorship arguably had a far more deleterious effect on Kim Ki-young's creative mind and its inner processes, rather than on the critical or transgressive quality of his completed films. In addition to his persistent issues with the state in relation to *Ban Geum-ryeon*'s script throughout the 1970s, his other project, *Transgression* (*Pagye*, 1974), which was meant to be an alternative project to *Ban Geum-ryeon*, ended up with only an audience of 17,320 over the nine days of its limited theatrical release, becoming one of the most disastrous commercial flops of the year.[10] Around this time, Kim began to turn his attention to producing pro-government, "National Policy Film (*gukchaek yeonghwa*),"[11] a genre through which producers and filmmakers were able to receive significant government rewards including the right to import lucrative foreign films.[12]

National Policy Films emerged following the second revision of the Motion Picture Law (1966). Under this revision, the Park regime again merged the existing film production companies from twenty-five to twelve for easier direct control over the industry. These twelve companies were required to produce various kinds of propaganda films that would promote the latest national aims and policies, and these were later labeled "National Policy Films."[13] In 1973, the Korean Film Commission (*Younghwa Jinheung Gongsa*), "Korea's only quasi-government film industry administrative body,"[14] was established and it made the production of National Policy Films more systematic and compulsory. The state endorsed and produced six National Policy Films during the 1970s through the organization while continuously pushing the film industry to join the march.[15] The existence of National Policy Films therefore functioned as a carrot and stick measure that the Park regime utilized to control disgruntled filmmakers, enticing them with considerable benefits that they otherwise couldn't earn.

The unlikely choices made by Kim Ki-young during this time, considering his status as "an auteur director with uncompromising vision,"[16] were a result of the combined force of this ever-increasing state regulation on film industry and the industrial recession provoked by the rapid growth of television. The number of televisions at home skyrocketed from 379,564 in 1970 to 2,014,927 in 1975 resulting a dramatic decrease in cinemagoers.[17] During this recession, Kim had to work as an "in-house" director taking on projects that the studio assigned to him. In this context, Kim responded in the following way to the comment by his former protégé Yu Ji-hyeong, that *Love of Blood Relations* (*Hyeoryugae*, 1976), his first National Policy Film, was "nothing like [one of Kim's] original films."

> I thought I was getting closer to my vision as a filmmaker, and what kind of films I should be making. However, as the tyranny of military regime became increasingly more severe under the Yushin system, on top of already downsizing film industry, all I could think about was how I was going to survive. We had to give in . . . either to make a living or keep our status as filmmakers. (189)[18]

What was arguably worse for Korean filmmakers was that the audience for foreign films, especially those from Hollywood, was increasing, and "nearly quadrupled," according to Yecies and Shim, in comparison to domestic films.[19] As filmmaking became more challenging both in terms of financing and logistics, Kim therefore chose to align with the Park regime to stay afloat, and produced three National Policy Films during the 1970s: *Love of Blood Relations*, *Soil* (*Heuk*, 1978), and *Water Lady* (*Sunyeo*, 1979).

Kim was not the only one who was steered onto such an unfortunate path. Some of the most significant filmmakers of the golden age of Korean cinema such as Shin Sang-ok, Yu Hyeon-mok, and Yi Man-hui also joined the National Policy Films directive or some other version of state propaganda production during the 1970s. Among the National Policy Film productions created by Korean auteurs, Kim Ki-young's work nonetheless stands out as the most peculiar. And perhaps this fact is not surprising considering his inclination toward outrageous subject matter and the unique visual representation commonly displayed within his "normal" films. In this respect, although Yu disregarded the *Love of Blood Relations* due to its lack of originality, I contend that Kim Ki-young's National Policy Films are actually "nothing like" the other productions fostered by the government. While standing out as "bastard children" within Kim's filmography, in the sense that they were not conceived freely by Kim's creative mind, these works still strongly depart from the conventional approaches to National Policy Films. Most significantly, even in these films, Kim never relinquished his signature tropes of powerful women, female sexuality, and the power of desire, elements which could hardly be considered de rigueur components of "propaganda film" in any context. Instead, he intermixes these personal concerns with the forced themes common to the state-led campaigns, conjuring up some of the most singular and bizarre versions of National Policy Film.

Soil and *Water Lady*, among the National Policy Films produced by Kim Ki-young, are the most conspicuous examples that demonstrate how the conventions of National Policy Film were transgressed via the director's ceaseless interest in the portrayal of women as powerful, transgressive central characters. By focusing on the paradoxes that predominate in *Soil* and *Water Lady*, this chapter will trace out how these collisions of authorial interest and state control do not just mark a particular juncture of Kim Ki-young's career, but to a larger extent, testify to the experiences of many other Korean filmmakers in the same period who were compelled to artistically succumb to the blunt force of political power. Yet despite this oppressive context Kim still somehow managed to meaningfully realize his unique interests and create some of the most unlikely propaganda cinema imaginable, within idiosyncratic films full of subversive and transgressive character.

II. THE DISFIGURATION OF "WISE MOTHER AND GOOD WIFE" IN *SOIL*

From 1966, the Grand Bell Award (*Daejongsang younghwaje*) began to develop the reward system of National Policy Films by supporting "anti-communist" films.[20] This is noteworthy because the Grand Bell Award was the most respected film award in Korea at the time. In relation to this, the film critic Yi Young-il testified that such film awards were directly manipulated by the Park regime and so the Grand Bell Award had unsurprisingly become a platform for pro-government campaign films during the period of Park's rule.[21]

The winners of the "anti-communist film" category were offered the rights to import foreign/Hollywood films, a contract which was far more lucrative than any reward available for domestic films. However, despite this kind of reward, the production of anti-communist cinema was never the predominant practice among film studios until the fourth revision of the Motion Picture Law(1973), or as some have called it, the Yushin Motion Picture Law.[22] This fourth revision dramatically strengthened film censorship while expanding the range of government rewards for various kinds of National Policy Films. Around this time, the terms for these films set by Park's government became more specified. The government set up the standard for National Policy Films as: "1. Any films that would promote the spirit of 'Yushin,' 2. Nationalist films that would motivate patriotism, 3. Any films that would promote the New Village Movement" (*Saemaul undong*).[23]

A number of Korean film historians have recognized roughly three subgenres of National Policy Films produced during the 1970s: anti-communist films; period epics featuring historically prominent figures; and, films themed on the New Village Movement.[24] The third group was itself an entirely novel category as such films specifically thematized the New Village Movement—a nationwide social project intended to rejuvenate rural Korea. This movement was actively pushed by Park Chung Hee in 1970 to help reduce the increasing disparity between cities and rural areas following rapid industrialization and urban migration in the 1960s, as for the first time in Korean history, the population of the countryside had dipped below that of the nation's cities.[25]

Hwang Hye-jin has argued that the New Village Movement was designed to achieve more than simply revive the rural economy. In fact, Park's government led the movement to earn votes from rural areas, which was his initial supporting ground until government led, city-focused-industrialization.[26] As Park's support in rural areas dramatically decreased, the Park government aggressively promoted the New Village Movement through which it promised two main agendas: the modernization of agriculture and funding for the export of local agricultural products.[27]

As with other National Policy Films focused on different programs, the state proactively utilized the medium to promote the New Village Movement. These films, called "New Village Films (*Saemaeul younghwa*)," were strongly encouraged by the state from 1971 to the late 1970s. Kim Ki-young's *Soil* was one such work that he produced in the hope that he could create National Policy Film "his own way while getting government perks."[28] *Soil* was based on the novel of the same title by Yi Gwang-su, which was serialized within the *Dong-A Daily* newspaper from 1932 to 1933. The film is set in the 1920s during the period of Japanese colonial occupation and centers on the peasant-born Heo Sung. In the story Heo loses his parents at an early age and is taken in by a friend of his father, the pastor of a church in Seoul. Growing up, Heo's brilliance captures the attention of a rich old man named Yun, who is one of the church members. Yun proposes that if Heo passes his upcoming bar exam, he will allow him to marry his daughter, Jeong-seon. Heo then passes his exam, becoming a lawyer and marrying Jeong-seon. However, it is clear this marriage is not the fruit of love, and that Heo married Jeong-seon to gain social elevation and Jeong-seon merely complied with her father's wishes. She quickly comes to despise her new husband and commits adultery, becoming pregnant by her paramour. Heo finds out, and indignantly refuses Jeong-seon's wish for a divorce. Instead, he wants to return to his rural home with her to start a new life. This has been Heo's desire since their marriage, as he wants to work for his village people and help them to regain and develop their land which was taken by the Japanese colonial government.

The majority of New Village Films begin with a newly married couple consisting of an urban woman and a rural man. The story then usually proceeds to trace out the achievements of the young wife as she leads the landowners and peasants to rejuvenate their poor rural village. In her analysis of *The Parade of Wives* (*Anaedeul ui haengjin*, Im Kwon-taek, 1974), Hwang argues that the "marriage" is therefore a significant plot element for these films, because it symbolizes the unification of old/countryside and modern/city, and the very promise of Park Chung Hee's New Village Movement.[29] Indeed, in *Soil* the peasant-born Heo marries the city-bred Jeong-seon, just as many New Village Films display a similar narrative. For instance, in *The Parade of Wives*, a New Village Film produced by the government-endorsed Korean Motion Picture Promotion Corporation, the coalition of city and country is represented by the opening marriage sequence of a Seoulite, Ji-sun, and a rural farmer, Yeong-du. Another quintessential New Village Film, *Mother* (*Oemoni*, Im Won-sik, 1977), also presents the story of an urban woman called Hong Yeong-ae, who willingly marries a divorcee war veteran living with five children in an underdeveloped rural area, in order to realize her vision of rural enlightenment.

In these films, the wife is the critical element that propagates the main theme of rural enlightenment and development. She is characterized as being of a much higher social status than her male counterpart, i.e., possessing a better family background and higher education, as exemplified through Jeong-seon in *Soil*. The woman's motive for this unrealistic union in New Village Film tends to be simply her passion for the betterment of the countryside, not love or romance, which would have made a more plausible reason. The wife is characterized by a capacity for infinite sacrifice and more importantly, her maternal nature. This perfectly serves to frame her in the role of "wise mother, good wife" (*hyeonmo yangcheo*), longstanding ideas that flourished during the colonial period that emphasized the woman's duty to dedicate her life to her husband and his children, and in this case, her country.[30] Here, the construction of a leading character based on the historically established discourse of a "wise mother, good wife" offered an efficient set up to convey the spirit of the New Village Movement. According to Eo Il-seon, throughout its national propaganda campaign the Park government repeatedly emphasized that the New Village Movement must not to be forced but voluntarily undertaken by the citizenry.[31] The healthy, young and beautiful heroine from the city in this regard was designed to function not only as an antithesis to the stereotype of the old and lazy rural man (who were often imagined as an obstacle for rural development),[32] but also as an object of desire that would entice rural men to willingly volunteer for the national enlightenment project.

Nonetheless, this type of "model wife" and the attendant gender dynamics common to most New Village Films is largely absent or debunked in *Soil*. While Jeong-seon is from an affluent family and well-educated, which superficially makes her a perfect fit for the "wise mother, good wife" profile, she transcends the major constituents of the trope because she loathes her husband and does not sanctify her marriage or motherhood. Jeong-seon's "unconventional" character as a wife is further accentuated by her suicidal behavior, as when she finds out about her pregnancy. She attempts to kill herself along with her unborn child by throwing herself under a train which causes her to lose a leg. Ultimately, Jeong-seon is a failure as a spouse, being neither a "wise mother" nor a "good wife," shortfalls which invalidate the discursive premise of the genre.

On the other hand, Yu-sun, Heo's childhood sweetheart, fulfills the ideals of such. Yu-sun never intended to leave her rural home and remained there to support her brothers and parents. Then, when Heo returns to the village, she cares for him and helps him rebuild the village, until he gets arrested by the Japanese authorities for leading the peasants to participate in his rural movement to develop the land that now belongs to the Japanese government. Therefore, in some sense, the dichotomy of Jeong-seon and Yu-sun seems to privilege the New Village Movement as the former—the disaffected nonconformist—ends up becoming a "cripple." However, Yu-sun is neither celebrated nor rewarded within the narrative for her piety, as she tragically dies by suicide after being raped by a member of the local authorities. The rural movement for emancipation and development is then ultimately accomplished neither by Yu-sun nor Heo but Jeong-seon, who ultimately takes over in the place of her incarcerated husband.

This resolution is of course befitting of the established trope of the New Village Film genre, as the successful rural movement in *Soil* is eventually realized by Jeong-seon, the metropolitan, high-status wife. However, she remains a (once) sexually fallen, "crippled" wife, burdened with a child conceived outside of her marriage. Yet interestingly the film does not vilify or punish Jeong-seon as "the fallen woman," and in the final sequence, Heo finally comes back to his rural home from prison and finds Jeong-seon living with her daughter. They promise a new life to each other and joyfully embrace the child who is now "their" daughter together. This happy ending of *Soil* not only transgresses the typical closure of New Village Film, but also disavows the traditional plot resolution usually imposed on the "fallen woman"; that the woman who "commits a sexual transgression, usually adultery," is ultimately punished for her sinful action.[33]

In most popular media such fallen women usually doom themselves at the narrative conclusion. For instance, in her research on US films of the 1930s featuring such female characters, Lea Jacobs argues that these films cannot have a happy ending, or if they did this was "designed to fulfill a didactic function."[34] The patriarchal discourse of such deviant women "getting what they deserve," remains something of an axiom within popular cinema, whereby the narrative punishment usually involves the fallen woman ending up tragically with a disease, in destitution, and/or suffering an early death (mostly by suicide).[35] To a similar extent within Korean cinema, the sexually fallen woman, such as the female protagonists in the 1970s' popular hostess films, usually encounter just such a disastrous fate through suicide (*Heavenly Homecoming Stars I* [*Byeoldeul ui gohyang*, Yi Jang-ho, 1974]; *26X365=0* [Ro Se-han, 1979]) or simply by going missing (*Do you Know Kkotsuni?* [*kkotsunireul asinayo*, Jeong In-yeop, 1977]). However, in *Soil* Jeong-seon not only is given a second chance, but also ultimately becomes the leader of the rural movement, rendering her a hero who protects "the soil" of people. This is a remarkable transformation from Yi Gwang-su's original novel since the novel explicates Heo Sung's sacrifice and achievements throughout the story.[36]

In particular, the inclusion of her daughter, conceived outside of marriage, into the new family in the final shot implies the strength of the newly formed matriarchal unit. *The Soil*'s extraordinary closure solidifies Kim's persistent interest in the portrayal of powerful female leads which is also hinted by its initial title, *Soil: The Things A Woman Loses and Finds* (*Yeoja ga ireun geot channeun geot*), as consistently shown in his prior films, including *the Woman* (女) series, blending this concern with the very tenets of the New Village Film genre. Ultimately *Soil* was not selected for the category for National Policy Films of 1978, no doubt in part because of its outrageous portrait of woman and marriage. And, perhaps in response, Kim's next New Village Film project, *Water Lady*, demonstrates a more explicit adherence to standard propaganda paradigms, but nonetheless, once again through his recurrent theme of "the super woman."

III. A FEMALE LEADER DETHRONES "*SANGI YONGSA* (A DISABLED WAR VETERAN)": THE REBUTTAL OF THE WAR VETERAN MYTH IN *WATER LADY*[37]

The Park regime's severe approach to the regulations and requirements for film production provoked soaring complaints from within the industry itself.

According to An Jae-seok, 56 percent of the respondents (which consisted of producers and directors) in the survey conducted for the summer issue of a film magazine, *The Era of Image* (*Youngsang sidae*, 1978), identified state control and censorship as the biggest cause behind the decline of Korean films.[38] In response to this collective antagonism, the Park government lowered the bar, shifting back to registration system from the more rigid, permission based system. As a result, more producers were able to legally register their companies. In 1978, six additional film companies, including Kim Ki-young's own, Sinhan Munye Film (*Sinhan munye yeonghwasa*), were registered, making a total of twenty film companies in South Korea.[39] *Water Lady* was the first project that Kim launched through this production company. Kim recounted the reason why he chose a National Policy Film to be his company's first project in the following passage:

> I came up with the idea for *Water Lady* in the late 60s. I wanted to make a film set in nature. Maybe I had been longing to get away from my excessively "expressionist style" and try the opposite, naturalism. I had a story about a disabled war veteran and a woman who has a stutter. I had pictured this young couple living in poverty in the countryside but then make a fortune after going through various kinds of hardship. I thought that this film had potential both for commercial success and the government reward given to quality national policy films (New Village Films).[40]

Although Kim mentioned that *Water Lady* had the dual goals of commercial success and government reward, I suspect that the production primarily aimed for National Policy Film reward, even more so than *Soil*. Notably, the film presents a proclamation at the opening, indicating that "1979" (the year of its production) is "the International Year of Children." This seemingly irrelevant statement comes with the logo (emblem) of the International Year of Children, followed by the information that the film is "specially" presented by Shin Han Literary Film Company. Although *Water Lady* is less focused on the issue of children than the concern of rural enlightenment, it nonetheless employs such tactics to present the film as "good public material" suitable for nomination.

Thematically, *Water Lady* focuses on rural enlightenment more overtly than *Soil*, an interest once again conveyed through the travails of a newlywed couple. The film starts with a war veteran, Jin-seok, coming home after getting a leg injury during the Vietnam War, which resulted in him permanently having a limp. He wants to settle down in his rural hometown as a farmer but lacks the money. The head of the village then tells him that the village provides agricultural funds for newlyweds. He then proceeds to set up a meeting for Jin-seok and potential bride Su-ok, who initially refuses to talk because of her severe stutter. They reluctantly marry each other and soon start farming.

Figure 7.1 Opening shot of *Water Lady*.

However, despite their hard work, the farming doesn't seem successful, particularly due to the disability of Jin-seok, who cannot endure heavy physical labor. Su-ok then takes over her family business of weaving bamboo baskets. Su-ok's remarkable weaving skills inherited from her mother, combined with Jin-seok's keen business insights finally come to fruition, making them one of the wealthiest families in the village. The couple, now with their expanded business, then help other villagers by providing them with well-paid jobs.

Compared to Kim's prior production *Soil*, *Water Lady* demonstrates a much more straightforward and conspicuous celebration of the New Village Movement. Moreover, the film explicates Park Chung Hee's other proclaimed achievements during his presidency through various characters and scenes, most notably through its employment of the disabled Vietnam veteran, Jin-seok. In fact, this was not unique to this film; it was rather a common practice utilized by filmmakers in the 1970s. Widely known as "pleasing set-ups" or "pleasing shots," according to Pak Yu-hui, many filmmakers occasionally inserted shots and backdrops of buildings and bridges newly built during the Park regime, or a certain characters who clearly represented Park's achievements in order to avoid severe censorship or to garner for a state reward.[41] Sending troops to Vietnam was a key part of Park Chung Hee's political agenda from the moment of his inauguration in 1961.[42] In so doing, Park legitimized his presidency internationally, supported the US government, and secured a substantial amount of funding from the US. The Park regime therefore actively utilized the deployment of Korean troops in Vietnam as part of their political campaigning, highlighting that this commitment helped in building the alliance between South Korea and the US. Jin-seok, therefore directly serves in the role of "pleasing character," living evidence of the Park government's "diplomatic" achievement.

Within the context of New Village Films, the Vietnam veteran is also considered a pivotal figure because he, as an incarnation of "public duty," symbolizes sacrifice, particularly as explicated through his disability.[43] Some of the most representative New Village Films, including the aforementioned *Mother*, also employ the trope of Vietnam War veteran with a disability as a major character who contributes to rural enlightenment. Like the paradigmatic "good mother and wise wife," the disabled veteran character also works effectively within New Village Films to represent the ideal of the worthy citizen, who self-sacrifices for the nation.[44] Nevertheless, Jin-seok's triumphant, upward narrative trajectory comes to a halt when he encounters Chu-wol. She is a paradigmatic femme fatale, or as Kelly Dong puts it, "a seductive interloper"—a character type Kim Ki-young frequently locates in his films amidst the crossfire of gender essentialism, class conflict, and psychosexual idiosyncrasies.[45] Chu-wol seduces Jin-seok for his money and lures him to kill his wife, plotting to have Jin-seok immediately arrested for this crime, so she could then take his money and go off with her own lover.

Jin-seok's downfall is preceded by a scene where their first tryst takes place. In this scene, Jin-seok comes to a massive bamboo forest and meets Chu-wol who has been hiding behind the trees. When Chu-wol spots him, she hides behind the bamboo tree, once the means for Jin-seok's affluence and social elevation, now disguising his imminent doom. As Jin-seok walks toward her, the camera cuts to bouncing bamboo trees in close-up, implying their sexual congress. After this meeting, Jin-seok is spellbound into doing virtually anything for Chu-wol, and easily agrees to kill his wife. However, when he takes Su-ok to the lake to murder her, he changes his mind. He and Su-ok then come back to the village where dozens of policemen and villagers are waiting to witness the fall of this former hero of the village. Now that his deception has been exposed Jin-seok begs for forgiveness from Su-ok but she refuses. And at this precise moment her stutter disappears, presumably because of the shock she had. Then Su-ok and her son leave Jin-seok behind and he slowly walks out of sight.

Figure 7.2 A tryst in the bamboo forest.

Figure 7.3 A tryst in the bamboo forest.

Water Lady offers a similar form of plot closure to *Soil*. First, the national myth of the disabled veteran is dismantled through Kim's signature tale of "dangerous liaisons," just as Jeong-sun's triumph effaces the paradigm of the "wise mother, good wife" in *Soil*. Simultaneously, the ending alludes to the fact that Su-ok will remain as the sole leader of her bamboo business on which the whole village is now dependent. Her capability as a new community leader and a matriarch is further strengthened by the fact her stutter is now gone, and the return of her son, after he had been forcefully separated from her because Jin-seok feared he might become a stutter too. Despite Kim Ki-young's ambition for this production as the inaugural project of his new company, *Water Lady*, like *Soil*, was unsuccessful, both at the box office[46] and in gaining government reward. Nonetheless these two films significantly signaled the progressive evolution of female representation within Kim's work. As if his Housemaid Trilogy and other similar female character-driven thrillers highlighted somewhat primitive, overly sexualized leading women who tended to be insidiously cunning and neurotically desperate for men's devotion, Kim's New Village films feature a self-fulfilled female leader/mother who is ultimately independent of her male spouse and/or the patriarchal system. In both the films examined here, the leading male is either rendered obsolete or a harmful figure for the family and community, and therefore subordinated to his wife (*Soil*) or removed entirely (*Water Lady*). This transition of female character development within Kim's work peaked in his construction of the super-wife characters with *An Experience to Die For*, a story about two wives who plan to murder each other's deceitful husbands. In this respect, *Soil* and *Water Lady* may not be remarkable as representative of "quality" National Policy Film or for their commercial achievement, but they are nonetheless significant in the director's career as they mark a dynamic shift toward the more progressive depiction of women in his work, an interest which has constituted the lifelong point of focus within Kim Ki-young's cinematic universe.

CONCLUSION: KIM KI-YOUNG'S EVERLASTING TALE OF WOMEN

Of course, I think that all women are nice and kind . . . But that is when they are still single. When men rip their hearts into pieces, they become demons and seek revenge. My wife said that her colleagues were taunting her that "your husband is playing with women again" and advised me that I should never ridicule housewives. When you provoke them, you will be beaten to death, so I'm trying to refrain from that (laughs). But the truth is, women, when their husbands die, live freely and happily for a good twenty years, but men don't even last two years after their wives die. Even if they manage to live longer, they are already as good as dead.[47]

Some have commented that Kim Ki-young's films are "grotesque melodramas" about women.[48] Indeed, Kim's filmography contains more than a dozen of films titled "(the deadly) woman" and/or led by female characters. More specifically, these characters tend to be a single woman who longs to become a wife, seeking out to register herself within the institution of marriage. She encounters a married man who promises her to take her as his new wife. But when this desire becomes frustrated, as in the Housemaid Trilogy (and subsequent remakes), this character transforms to an omnipotent murderess who brutally punishes (and often kills) the man and his entire family. For Kim, as he mentions above, marriage, or "the man in it," dehumanizes the woman and turns her into "a demon." Kim (and many cinemagoers at the time) loved his own fable of domestic horror, *The Housemaid*, to the degree that he remade it four times over nearly three decades.

Kim's persistent study of such demonic women was, however, interrupted by the Yushin System and the government's subsequent approach to film regulation in the 1970s. This served to oppress the Korean film industry through severe censorship and the direct reinforcing of propaganda film or National Policy Film, as the "correct" subject material for any professional director to undertake. Nevertheless, *Soil* and *Water Lady*, which were ostensibly produced in support of the Park regime's New Village Movement, are here highlighted for the transgressive and subversive character of their female leads, a quality that is external both to the wider canon of propaganda films and Kim Ki-young's prior oeuvre, but emerges from somewhere between the established discursive concerns of these two constellations. Jeong-sun and Su-ok, the heroines in *Soil* and *Water Woman* respectively, are the "hybrid" figures that result from this new nexus of concerns, neither character being a seductress nor murderess, but a self-made community leader who takes charge of the village by replacing her "incapable" husband. Kim Ki-young's focus on a somewhat mythic idea of "Über Woman" in these works sees the main female protagonist refigured from murderess to leader. This transformation does not simply function to convey the message of the New Village Movement, but more importantly serves to present audiences with fully fledged agents of autonomous femininity.

There has not been enough research dedicated to Kim Ki-young's National Policy Films, either in Korean or English, not to mention the larger topic of Korean National Policy Films per se. I suspect this has to do with scholars and critics' common dismissal of Kim Ki-young's "self-admitted failures," a term for once he himself used to describe *Water Lady*.[49] Yet, these films still offer meaningful material evidence to demonstrate how a regulative force could function constructively, in that it helped to shape highly innovative examples of film form, narrative, and representational strategy.[50] It is my contention that Kim created some of the most progressive female characters of his oeuvre through his output for National Policy Film, and that this development would not have been possible without such forced external provocation. Relative to the bigger picture of Korean film, this study hopefully indicates the need to properly evaluate the wider range of National Policy Films produced by other auteurs of Korean cinema, and treat such as a viable artistic texts through which meaningful disparities and paradoxes might become unraveled.

NOTES

1. In 1972, Park Chung Hee's military regime enacted the Yushin Constitution to guarantee his lifetime presidency, and also heightened the censorship of all media, including television, radio, and film in an effort to suppress public criticism of his dictatorship. As part of the Yushin Constitution, the Park Chung Hee government revised the Motion Picture Law (the fourth amendment) in 1974. Under this amendment, the government maximized its control over cinema, appointing the Minister of Public Information and Culture to oversee the implementation and application of most film-related rules.
2. Geum Dong-hyeon and Kim Kyeong-mi, "Demystification of Sublime: Kim Ki-young's *Soil* [Sunggo ui talsinbihwa: Kim Ki-young ui heuk biteulgi]," *The Korean Language and* [*Literature Eomunhak*] 143 (2019): 361.
3. Yu Ji-hyeong, *Conversation for Twenty-Four Years* [Isipsanyeon ui daehwa: Kim Ki-young gamdok inteobyu] (Seoul: Sun Publication, 2008), 160–2.
4. The initial title for the film was "Geum Byung-mae"; it was later changed to "Ban Geum-ryeon" upon its release, quoted in Jeong Ji-yeon, "The Film of August II," August, 2020, accessed October 10, 2021, https://www.kmdb.or.kr/story/10/5434.
5. Yi Man-hui was arrested and interrogated by KCIA for his depiction of North Korean soldiers as "humane" in his *The Seven Female POWS* (*Chirin ui yeoporo*, 1965).
6. Kim Seung-gyeong, "A Release of Censorship Documents of The March of Fools," August, 2018, accessed October 15, 2021, www.kmdb.or.kr/story/180/4769.
7. Park Yu-hui, "A Study on the Dynamics of Film Censorship and Representation of Sentiment during the Park Chung Hee Regime [Park Chung Hee jeongkwongi yeonghwa geomyeol kwa kamseong jaehyeon ui yeokhak]," *The Critical Review of History* [*Yeoksa bipyeong*] 99 (May 2012): 43.

8. Brian Yecies and Aegyung Shim, *The Changing Face of Korean Cinema: 1960–2015* (New York: Routledge, 2016), 19–20.
9. Ibid., 21.
10. Yu, *Conversation for Twenty-Four Years*, 174.
11. Yecies and Shim, *The Changing Face*, 109.
12. O Jin-gon, "A Study on the Ambivalence of Korean National Policy Film in the 1970s -Focusing on *When Wild Flowers Blossom* (1974) [1970nyeondae hanguk gukchak yeonghwa ui yanggaseong kwa kyunyeol yangsang e gwanhan yeongu]," *The Study of Contemporary Cinema* [*Hyundae yeonghwa yeongu*] 15, no. 1 (January 2019): 79.
13. Hwang Hye-jin, *Study on Korean Film in the 1970s during the Revitalizing Reform System* [*1970nyeondae Yushin chejegi ui hanguk yeonghwa yeongu*]. Doctoral diss., Dongguk University, 2003, 36.
14. Yecies and Shim, *The Changing Face*, 107.
15. These National Policy Films include: *Testimony* (*Jeungeon*, Im Kwon-taek, 1973), *When Wild Flowers Blossom* (*Deulgukhwaneun pieotneunde*, Yi Man-hui, 1973), *Won't Cry* (*Ulji aneuri*, Im Kwon-taek, 1974), *The Parade of Wives* (*Anaedeurui haengjin*, Im Kwon-taek, 1974), *A Spy Remaining Behind* (*Jallyu cheobja*, Kim Si-hyeon, 1975), *The Tae-Baek Mountain* (*Taebaek sanmaek*, Kwon Yeong-sun, 1975). Eo Il-seon, "An Analysis of the Enlightenment Movies under the Yushin System [Yushin chejeha ui kyemong yeonghwa bunseok]," *The Journal of the Korean Entertainment Association* [*Hanguk Entertainment Hakhoe Nonmunji*] 8 (August, 2014): 49. Because of low box office returns for these national policy films, in 1975 the regime ceased production of feature films, wrapping up all its outstanding projects. Yecies and Shim, *The Changing Face*, 112.
16. Ku Hyeon-kyeong notes that Kim became isolated from the film industry because he was too stubborn and uncompromisingly pushing his ideals when making a film. *A Study in Conversion of Media from Novel to Movie with Special Reference to Ieodo written by Yi Cheong-jun and Ieodo directed by Kim Ki-young* [*Soseol eso yeonghwa ro maeche jeonhwan yeongu*], Master's diss., Keonguk University, 2010, 14.
17. Eo, "An Analysis," 53.
18. Yu, *Conversation for Twenty-Four Years*, 189.
19. Yecies and Shim, *The Changing Face*, 107.
20. Hwang, *Study on Korean Film*, 52–3.
21. Kim Se-jin, *A Study of Propaganda Patterns on 1970s Korean National Policy Film* [*1970nyeondae hanguk gukchaek yeonghwa ui seonjeon hyeongsik yeongu*], Master's diss., Hanyang University, 2006, 20–1.
22. Eo, "An Analysis," 8.
23. O Jin-gon, "A Study of the Characteristics of the Korean Excellent Films in the 1970s [1970nyeondae hanguk 'usuyeonghwa' ui sidaejeok teuksuseong gochal]," *The Journal of Humanities* [*Inmoonhak Yeongu*] 47 (2014): 18.
24. According to Son Jeong-weon and Kim Dong-Wan, Park Chung Hee personally initiated the Saemaul movement (hereafter, the movement) in 1970 as a rural community development initiative. The movement's original aims were economic development and the cultural modernization of rural areas, provoked by disparities between cities and rural areas in result of rapid industrialization during the 1960s. To address this cultural lag, the Park regime-led New Village Movement has arguably been its largest and most aggressive intervention into rural society. Son Jeong-weon and Kim Dong-Wan, "South Korea's Saemaul (New Village) movement: an organizational technology for the production of developmentalist subjects," *Canadian Journal of Development Studies* 34, no. 1 (2013): 23.

25. Kim Seong-jo, "The South Korean New Village Movement: Representation and Globalization [Yeoksahak ui siseon eso bon saemaeul undong ui jaehyeon gwa segyehwa]," *The Dongbang hakji* 193 (December 2020): 309.
26. Hwang, *Study on Korean Film*, 63.
27. Ibid., 63.
28. Yu, *Conversation for Twenty-Four Years*, 208–9.
29. Hwang, *Study on Korean Film*, 63.
30. "Hyeonmo yangcheo (wise mother, good wife)" is a traditional idea for womanhood that arose in the eighteenth century. According to Choi Hye-wol, this was arguably the most influential gender ideology in modern Korea. The idea was "refashioned and reconstituted under the influence of the ideology of domesticity promoted by American Protestant women missionaries and the Meiji gender ideology of *ryosai kenbo*, which transpired through Japanese colonial policies in Korea." Choi Hye-wol, "'Wise mother, good wife': A Transcultural Discursive Construct in Modern Korea," *The Journal of Korean Studies* 14, no. 1 (Fall, 2009): 1.
31. Eo, "An Analysis," 54.
32. Ibid., 54
33. Lea Jacobs, *The Wages of Sin: Censorship and the Fallen Woman Film, 1928–1942* (Los Angeles: University of California Press, 1997), 76.
34. Ibid., 76.
35. The argument is based on these scholarly works: Nina Attwood, *The Prostitute's Body: Rewriting Prostitution in Victorian Britain* (London: Pickering & Chatto, 2011); Nina Auerbach, "The Rise of the Fallen Women," *Nineteenth-Century Fiction* 35, no. 1 (June 1980).
36. Kim Ki-young's *Soil*'s initial title was *Soil: The Things A Woman Loses and Finds* (yeojaga ileungeot chatneungeot) which establishes the pivot of this film as the woman; Yi Mi-na, "A Study of Screen Adaptations of the novel, *Soil* by Yi Gwang-su [Yi Gwang-su soseol, Heuk ui younghwahwa yangsang kwa gochal]," *Chunwon Research Journal* [*Chunwon yeonguhakbo*] 13 (December 2018): 312.
37. *Suneyo* has several different versions of English titles. KMDB (Korean Movie Database) indicates "Woman of Water," some other sources title as "Water Woman."
38. An Jae-seok, *A Study on the 'Youngsang Sidae as Young Cinema Movement [Cheongnyeon yeonghwa undong euroseoui 'yeongsangsidae' e daehan yeongu]*, MA diss., Chungang University, 2001, 12.
39. Seong Ha-hun, "The Termination of Pre-Censorship after 76 years," July 20, 2021, accessed October 29, 2021, http://star.ohmynews.com/NWS_Web/OhmyStar/at_pg.aspx?CNTN_CD=A0002673579&CMPT_CD=P0010&utm_source=naver&utm_medium=newsearch&utm_campaign=naver_news.
40. Yu, *Conversation for Twenty-Four Years*, 237–9.
41. Pak, "A Study on the Dynamics of Film Censorship," 83.
42. Ham Gyu-jin, "What If Park Chung-hee Didn't Send Out Troops [. . .]," March, 2010, accessed October 11, 2021, http://h21.hani.co.kr/arti/special/special_general/26884.html.
43. Kim, *A Study of Propaganda Patterns*, 64–5.
44. Ibid., 64–5.
45. Quoted in Kelly Dong, "Transgressions in Dark Age: The Films of Kim Ki-young and Yi Hwa-si," *Cinema Scope*, accessed October 20, 2021, https://cinema-scope.com/features/transgressions-in-the-dark-age-the-films-of-kim-ki-young-and-Yi-hwa-si/.
46. *Water Lady* was initially released at the Jeonju Theater (*Jeonju geukjang*) located in Jeon-ju, but because of its low sales it didn't receive a wide release in major cities including

Seoul. Korean Movie Database (KMDB), accessed October 22, 2021, https://www.kmdb.or.kr/db/kor/detail/movie/K/03334.

47. Yi Jae-lim, "Kim Ki-young—A Legendary Filmmaker Defined by Women," *Joongang Daily*, May 27, 2021, accessed October 23, 2021, https://koreajoongangdaily.joins.com/2021/05/27/culture/features/Kim-Kiyoung/20210527193400425.html.

48. Quoted in the description of *Woman of Fire* on Harvard Film Archive, accessed October 25, 2021, https://harvardfilmarchive.org/calendar/woman-of-fire-2017-02.

49. Jang U-seok, "The Director of *The Housemaid* and *Carnivorous Animal*, Kim Ki-young (Hanyeo, Yuksik dongmul Kim Ki-young eul mannada), *Yeongnam Daily*, May 6, 2021, accessed October 29, 2021, https://www.yeongnam.com/web/view.php?key=20210506010000678.

50. Jacobs, *The Wages of Sin*, 23.

CHAPTER 8

Rediscovering Kim Ki-young: The Rise of the South Korean Auteur on the Film Festival Circuit

Jason Bechervaise

INTRODUCTION

Domestically South Korean cinema has seen remarkable growth over the last two decades. Prior to the COVID-19 pandemic, audiences on average saw four films per year while admissions to Korean films have surpassed 100 million a year since 2012. In 2019, box office sales in Korea made it the fourth biggest market in the world after North America, China, and Japan.[1] Overseas, the unprecedented success of *Parasite* (*Gisaengchung*, Bong Joon Ho, 2019) has underscored Korea's growing cinematic profile on the world stage. It also reconfirms how reliant the industry is on the Korean auteurs to drive its sales. Festivals, of course, have played a crucial role in this regard as *Parasite* illustrates, having won the *Palme d'Or* at the Cannes Film Festival in 2019 before going on to win Best Picture at the Academy Awards in February 2020.

More than twenty years earlier Kim Ki-young was a precursor to what would ultimately later follow. In 1997, the Busan International Film Festival (BIFF) curated a retrospective of his work that screened eight of his works.[2] The festival, which was then in its second year, had programmed a section dedicated to older Korean films that continued through its subsequent editions until 2019. Today the festival is renowned for its extensive focus on new discoveries, as evidenced by the exposure it afforded Park Jung-bum's *The Journals of Musan* (*Musan ilgi*, Park Jung-bum, 2011) or more recently Kim Bora's *House of Hummingbird* (*Beol-sae*, Kim Bora, 2018). However, one of the most interesting areas of the festival programming in its infancy was the showcasing of established and "forgotten" filmmakers, and a prime example of this concern was the Kim Ki-young retrospective titled "Kim Ki-young: Rediscovering a Director from the Past." Soojeong Ahn writes in her text on the festival, *The*

Pusan International Film Festival, South Korean Cinema and Globalization, that through this retrospective, Kim became the first South Korean filmmaker to receive international recognition.[3] The Berlin Film Festival just four months later also put together a retrospective of Kim's work following the enthusiasm in Busan, screening four of his films in the forum section.[4] After all, as Nikki J. Y. Lee notes when writing about the "transnational auteur" Park Chan-wook, "international film festivals strive to 'discover' and present 'new' cinemas and new auteur directors, so as to feed distributors', journalists', and audiences' desires for something fresh and exciting."[5]

While directors from the so-called New Wave movement, such as Park Kwang-su and certainly Im Kwon-taek, had gained exposure at festivals in Europe—with, for instance, *The Surrogate Woman* (*Ssibaji*, Im Kwon-taek, 1986) invited to Venice, where Kang Su-yeon won Best Actress in 1987—the newfound attention surrounding Kim's work marked a first for a Korean filmmaker. Chris Berry states that the "'heat' has been generated by the PIFF [it was changed to BIFF (Busan International Film Festival) in 2011] retrospective the likes of which I have not seen before around Korean cinema."[6] Today, this might sound unusual given the heights Korean cinema has reached since then. However, if we place this retrospective into a wider body of work from Korean auteurs, it soon becomes clear that they share much in common with how Korean cinema has been propelled into the international spotlight with film festivals playing an integral part.

This discussion will, therefore, focus on the rediscovery of Kim Ki-young through the Busan and Berlin Film Festivals and how this is closely connected to the wider relationship between film festivals and the Korean auteur. My central argument is that the spotlight of Kim's work at these festivals underlines the canonization of the auteur at festivals and how they remain a crucial platform from which Korean cinema is able to lure audiences from overseas. The success of Park Chan-wook, Bong Joon Ho, and Kim Jee-woon as they continue to propel Korean cinema onto the world stage further strengthens this point. As such, this argument will also make reference to these filmmakers as established auteurs.

THE FILM FESTIVAL CIRCUIT AND ITS RELATIONSHIP TO THE AUTEUR

To begin it is necessary to examine the role of the auteur at festivals and how this has evolved over the years both locally and internationally. Ultimately, film festivals are a western construct. As Stringer writes, "it is necessary to underline the core observation that the film festival is originally a European phenomenon; it is a creature of the European region that went global."[7] Indeed, the world's first festival was held in Venice in 1932. Later Berlin (founded in 1951), Cannes (established in 1946) along with Venice would become the "big three" and remain the most influential film festivals in Europe. Marijke de Valck argues that there are three central phases in how the European film festival landscape has developed. The first phase occurred between the launching of Venice in 1932 and 1968 when the initial festival format was being reorganized, disrupting both Venice and Cannes. The early 1970s saw film festivals as showcases for national cinemas such as Locarno. The second phase, during the 1970s, consisted of independently organized festivals that worked to protect cinematic art and further establish relationships with the wider film industry. The final phase, the creation of the festival circuit in the 1980s, came with film festivals being established across the globe as the phenomenon became professionalized and institutionalized.[8] The Busan Film Festival, of course, would later play a crucial role on the festival circuit, both having its roots entrenched into the local film industry and also launching in 1996 when the festival model was being proliferated far and wide. Busan was not the only festival to launch in Korea in the late 1990s and early 2000s. The Bucheon Fantastic Film Festival (BIFAN) had its first edition in 1997 while the Jeonju International Film Festival was established in 2000. The growth of these festivals along with several others correlates with the rise of the Korean Film Industry.

Before this discussion turns to Busan and the Kim retrospective, it is important to establish the relationship between festivals and auteur cinema. Central to this, undoubtedly, is the Cannes Film Festival, an event that has a very compelling if somewhat unexplored relationship to Korean cinema. Although there has recently been a trend in which the festival has invited genre films from Korea following the tremendously successful *Train to Busan* (*Busanhaeng*, Yeon Sang-ho, 2016) Cannes has remained largely focused on the auteurs. Im Kwon-taek won Best Director for his film *Chihwaseon* (*Chwihwaseon*, Im Kwon-taek, 2002) in 2002, Park Chan-wook's *Oldboy* (*Oldeu boi*, Park Chan-wook, 2003) brought home the Grand Prix in 2004, Lee Chang-dong secured his first award in Cannes with Best Screenplay for *Poetry* (*Si*, Lee Chang-dong, 2009), while Hong Sang-soo has been invited to the festival numerous times and won the *Prix Un Certain Regard* for *Hahaha* (Hong Sang-soo, 2010) in 2010. Kim Ki-young's *The Housemaid* (*Hanyeo*, Kim Ki-young, 1960) was screened in the Cannes Classics Section in 2010 following its restoration. It was the same year Im Sang-soo's remake of the film (same name) was selected in competition. Nine years later Bong Joon Ho would make history at the festival with *Parasite*; a film that has seen comparisons made to *The Housemaid* given the narrative focus on social critique, the focus on family and the home invasion.

Bong, who has long cited Kim as a major influence, first made an impression at Cannes when his third feature, *The Host* (*Gwoemul*, Bong Joon-ho, 2006), was invited to Directors' Fortnight (*La Quinzaine des Realisateurs*) in 2006. This sidebar was founded in 1969 by the French Directors Guild that would transform the festival into an event that placed more of an emphasis on the director and festival curator. It came in response to protests in Paris against the decision to remove the founder of La Cinémathèque française, Henri Langloise, that spread to Cannes. This followed anti-government and anti-establishment strikes throughout France in May and June 1968. The festival was suspended allowing it to usher in a new era transforming the festival into an organization that was more politically independent.[9] The Directors' Fortnight signified its growing attention on the auteur. Dorota Ostrowska writes:

> For the first time the figure of the auteur was acknowledged as the key and independent agent in the creative process of filmmaking and film festival exhibition. Films of specific directors were deemed "auteur films" and sought out for screening at the festival. The increasing importance of directors in the context of the festival also meant a much more personal and direct relationship between individual artists and festival programmers with the filter of the national boards and producers' associations being removed or its role significantly limited.[10]

Instrumental to the creation of the director's sidebar were French filmmakers such as Jean-Luc Godard and François Truffaut who led the French New Wave that emerged in the late 1950s. It was not just directors who wielded influence; theorist André Bazin, who co-founded *Cahiers du cinéma* in 1951, wrote extensively about film, realism and the auteur. In his article "La Politique des auteurs" (1957) he summarized auteurism as "choosing in the artistic creation the personal factor as a criterion of reference, and then postulating its permanence and even its progress from one work to the next."[11] The *Cahiers du cinéma* writers distinguished auteurs from metteurs-en-scène through their use of mise-en-scène. The latter do not use mise-en-scène to convey a particular style; rather they are seen as technicians, as opposed to auteurs such as Alfred Hitchcock or Jean Renoir, whose oeuvre's distinctive characteristics would have a lasting impact on cinema.

The launching of the Directors' Fortnight would reflect wider changes at the festival with a focus on new talent from different areas of the globe and the role of festival director as a curator. Gilles Jacob, the first delegate general of the Cannes Film Festival, transformed the main competition and established Un Certain Regard in 1978.[12] Darota Ostrowska writes, "These changes to the festival were intensified in the early 1990s and culminated in the emergence of a new category of films, the 'Cannes film,' which paved the way for a 'festival film.'"[13]

Berlin and Venice have followed Cannes's lead in showcasing auteur cinema albeit with different tastes. The latter is now very much part of the awards season together with festivals in North America, most notably Toronto and Telluride. Other festivals in Europe such as Rotterdam, San Sebastian, and Edinburgh have tended to also focus on discoveries akin to Busan.

THE BUSAN INTERNATIONAL FILM FESTIVAL KIM KI-YOUNG RETROSPECTIVE

Turning now to the retrospective itself. In Ahn Soojeong's book on the Busan Film Festival, she examines the re-circulation of Korean films at BIFF. She notes how the history of screening classic films is different compared to many other countries in the West. Korea's turbulent history undoubtedly has had an impact on the availability of prints.[14] Kim Ki-young's work is no exception. Of the thirty-two feature films he directed, only twenty-three have prints preserved while some are incomplete. His feature debut, for example, *Boxes of Death* (*Jugeom ui sangja*, 1955), that was produced through the United States Information Service (USIS), was lost until it was discovered in 2009 but is missing an audio track. It was the first film in Korea to use the Mitchell camera and synchronous sound.[15] Four of Kim's features: *Yangsan Province* (*Yangsando*, 1955), *A Touch-me-not* (*Bongseonhwa*, 1956), *The Sea Knows* (*Hyeonhaetan eun algoitta*, 1961) and *Goryeojang* (1963), are also incomplete.

Ahn also notes the role played by film libraries in Europe (Berlin, London, Paris), dating back as early as the 1930s, in functioning "articulations of nation, film and educated citizenship,"[16] referring to the work of Haidee Wasson's *Museum Movies: The Museum of Modern Art and the Birth of Art Cinema*. The Korean Film Archive (KOFA) came significantly later. It was founded in 1974 as the Korean Film Storage Center. This was the year after the Korean Motion Picture Promotion Corporation (KMPPC) was created. KMPPC became the Korean Film Commission in 1999 before being renamed The Korean Film Council (KOFIC) in 2004. The two governmental organizations are interlinked. Both KOFA and KOFIC were founded in the 1970s when Korean cinema had entered a steep decline as the Yushin System under President Park Chung Hee had brought further suppression to wider society and to the film industry. The government responded to the drop in film admissions by making several revisions to the Motion Picture Law in the 1960s and 1970s. Enacted in 1962 shortly after Park's military coup in May 1961, the Motion Picture Law was used as a tool by the government to ensure films propagated its nationalist agenda. Film companies had to be registered but in order to do so a company would need to own a studio of at least 2,000 square meters along with equipment such as 35mm or 70mm camera. The registered companies also had to produce at least fifteen films per year along with "quota quickies."[17] This resulted in a vast number of films being made. In 1969 alone, 233 Korean films were produced. But the further revisions did not solve the underlying problems facing the industry with the government tightening its grip as it entered a recession in the 1970s (admissions in 1969 surpassed 178 million but dropped to 70 million in 1976). Yet it is probably no coincidence that these organizations were formed within twelve months of each other as the government drew up measures to help the rapidly declining film industry.

The KOFA, however, was not in receipt of government funding to preserve prints until 1994.[18] During the 1990s, under civilian governments—Kim Young-sam and then Kim Dae-jung—the attitude towards the Korean film industry changed dramatically. In 1994 President Kim Young-sam was shown a videotaped report by the Presidential Advisory Council on Science and Technology about the media sector that included the global success of *Jurassic Park* (Steven Spielberg, 1993), in which sales related to the film were explained as being equivalent to the exporting of 1.5 million Hyundai Cars, more than double the amount sold overseas in 1992.[19] Kim became convinced that the media sector needed support. It marked the beginning of a different relationship between government and the Korean film industry.

Realizing that the government needed to support it rather than seek to control it, both KOFA and KOFIC would become important institutions in promoting and preserving Korean cinema. KOFA would focus on Korean films prior to 2000, while films made later would largely fall under KOFIC's remit. Although Ahn is correct to state film preservation in Korea came much later, what both organizations have achieved over the last three decades is remarkable. KOFA's YouTube channel now features over a hundred Korean films with English subtitles (available to watch for free) including four of Kim's films, while the Korean Film Council continues to support the industry in a variety of ways. Indeed, without KOFA and KOFIC it is highly doubtful that the BIFF would have become the festival it is today, bringing together both past and present Korean cinema to both local and global audiences.

Ahn writes how the effort behind the establishment of the first retrospective in 1996, "Redefining Korean Cinema in 'Our Own' Critical Perspective: Korean New Wave Retrospective From 1980 to 1995" is "linked with the desire of the Korean film industry to "break through" into the global market.[20] However, it was not until the Kim Ki-young retrospective a year later that the festival achieved this breakthrough, as underlined by Chris Berry's aforementioned essay "Introducing 'Mr. Monster.'"

Following this retrospective Kim was viewed as one of the first Korean auteurs to establish himself on the global stage. "Critics from around the world delighted in films like *Killer Butterfly* (*Salinnabi reul jjotneunyeoja*, 1978) and *Insect Woman* (*Chungnyeo*, 1972) movies which quickly established Kim as a fully-fledged auteur in the Russ Meyer/Roger Corman scheme of things," was, for instance, the reaction of one writer.[21] The title of the article by James Havis Richard is quite telling: "A Star Is Born—Aged 78." It was considered a weak year for Korean films the year of the Kim retrospective at Busan. However, as Chris Berry writes, "there was an unexpected happy ending. 'Mr. Monster' came to the rescue."[22] This is reaffirmed by Richard. "The new discovery at this year's 2nd Busan International Film Festival was not to be found in the New Currents section, a competitive event for new Asian directors. Instead, it was the name of 78-year-old Kim Ki-young."[23]

Interestingly, there were some concerns about holding a Kim Ki-young retrospective at Busan owing to his "excessive" style, with organizers unsure whether his work would resonate with international and local audiences. Although Kim was seen as part of the "big three" during the 1960s Golden Era, together with Yu Hyeon-mok and Shin Sang-ok, his place in the industry gradually grew less secure, most notably during the tumultuous 1970s. As restrictions were placed on who could own a studio, he was forced to work with other production companies having lost his own. He continued to make films but embarking on projects based on literary works that were made to reach the national film quota system he became more isolated.[24] These features, though, which included *Promise of the Flesh* (*Yukche ui yaksok*, Kim Ki-young, 1975) and *Ieo Island* (*Ieodo*, Kim Ki-young, 1977) would later attract notice. The former screened in Busan in 1997 while the latter was part of both retrospectives, in Busan and Berlin. During the 1980s and early 1990s he became even more reclusive before his rediscovery. Kim even chose not to release his last film, *An Experience to Die For* (*Jugeodo joeun gyeongheom*, Kim Ki-young, 1990). The film premiered at BIFF in 1998 months after Kim's untimely death, the year after his retrospective. The print was then left in his garage and received a posthumous release in July 2021 after the film's star, Youn Yuh-jung, won an Academy Award for her supporting role in *Minari* (Lee Isaac Chung, 2020).

The screening of Kim's films at BIFF, therefore, was overdue despite the concerns some at the festival had. In fact, the issues over "excess" proved to be a defining characteristic of work that appealed to the international guests at the festival. Berry states "it is somewhat surprising to note that in a cinema of excess, Kim Ki-young is more excessive than most."[25] He argues that when it comes to Korean cinema there are two major characteristics: realism and excess.[26]

Over the last twenty years, realism has no longer been a trait associated with Korean cinema except for the work of Lee Chang-dong and Im Kwon-taek. Even Lee, however, made a departure from realism with his latest feature *Burning* (*Beoning*, Lee Chang-dong, 2018). Im has been less active over recent years with his 102nd film, *Revivre* (*Hwajung*, Im Kwon-taek, 2015), released seven years ago. Directors over the last two decades have focused more on genre to tell their stories. Park Chan-wook, Bong Joon Ho, and Kim

Jee-woon are such examples. Certainly, in the late 1980s and early-to-mid 1990s, realism was prevalent in much—though not all—Korean cinema with its roots in the 1960s evident in many films, not least *Aimless Bullet* (*Obaltan*, Yu Hyeon-mok, 1960).

At the time of the Kim Ki-young retrospective in Busan, Korea's film industry was in the midst of significant transformation. The "New Wave" or "New Korean Realism" group of filmmakers led by Park Kwang-su were becoming less influential as a new generation was being nurtured. As Darcy Paquet contends, it is probably not a coincidence that almost all the "New Korean Cinema" auteurs made their debuts between the years of 1996 and 2000.[27] Only Park Chan-wook made his debut earlier but even Park only really established himself as filmmaker after *Joint Security Area* (*Gongdong gyeonbi guyeok jeieseuei*, Park Chan-wook, 2000), released in 2000.

Berry's observations on "excess" and Kim's distinctive style thus warrants further attention given how Korea's auteurs have also uniquely expressed Korean culture and society through their films. Berry concludes his essay by stating "we may yet find that Kim Ki-young, the maverick Mr. Monster, comes to signify Koreanness."[28] Referring to some of the films screened in the retrospective, Berry highlights their "unrealistic" quality: such as the use of camera angles, shadows, and lighting in *The Housemaid* (Kim made a conscious effort to learn as much about lighting as possible, studying it himself). Berry also makes reference to the "over-the-top" sex scenes in *Killer Butterfly*, *The Insect Woman*, and *Woman of Fire '82* (*Hwanyeo 82*, 1982),[29] making a contrast to the realism found in early Korean cinema: "if restraint and realism are desired, Kim Ki-young is not your man."[30] Examining the mise-en-scène of films, Berry argues "Kim Ki-young's films focuses excessively on the fetishistic trappings of American consumer culture in Korea,"[31] using *The Housemaid* and *The Insect Woman* as examples.

Of the eight films screened at the Busan retrospective, *The Housemaid* remains Kim's most famous feature—it was the first Korean film to be remastered and to be part of the Korean Film Archive's Blu-ray collection. But many of his films have since become sought after. In addition to *The Housemaid*, the festival also screened *The Insect Woman*, *Ieo Island*, *Woman of Fire '82*, *Yangsan Province*, *Promise of the Flesh*, *Carnivorous Animals* (*Yuksik dongmu*l, 1984), and *Killer Butterfly*. Four months later, Berlin would show *The Insect Woman*, *The Housemaid*, *Woman of Fire '82*, and *Ieo Island* in the Forum section that also screened nine other Korean titles. *Ieo Island* would later be a further addition to the Korean Film Archive's Blu-ray collection and *Killer Butterfly* would be released on Blu-ray under the title in the US in 2019 through Mondo Macabro. Ultimately following Busan, Kim's films would screen at festivals throughout much of the world as Korean cinema was gathering more and more attention. There was a Kim Ki-young retrospective at the cinematheque in Paris in 2006 that screened eighteen of his films. *Killer Butterfly* formed part of a program at the Far East Film Festival in Udine that focused on 1970s Korean cinema. More recently in 2019, *Goryeojang* was invited to the London Korean Film Festival, which again signifies the importance of Korean cultural centers and government funding in promoting Korean auteurs and their work. It was also quite fitting that Youn Yuh-jung in her Academy Award acceptance speech expressed her gratitude towards Kim Ki-young for giving her an opportunity to work in film. This came a year after *Parasite* had won the historic Best Picture Award further elevating Kim Ki-young's status as not just a Korean filmmaker, but a leading national auteur.

THE KOREAN AUTEUR AND THE FESTIVAL CIRCUIT

This brings the chapter back to the relationship between the Korean auteur, the festival circuit and Korean cinema on the world stage. As the discussion above has made reference to, the growth of the Korean film industry globally has correlated with the rise of the Korean auteur. Kim Ki-young has been a forerunner, after having been (re)discovered by critics and programmers in Busan. As Berry notes at the time of writing his essay on the Kim Ki-young retrospective, Korean cinema had yet to establish an image on the international art-house circuit.[32] Although Korean films had been invited to the "big three" festivals in Europe prior to 1997—Kang Dae-jin's *The Coachman* (*Mabu*, 1961) was part of the main competition at the Berlin Film Festival as far back as 1961 winning the Silver Bear Extraordinary Prize—no Korean filmmaker had generated the kind of enthusiasm Kim had created in Busan in 1997.

The local reaction was conversely a muted affair according to Ahn Soojeong.[33] The Korean press failed to pay much attention to the retrospective and were not even aware of its success. There was even criticism of the poor attendance (the retrospectives tend to attract fewer people compared to the more high-profile world premieres). Even local critics appeared confused by the international reaction.[34] Ahn cites Korean critic Lee Dong-jin: "The popularity of Kim's films to the western film professionals conversely reflects that we don't have any representative Korean *auteur* available at the moment to show to the global market."[35]

As Ahn states, "it illustrates the BIFF had failed in establishing its own aesthetic norms and tended to lead on such international aesthetics already sanctioned by Western festivals."[36] This discussion above has demonstrated how festivals are a western phenomenon and Cannes, in particular, has thrived with its auteur-driven curating. Other festivals such as Venice and Berlin followed suit, while other festivals on the circuit continue to follow, at least to a certain degree, Cannes's lead. This is not to say Busan has not developed its own signature programming—I would argue that the retrospective is reflective of its dedication towards promoting and supporting the Korean film industry primarily, and also the wider Asian film sector that is at the core of BIFF's choice of programming. International guests, by and large, attend Busan to watch Korean and Asian films. As such, its roots are tied to national and regional interests.

Busan has retained a strong emphasis on Korean cinema in a variety of ways. The festival's Korean cinema sections (panorama, vision, and the retrospective), its New Currents signature program (that invariably includes films by debut Korean filmmakers), have turned the festival into a place of discovery; mirroring in some respects also the Sundance Film Festival in the US. The industry arm of the festival that is now called the Asian Contents and Film Market was launched in 2006 as the Asian Film Market (AFM). It has become one of the leading industry events in Asia, and despite the pandemic is set to continue to be, as AFM shifts to include streaming and series content as its current name suggests. Even in its earlier years its focus on the industry was evident with the Promotion Project Plan (PPP) that was launched in 1999 and later changed to the Asian Project Market in 2011 that supports emerging Asian film directors including those from Korea. In short, the timing of when Busan emerged along with Korea's two other major festivals strongly suggests a link between the festival and so-called New Korean cinema.

Indeed, the link between festivals and national film industries has long been evident in Europe. Cannes continues to showcase French auteurs and is highly influenced by its local industry. The fact that Netflix films are essentially barred from competition following pressure from French exhibitors is characteristic of this. Interrelated to the idea that a festival is closely connected with national cinema is art cinema. David Bodwell argues that festivals provide a space for films that have been produced outside the studio system. "Festivals are the major clearing house for art cinema."[37] He also points to the emergence of Japanese, Korean, and Chinese filmmakers in the 1990s and 2000s as a "replay at an accelerated pace the trajectory of art cinema."[38] After all, festivals have been crucial in enabling national cinemas to develop an international profile and interest despite the omnipresent Hollywood industry. Rosalind Galt and Karl Schoonover suggest that "art cinema's specificity emerges in a relationship between the *art* and *global*."[39] In this regard Galt and Schoonover view them as being "mutually dependent" with a common idea of the "global," speaking "to the international address, distribution, audience and aesthetic language of art cinema."[40]

Central to how art cinema is distributed and consumed is the notion of the auteur, something that has proved to be an effective form of programming in Europe. Turning back to the work by French critics and New Wave filmmakers of the 1960s, there was an unambiguous intent in championing auteur cinema that paved the way in which Cannes would subsequently head with the founding of Directors' Fortnight, and the changes to the official selection that followed in later years. Chris Berry's impressions of Kim Ki-young's use of mise-en-scène and his striking aesthetic or "excess" echoes André Bazin's thoughts on the auteur and the importance he and his contemporaries placed on mise-en-scène. Unlike the discovery of a new filmmaker who has directed one, or perhaps two, feature films, and who demonstrates the potential of becoming an auteur, Kim's career was extensive by 1997 having helmed thirty-two films. Consequently, he had a whole body of work to be explored. This allowed academics like Berry, along with critics, programmers, and audiences to delve into his films and ascertain his stylistic traits. Berry's essay is, therefore, evidence of the impact Kim's film had and its place in the history of Korean cinema.

The showcasing of an auteur at a festival is not just reducible to a series of screenings. There is an interaction between the director with the audience and professionals from the industry through press conferences, Q&As, and masterclasses. Cindy Hing-Yuk Wong states "the director becomes an event."[41] As such, Kim also attended Busan, participating in the festival, and it was the director himself who became the festival's central draw for international guests. Yet while the auteur can take part and converse with attendees, he/she cannot completely control the discourse."[42]

The festival itself also contributes to this with its own material. The year of the Kim Ki-young retrospective would be the first year the BIFF would publish a book based on the contents of the event; it was titled *Kim Ki-Young: Cinema of Diabolical Desire and Death* (1997).[43] The discourse surrounding his films in this text considers him as a "non-conformist auteur,"[44] adopting an "aesthetics of excess,"[45] heavily engaged with addressing the "frustrated male sexual fantasy."[46] Through such analysis, this book was able to capture some of the discourse that emerged from the critical commentary offered by the festival's overseas guests. In the preface, Kim Dong-ho, former director of the Busan Film Festival, wrote: "Kim Ki-young depicted this turbulent period [the 1960s and 1970s] by visualizing and dramatizing these social issues and controversies through a discourse of sex [. . .] He succeeded in constructing psychological dramas with an expressionistic style rare in Korean cinema." Crucially, this provided audiences who lacked an understanding of the Korean cinema industry or wider Korean society with an insight into the films' complex themes. Kim also stressed the link between the festival and "rediscovery," by stating the festival "presents this retrospective to develop more specialized studies of Korean film history through the rediscovery of lost films and the restoration of damaged films," thereby reinforcing the link between the festival and the work conducted by the Korean Film Archive.[47]

The discourse surrounding Kim's work continued well beyond his passing, which tragically occurred when his house burned down just six days before the Berlin Film Festival in 1998. If anything, his death added to the urgency of rediscovering his films and addressing their significance. Still, it would not be until years later when the younger auteurs (those who were born in the 1960s, then went to university in the 1980s, and entered the Korean film industry in the 1990s) were securing festival invitations that the significance of Kim's retrospective would become further apparent.

A case in point is Park Chan-wook. In Marc Raymond's compelling essay "From Old Boys to Quiet Dreams: Mapping Korean Art Cinema Today," Raymond charts and theorizes how Korean cinema has operated in both domestic and overseas film festivals. His argument concerns the emergence of the Korean auteurs through an analysis of how Park Chan-wook and Lee Chang-dong were established at film festivals. When examining Park, who worked as film critic in the 1990s and was well-versed in literature as well as cinema, Raymond underlines the importance of Park championing the films of Kim Ki-young and that it "provided an important antecedent to Park's eventual rise in the 2000s."[48] Park was particularly fond of Kim's films made during the 1970s, features Kim himself had lost faith in. The expressionistic style of the work by both Kim and Park demonstrates the influence the former had on the latter. Crucially, as Raymond contends, the celebrating of Kim's films through the Busan retrospective and by Park himself is "part of a broader movement of Korean cinema as a whole to construct itself in the areas of both national and world cinemas."[49] What was achieved through the retrospective and then later at Berlin was indicative of a journey Park would later embark on. "The shaping of this space," Raymond argues, is "where cult cinema could negotiate between the popular and art cinema."[50] Indeed, the fascination surrounding Kim's stylistic excess as an auteur would be repeated in 2004 when Park's *Oldboy* won the Grand Prix in Cannes, and this is particularly so given how the film was received overseas with significant attention paid to the film's "grotesque" violence and excess. The UK DVD label Tartan branded many of Park's films under its "Asia Extreme" label, including *Sympathy for Mr. Vengeance* (*Boksu neun naui geot*, 2002) and *Lady Vengeance* (*Chinjeolhan geumja ssi*, 2005). This auteurial path to international establishment was not just limited to Park. Kim Jee-woon's *A Tale of Two Sisters* (*Janghwa, Hongryeon*, 2003) and *A Bittersweet life* (*Dalkomhan insaeng*, 2005) were similarly branded as the genuine work of an auteur, along with several Kim Ki-duk films such as *The Isle* (*Seom*, 2000) and *Bad Guy* (*Nappeun namja*, 2001).

Toward the end of the documentary on Kim Ki-young directed by Kim Hong-joon, in which Korean filmmakers were interviewed about his work, Kim Jee-woon says "some of the cinematic DNA was passed on to the next generation."[51] Here he was comparing his own work to films such as *Woman of Fire*. And, in this regard, the dramatic and expressionist use of the house and stairs in *A Tale of Two Sisters* echoes the stylistic excess of Kim that is referenced in the documentary. There are, no doubt, many other thematic and conceptual connections between the work of Kim Ki-young and the next generation of filmmakers. Many of Park Chan-wook's films are reminiscent of Kim's work, as with Park's stylization and his focus on female characters and sexuality in films such as *Lady Vengeance* (*Chinjeolhan Geumjassi*, Park Chan-wook, 2005), *Thirst* (*Bakjwi*, Park Chan-wook, 2009) and *The Handmaiden (Agassi*, Park Chan-wook, 2016). Bong Joon Ho has also been heavily influenced by Kim, as can be seen through *Parasite* and its parallels with *The Housemaid*. The use of smell that is a prominent motif in *Parasite* also appears in *Woman of Fire* and the breakfast scene in the epilogue of *Memories of Murder*, with all its western decor and food, is perhaps a reference to a similar scene in *Woman of Fire '82*. On the Korean DVD of *The Housemaid*, Bong also takes part in a film commentary with film critic Kim Yeong-jin, in which Kim refers to how Bong describes it as the "*Citizen Kane* of the Korean world." Bong's father (Bong Sang-gyun) designed the opening film titles for *The Housemaid* illustrating a personal connection to the film.[52]

Nonetheless, it is also true that after having established a cinematic reputation abroad, like Kim Ki-young has done, the reaction domestically and internationally can be different. More recently in Korea, Kim's films have generated interest due to Youn Yuh-jung's Academy Award and her acceptance speech. In the week that followed, Kim even made it into the top ten of the portal site Naver's most searched "film person,"[53] a rare event for a deceased filmmaker who made films decades ago. Nevertheless, as the local reaction after the retrospective suggests, Kim's films did not generate the same levels of enthusiasm until later, as Park Chan-wook, Bong Joon Ho, the Korean Film Archive, and other film festivals continued to champion his work.

Although Park Chan-wook, Bong Joon Ho and Kim Jee-woon had established themselves as talented filmmakers in Korea, and even "commercial auteurs," their status as auteurs in the sense that Bazin would define the term was solidified by their success overseas, and chiefly within film festivals. For Lee Chang-dong, Hong Sang-soo, and Kim Ki-duk, who died in 2020 due to complications from COVID-19, the contrast is even more stark; this is especially true for Kim Ki-duk, who remains loathed in Korea, even after his death, due to allegations of sexual assault against him, but who is largely admired in the West. Hong Sang-soo is another case in point. Despite being extremely prolific compared to his peers with twenty-six films to date (and counting), he continues to secure festival invitations and win awards at Europe's top festivals. In 2021 his work *Introduction* (*Inteurodeoksyeon*, Hong Sang-soo, 2021) won the Silver Bear for Best Screenplay at Berlin, while in Korea, his film output is largely ignored outside the cinephile community and it is his private life that attracts all the mainstream attention. As for Lee Chang-dong, *Burning* (2018) encapsulates how his films can be embraced by the critics at a major festival, with the work having broken *Screen International's* "jury grid" record,[54] but then failing to strike a chord with audiences at home. It even became the first Korean feature to be shortlisted for the Academy Award for Best International Feature in 2019.

CONCLUSION

This chapter has attempted to examine the rediscovery of Kim Ki-young on the festival circuit and how it relates to the rise of the Korean auteur at film festivals. In exploring the origin of festivals in Europe and its relationship to the development of the idea of the cinematic auteur, this essay has argued that this trajectory can be directly linked to the rediscovery of Kim in Korea, and the development of local film festivals in this context. The Busan International Film Festival, of course, emerged, like the Korean film industry, under a unique set of circumstances in the 1990s as the government sought to promote and support the nation's motion picture industry. How the festival has mirrored the growth of Korean cinema along with its auteurs is testament to how they are all closely connected. Yet, the success of the festival globally, as the Kim retrospective illustrates, is also linked to the western phenomenon of the film festival in its focus on auteur programming. This has been manifested in the discovering, or "rediscovering," of filmmakers, but also nurturing and celebrating them. It has since discovered numerous Korean directors and used the retrospective to shed light on the careers of other auteurs including Shin Sang-ok and Yi Du-yong.

The timing of the retrospective was also extremely significant, as it preceded the growing prominence of Korean auteurs at prestigious festivals in Europe that came a few years later. Attention was given to Kim's use of style, his excess, and his "Koreanness"— characteristics that can be seen in the work of Park Chan-wook, Bong Joon Ho, Kim Jee-woon and others. During the 1980s and early 1990s, Korean cinema both locally and internationally was at least to some degree associated with the realist aesthetic and storytelling that has been evident in Korean films since the 1950s. Im Kwon-taek, who was one of Korea's most prominent filmmakers on the festival circuit during the 1980s, 1990s, and early 2000s, was certainly widely respected and revered, but did not generate the same kind of enthusiasm among international guests in the same way that Kim Ki-young did in 1997. While both filmmakers, one could argue, conveyed an idea of "Koreanness" in their films, they had starkly different styles. Im, in his later work, frequently adopted the long take while Kim used unusual camera angles and lighting as he experimented with genre convention. Ultimately the films of Kim would share more in common with Park Chan-wook and his generation that also came to resonate on the festival circuit.

Therefore, the Busan retrospective and then the screening of four of Kim's films in Berlin were a consequence of the changes that were happening in the local industry with festivals seeking to promote Korean cinema globally. In so doing, they served as an indication of what was to come, with major festivals curating their Korean selections with a focus on Korea's most high profile filmmakers underscoring the importance of Kim Ki-young as a leading Korean auteur.

NOTES

1. Patrick Frater, "Korean Movies Lose Box Office Crown, for the First Time in a Decade," *Variety*, January 5, 2022, accessed Febrary 10, 2022, https://variety.com/2022/film/asia/korea-box-office-local-movies-lose-crown-in-2021-1235146984/.
2. These were as follows: *Carnivorous Animals* (*Yukshik dongmul*, 1985), *The Housemaid* (*Hanyeo*, 1960), *Insect Woman* (*Chungnyeo*, 1972), *Ieo Island* (*Ieodo*, 1977), *Promise of the Flesh* (*Yukcheui yaksok*, 1975), *Killer Butterfly* (*Salinnabireul jjotneun yeoja*, 1978), *Woman of Fire '82* (*Hwanyeo '82*, 1982), *Yangsan Province* (*Yangsando*, 1955).
3. Soojeong Ahn, *The Pusan International Film Festival, South Korean Cinema and Globalization* (Hong Kong: Hong Kong University Press, 2011), 110.
4. These titles were: *The Insect Woman*, *The Housemaid*, *The Woman of Fire' 82*, and *Ioe Island*.
5. Nikki J. Y. Lee, "Salute to Mr. Vengeance!: The Making of a Transnational Auteur Park Chan-wook," in *East Asian Cinemas: Exploring Transnational Connection on Film*, ed. Leon Hunt and Wing-fai Leong (London: I. B. Tauris, 2008), 209.
6. Chris Berry, "Introducing Mr. Monster: Kim Ki-young and the Critical Economy of the Globalized Art-House Cinema," in *Korean Film Directors: Kim Ki-young*, ed. Hong-joon Kim (Seoul: Korean Film Council, Seoul Selection, 2007), 43.
7. Julian Stringer, "Film Festivals in Asia: Notes on History, Geography and Power from a Distance," in *Film Festivals: History, Theory, Method, Practice*, ed. Marijke de Valck (London: Routledge, 2016), 34.
8. Marijke de Valck, *Film Festivals: From European Geopolitics to Global Cinephilia* (Amsterdam: Amsterdam University Press, 2007), 19–20.
9. Dorota Ostrowska, "Making Film History at the Cannes Film Festival," in *Film Festivals: History, Theory, Method, Practice*, ed. Marijke de Valck (London: Routledge, 2016), 24–5.
10. Ibid., 25.
11. Robert Stam, *Film Theory* (Malden, MA: Blackwell, 2000), 84–5.
12. Ostrowska, "Making Film History at the Cannes Film Festival," 27.
13. Ibid., 27.
14. Ibid., 109.
15. Hong-joon Kim, *Korean Film Directors: Kim Ki-young* (Seoul: Korean Film Council, Seoul Selection, 2007), 109.
16. Ahn, *The Pusan International Film Festival*, 110.
17. Production companies could import one film (usually lucrative Hollywood titles) for every three Korean films produced.
18. Ibid.
19. Darcy Paquet, *New Korean Cinema: Breaking the Waves* (London: Wallflower Press, 2010), 34.
20. Ibid., 34

21. James Havis Richard, "A Star Is Born—Aged 78," Moving Pictures MIFED 1997 Special (November) 1997), cited in Ahn, *The Pusan International Film Festival*, 117.
22. Berry, "Introducing Mr. Monster," 41.
23. Richard, "A Star Is Born," 117.
24. Yi Yeon-ho, "Introduction," in Kim, *Korean Film Directors*, 24.
25. Berry, "Introducing Mr. Monster," 44.
26. Ibid., 44.
27. Paquet, *New Korean Cinema*, 66–7.
28. Berry, "Introducing Mr. Monster: Kim Ki-young," 56.
29. Ibid., 44–6.
30. Ibid., 46.
31. Ibid., 46.
32. Ibid, 52.
33. Ahn, *The Pusan International Film Festival*, 110.
34. Ibid., 110.
35. Lee Dong-jin, "Toward the New Centre in Asia," *Chosun ilbo*, November 10, 1997, cited in *The Pusan International Film Festival, South Korean Cinema and Globalization* (Hong Kong: Hong Kong University Press, 2011), 118.
36. Ahn, *The Pusan International Film Festival*, 110.
37. David Bordwell, "The Art Cinema as a Mode of Film Practice," in *Poetics of Cinema* (New York: Routledge, 2008), 160.
38. Ibid., 161.
39. Rosalind Galt and Karl Schoonover, "Introduction," in *Global Art Cinema: New Theories and Histories*, ed. Rosalind Galt and Karl Schoonover (Oxford: Oxford University Press, 2010), 20.
40. Ibid., 20.
41. Cindy Hing-Yuk Wong, *Film Festivals: Culture, People, and Power on the Global Screen* (New Brunswick, NJ: Rutchers, 2011), 126.
42. Ibid., 127.
43. Kim Dong-ho, ed., *Kim Ki-young: Cinema of Diabolical Desire and Death* (Pusan: Pusan International Film Festival, 1997).
44. Yi Yeong-il, "Diabolical Desire," in Kim, *Kim Ki-young*, 18.
45. O Yeong-suk, "Imagination of Excess or Heresy," in Kim, *Kim Ki-young*, 30.
46. Yim Kyeong-hun, "Frustrated Male Sexual Fantasy," in Kim, *Kim Ki-young*, 42.
47. Kim Dong-ho, "Preface," in Kim, ed., *Kim Ki-young: Cinema of Diabolical Desire and Death*, 5.
48. Marc Raymond, "From Old Boys to Quiet Dreams: Mapping Korean Art Cinema Today," in *Film Criticism* 2 (2018): 1.
49. Ibid., 1.
50. Ibid., 1.
51. *Two or Three Things about Kim Ki-young* (*Gamdokdeul Kim Ki-young eul malhada*, Kim Hong-joon, 2008), The Korean Film Archive Blu-ray Collection.
52. Kim Hyeon-rok, "Bong Joon Ho, 'My Father Participated in the Late Director Kim Ki-young's *The Housemaid*,'" *Star News*, January 10, 2007.
53. Jason Bechervaise, "Kim Ki Young is now appearing in the top 10 of Naver's film person ranking," *Twitter*, May 4, 2021, accessed February 13, 2022, https://twitter.com/jasebechervaise/status/1389405512668651521?s=21.
54. Ben Dalton, "'Burning' Sets Record Score in History of Screen's Cannes Jury Grid," Screendaily, May 18, 2018, accessed February 13, 2022, https://www.screendaily.com/news/burning-sets-record-score-in-history-of-screens-cannes-jury-grid/5129480.article.

Appendix

Script: *The Sea Knows* (Scenes lacking sound) from Kim Hong-joon, ed., *Kim Ki-young Screenplay Collection II* [*Kim Ki-young sinario seonjib 2*] (Korean Film Archive, 2008).
Translation: Song Won-jeong
Minutes from *The Sea Knows*, YouTube channel of Korean Classic Film. (1:00:07)

126. VISITING ROOM

(Aroun enters the visiting room.)
(Gyeong-hui stands up seeing him.)

Gyeong-hui	Sir!
Aroun	How did you get here?
Gyeong-hui	You didn't answer the letters I wrote.
Aroun	They don't allow communication with the outside here.
Gyeong-hui	What happened to my letters, then?
Aroun	They became a knife of the military police to cut off my head.
Gyeong-hui	Oh!
Aroun	The fact that they allowed this temporary release is even more suspicious.
Gyeong-hui	But I asked for it.
Aroun	Anyway, let's get out of here.

(Aroun takes Gyeong-hui out.)

127. TEA HOUSE

(Aroun and Gyeong-hui are having tea.)

Aroun	What did you write in those letters?
Gyeong-hui	That your mother prays for you every day with a bowl of water.
Aroun	And?
Gyeong-hui	That you are a hero to us students, for standing up against Government General Goiso.
Aroun	For those words, hundreds of military police would come looking for you.
Gyeong-hui	I figured an escape route for you, to North Gando.
Aroun	Gyeong-hui, you are something beyond imagination.

(A military police officer approaches Aroun. Aroun stands up.)

| Police | Identification! |

(Aroun shows his identification to the military police.)
(The military police officer leaves.)

| Gyeong-hui | Sir, please don't let me down. |
| Aroun | We have to be prepared, now that the military police saw the letters. Let's get to somewhere to ditch them. |

127A. DOWNTOWN NAGOYA

(A tram passes by the downtown.)

130. HIDEKO'S HOUSE, ROOM

(Hideko's mother puts tea in front of Aroun and Gyeong-hui.)

Hideko's Mother	Is this your fiancée?
Aroun	She's a younger sister of a friend.
Hideko's Mother	I heard that the Busan-Shimonoseki ferry sank down the other day.
Gyeong-hui	That's why it was so terrifying to cross Hyeonhaetan.

Hideko's Mother	A girl's determination is fierce. They would go through everything for the ones they've Joseon.
Gyeong-hui	I guess a girl's mind can only be read by another girl.

(Aroun drinks tea.)

Hideko's Mother	Aroun san, you are a happy man. Excuse me for a second.

(Hideko's mother leaves the room.)

131. HIDEKO'S HOUSE, KITCHEN

(Hideko is preparing food. Hideko's mother approaches her.)

Hideko's Mother	A Josenjin's match can only be another Josenjin. It's time for you to give up, Hideko
Hideko	Why would he bring her here? To prove their innocence, perhaps?
Hideko's Mother	Forget about it. A girl crossed Hyeonhaetan, risking her own life.

132. HIDEKO'S HOUSE, KITCHEN (LATER)

(Aroun comes out of the room.)

Aroun	Please take care of her.
Hideko's Mother	Why, are you going somewhere else?
Aroun	I'm going to stay at a nearby inn.
Hideko	But, wouldn't the girl be upset if you don't sleep with her?
Aroun	Why would she be upset?
Hideko	Because it's a privilege for a young couple.
Aroun	I'm heading out.

(Aroun leaves the place.)

Hideko's Mother	Hideko, how rude!

132A. IN FRONT OF HIDEKO'S HOUSE (NIGHT)

(Aroun leaves the house and starts to walk.)

133. BEDROOM, HIDEKO'S HOUSE

(Hideko and Gyeong-hui sit together.)

Hideko	How long have you known Aroun san?
Gyeong-hui	When he came back for summer wearing a high-school hat.
Hideko	That's when you fell for him? Mine was when my big brother brought a recruit in a military hat, who was heading for the prostitutes.
Gyeong-hui	That's when you fell for him?
Hideko	It was a weird sensation, back then.
Gyeong-hui	Don't think about marrying him.
Hideko	Why?
Gyeong-hui	Different nations, that's why.
Hideko	Our child will transcend such division.
Gyeong-hui	It's a tragedy.
Hideko	Tragedy is when you conceive a male seed without love, like a herd of cows or horses.
Hideko	He must be alone in that inn, shouldn't someone console him?
Gyeong-hui	It's not something an educated lady would do.
Hideko	Education always requires sacrifice. I'm going.

(Hideko leaves the room.)

(1:23:32)

172. MILITARY TERRITORY

(A soldier plays a morning bugle for morning roll call.)

173. BARRACK

(Soldiers wake up.)

Sound	Wake up! Get ready for the departure!

(Inoue enters the barrack.)

Inoue	Attention! The dispatch is postponed. The bombing last night took our transport ship.*

(Soldiers cheer in joy.)

Inoue	Good. No good in going to a war without telling the family. You will have a day release instead. Go home and have a good cry with your mothers or with your girls.

(Inoue walks to Aroun.)

Inoue	Aroun, you lucky bastard, where would you be if you had to leave without seeing that chick one more time?

(Aroun smiles awkwardly out of embarrassment.)
(Inoue walks out of the barrack.)

(Translator's notes: Inoue speaks in a strong southern accent.)

174. IN THE CAR

(Inoue and Aroun are in a moving car.)

Inoue	You son of a bitch, falling for a Japanese girl.
Aroun	Less burden to die on when you think of girls.
Inoue	But try not to when you're out there. They say bullets will come looking for you.

175. HIDEKO'S HOUSE, ROOM

(Hideko gets up seeing Aroun.)

Hideko	Aroun san!

(Aroun walks into the room.)

Aroun	Hideko!

(Hideko bows to Aroun.)

Hideko	I thought I'd never see you again.
Aroun	I could have been on the boat right now if it wasn't for the bombing yesterday. I met this American prisoner. It means that the war's about to come to an end.

Hideko	Will Japan lose?
Aroun	Yes, but I still want to be a great Japanese soldier for Hideko san.
Hideko	No need to fight a losing war. What are we to stop a war that's already lost?
Aroun	Hideko!
Hideko	Fight for your life if you care about your nation for just one bit! But why would you sacrifice your life for the Japanese, let alone bear all the punishment? Let's run away.
Aroun	We'll be shot if the military police find out.
Hideko	Then we'll die together if you don't want to run. So that we'll have no sorrow or regrets.

(Hideko cries in Aroun's arms.)
(Hideko's mother enters the room.)

Hideko's Mother	Hideko! Since when have you made yourself this miserable? Are you to give up your soul to a Korean after your body?
Hideko	Think, mother, please. This man is Korean. Do you think he should die in vain for Japan? Or should he live to feed his wife and child?
Hideko's Mother	*(Shocked)* A child?
Hideko	Japan is trying to deceive us. Japan will lose this war. How can I let him walk on death row knowing all that?
Hideko's Mother	That's why I told you to pick a man after the war.
Hideko	I don't have a choice now.

(Hideko's mother sighs.)

Hideko's Mother	Let the child see its father's face.
Hideko	Mother!

(Hideko and Aroun rise.)

Hideko's Mother	There's no choice. Better to live as a coward than die. Run. Follow your husband, to the end of the world. Let the world know that a Japanese girl never betrays her husband.
Hideko	Mother!

(Hideko hugs her mother in tears.)

Hideko's Mother	I blame the planes for dooming Japan and making us people without a nation.

176. THE AIR

(Planes fly in the cloud.)

177. IN FRONT OF THE DUGOUT (NIGHT)

(A military truck stops.)
(Inoue jumps out of the truck as a bomb goes off nearby.)
(Inoue dives into the dugout.)

178. IN THE DUGOUT

(Dust falls over Inoue.)
(Inoue looks around, sees a man's leg stuck out from a pile of dirt.)

Inoue   Horrid! As though I'm in a butcher's!

Index

Note: Illustrations are indicated by page numbers in bold.

Academy Awards, 35, 107, 146, 152, 154, 158, 159
adultery, 9, 73, 76, 77, 2, 86, 94, 95–6, 134, 135–6
agency, 56, 108, 109, 116
Ahn, Soojeong, 146–7, 150, 151, 154
Aimless Bullet (1961), 53, 65, 88, 153
An Jae-seok, 137
An, Jinsoo, 53, 54
An Seong-gi, 8
Anarchist from Colony (2017), 55
animals, 9, 41–2, 75, 77–81, 91, 97, 98, 101–3, 104
anti-communism, 7, 25–9, 36, 132–3
anti-war sentiment, 51, 54, 57, 64, 65–7
anxiety, 24, 75, 86
appropriate Koreanness, 92–3, 105
April Revolution, 5, 47, 87–8
Army (1944), 40
art cinema, 2, 154, 155, 157
Ashby, Christine, 108
Asia Pacific War, 6, 8, 29, 65–6
Asian Film Festival, 73
Asian Film Market (AFM), 155
Assault of Justice, An (1951), 19

auteurship, 3–4, 5, 10–12, 21–2, 24–6, 30, 52, 131, 132, 146–60
authoritarianism, 8, 65, 95, 104
Autobiography of a Jeep (1943), 23, 24
awards, 8, 35, 73, 132–3, 146, 148, 149–50, 152, 154, 158–9

Bad Guy (2001), 157
Bae Seok-in, 22, 54
Ballad of Narayama (Fukazawa), 35, 37–8, 42
Ballad of Narayama (1958), 34–6, 37, 38–40, 42, 44–8
Ballad of Narayama (1983), 34–6, 37, 40–1, 44–8
Ban Geum-ryeon (1974/1981), 10, 129, 130
Bazin, André, 149, 156, 158
Berlin International Film Festival, 3, 147, 148, 149–50, 152, 153, 154, 156, 158
Berry, Chris, 2, 147, 151, 152, 153, 154, 156
binary oppositions, 74–5, 76, 97
biopolitics, 9, 47, 105
Bird of a Feather (1961), 25
Bittersweet Life, A (2005), 157

Bloch, Ernst, 6
Bodwell, David, 155
Bong Joon Ho, 3, 74, 147, 148, 152–3, 158, 159
"Boycott Japan" movement, 51
Boxes of Death (1955), 7, 21, 25–9, 26–7, 129, 150
Bridges at Toko-Ri, The (1954), 28, 54
Brueggeman, Brenda, 123
Bucheon International Fantastic Film Festival (BIFAN), 3, 148
Buddhism, 36, 37, 40, 43, 44
bunraku theater, 38, 40
Burning (2018), 152, 158–9
Busan, 7, 18, 21, 29
Busan International Film Festival (BIFF), 2, 3, 11, 146–7, 148, 150–7, 159–60

Cahiers du cinéma, 149
Cannes Film Festival, 146, 148–9, 154, 155–6, 157
cannibalism, 9, 10, 42
capitalism, 34, 36, 105
Carnivorous Animals (1984), 8–9, 91–4, 95, 97–8, 102, 105, 153
castration complex, 94–5
censorship, 3, 8, 10–11, 53, 54, 65, 87, 108, 129–30, 133, 137, 138, 141
Chang Myon, 53
Cheon Hak-beom, 22
Cheu, Johnson, 118–19
Chihwaseon (2002), 148
China, 2, 36, 146, 155
Choe Gi-suk, 37
Choi, Chungmoo, 84
Chorus of Trees, The (1968), 55
Chun Doo-hwan, 104
Chung, Lee Isaac, 107
Chūō kōron magazine, 37, 38
cigarettes, 75, 83, 85, 86, 88, 103
Cinémathèque française, La, 149
cinematography, 39, 73, 115
class, 6, 37, 76, 80–1, 88, 92, 93, 108, 119, 123, 124, 125, 130, 139

classic films, 2, 4–5, 125, 150
Coachman, The (1961), 88, 154
Cold War, 6–7, 25–9, 36, 97
colonialism, 5, 6, 10, 17–18, 29, 34–6, 51–5, 84, 113, 133–4
"comfort women", 52, 67
common-sense morality, 36, 39–40, 42, 47
communism, 7, 25–9, 36, 39, 53, 65, 132–3
Complete History of Korean Cinema (Yi), 22
Confucianism, 35, 37, 43, 45
consumption, 87, 105, 153
costumes, 85, 86, 98
counter-hegemony, 36
Country Plan for Korea report, 29
COVID-19 pandemic, 4, 107, 146, 158
Crossley, Nick, 123

Daehan News, 21
Daughter of the Governor General, The (1965), 55
Davis, Lennard J., 111, 115, 125
de Valck, Marijke, 148
deafness, 117–24
decadence, 44, 87–8
Defiance of Teenager, A (1959), 8
Deleuze, Gilles, 99–101, 102
democracy, 3, 5, 38, 43, 48, 65, 74
desire, 9, 56, 75, 77–8, 80, 82, 83, 86–7, 92, 95, 108, 116, 132
despair, 65, 66
Diary of a Sergeant (1945), 23
Diary of Three Sailors (1955), 21, 22, 23–4, **24**
dictatorship, 5, 8–9, 34, 43, 74, 87, 129
difference, 92–3, 98–101, 104
Difference and Repetition (Deleuze), 99–101
digitization, 5
Directors' Fortnight, 148–9, 156
disability, 9, 43, 81, 102, 107–25, 135, 137–40
Do You Know Kkotsuni? (1977), 136

documentary films, 2, 7, 18, 21, 22–5, 108, 157–8
Dokdo/Takeshima islands, 52, 67
Dong, Kelly, 139
Double Suicide (1969), 40
dreams, 75–7, 78–9, 101–2
dubbing, 22

economic crisis, 3, 87
Edinburgh Film Festival, 150
ego, 83
Elegy of Ren (1969), 10
entertainment value, 26–8, 64
Eo Il-seon, 135
Epstein, Jean, 103
Era of Image magazine, 137
espionage, 61–2, 63
ethnography, 40, 46
eugenics, 111, 113–14
European cinema, 8, 22, 26, 28
excess, 2, 5, 8, 26, 42–3, 77, 152, 153, 156, 157, 159
Experience to Die For, An (1990), 129, 140, 152
expressionism, 24, 28, 45, 74, 156, 157
extimacy, 77–8

fallen women, 135–6
fantasy, 76–8; *see also* sexual fantasy
Far East Film Festival, 154
female audiences, 65, 66
female costumes, 85, 86, 98
female voice, 107–25
femininity, 74, 81, 83, 91–2, 94, 96–7, 104, 108
feminism, 3, 124–5
femmes fatales, 74, 94, 109, 139
fertility, 80, 92, 105; *see also* reproduction
Fighting Men, 23
filial piety, 35, 36–7, 43, 45
film distribution, 54, 155
Film Law *see* Motion Picture Law
film libraries, 150

film regulation, 129–37, 141–2, 150; *see also* censorship
film studios, 18–20, 129, 133, 150, 152; *see also* production companies
Fires on the Plain (1959), 54
First World War, 23
Fischer, Susan, 119–20
folk tales, 35, 36–8, 41, 45
Foucault, Michel, 35
frame narratives, 76, 101
French Directors Guild, 149
French New Wave, 149, 155–6
Freud, Sigmund, 9, 24, 74, 75, 77, 81, 83, 95, 98
Fujitani Takashi, 54–5
Fukazawa Shichirō, 35, 37–8, 40, 42
Fury in the Pacific (1945), 23
Fūryū mutan (Fukazawa), 38

Galt, Rosalind, 155
Garland-Thomson, Rosemary, 110, 118, 125
gaze, 75, 79–80, 110, 118–19, 122
gender, 12, 74–5, 81–3, 88, 91–106, 107–25, 135–6, 139–42; *see also* femininity; masculinity
German Expressionism, 28
geronticide, 36–8, 43–5, 47
Geumcheon case, 74
Godard, Jean-Luc, 149
golden age (of Korean cinema), 22, 131, 152
Gong Midori, 54, 56
Gong, Qunhu, 119–20
Goryeojang (1963), 10, 10, 23, 34–6, 37, 41–8, 92, 150, 154
Grand Bell Award, 132–3
Grand Prix, 148, 157
Greater East Asian Co-Prosperity Sphere, 64
grotesque, 2, 8, 9–10, 27, 73, 94, 141, 157
Gwangju Democratization Movement, 74

Ha Gil-jong, 129, 130
Hahaha (2010), 148
Han Un-sa, 52
hanbok, 85, 86
Hand of Fate (1954), 36
Handmaiden, The (2016), 158
Harp of Burma (1956), 54
Hearst Metrotone News, 22
Heavenly Homecoming Stars (1974), 136
hegemony, 36, 39, 111
Higson, Andrew, 18
Hitchcock, Alfred, 149
Holiday (1968), 130
Hollywood, 3, 22, 28, 30, 36, 54, 131, 133, 136, 155
Hong Hae-seong, 6
Hong Sang-soo, 148, 158
horror, 24, 45
Host, The (2006), 148
House of Hummingbird (2018), 146
Housemaid, The (1960), 2, 9, 23, 34, 51, 53, 65, 73–88, 92–6, 99, 101–2, 105, 107, 141, 148, 153, 158
Housemaid, The (2010), 3, 108, 148
Human Condition: The Road to Eternity (1959), 54
humiliation, 58, 60
Hwang Hye-jin, 133, 134
hybridity, 6, 30

I Am a Truck (1953), 7, 21, 22, 23, 24–5, 101
Ichikawa Kon, 54
id, 83
Ieo Island (1977), 9, 10, 92, 152, 153
Im Kwon-taek, 10, 147, 148, 152, 159
Im Sang-soo, 3, 148
imaginary order, 75, 76, 80–1, 87
Imamura Shōhei, 34, 36, 40–1, 44–8
IMF financial crisis, 3
imported films, 23, 130, 131, 133
impotence, 91, 94, 95
independent filmmaking, 7, 11, 108
industrialization, 104, 133
Insect Woman (1972), 8–9, 91, 92–4, 95, 97, 101, 102, 105, 151, 153

insects, 91, 102
interethnic romance, 12, 51–67
Introduction (2021), 158
Ishikawa Seji, 54
Isle, The (2000), 157
Italian neo-realism, 8, 28

Jacob, Gilles, 149
Jacobs, Lea, 136
Jang Sun-woo, 74
Japan
  art and culture, 6, 29, 39, 51, 57, 64
  boycotting of, 51
  cinema audience numbers, 146
  colonial occupation of Korea, 5, 6, 17–18, 29, 34–6, 51–5, 133–4
  customs and traditions, 29, 35, 36–8
  film, 29, 34–6, 38–41, 44–8, 54, 155
  filming in, 54
  Imperial Army, 52–3, 55, 57, 58, 63–4
  Kim's time living in, 6, 54
  Korean–Japanese romance, 51–67
  representations of in film, 54, 56–7, 65
  territorial disputes with Korea, 52, 67
  wartime use of "comfort women", 52, 67
Japanese Tragedy (1953), 40
Jeong, Ju-yong, 19
Jeonju International Film Festival, 148
Jinhae, 18–19
Jinmu Emperors of Northeast, The (Fukazawa), 40
Jo Baek-bong, 19
Joint Security Area (2000), 153
jokes, 77
jouissance, 82
Journals of Musan, The (2011), 146
Jung Il-sung, 54
junshoku films, 29
Jurassic Park (1993), 151
Justice (1945), 23

kabuki theater, 38
Kang Dae-jin, 154
Kang Su-yeon, 147

INDEX   173

Killer Butterfly (1978), 151, 153, 154
Kim Bong-su, 19
Kim Bora, 146
Kim Dae-jung, 151
Kim Deok-jin, 115
Kim Dong-ho, 156
Kim, Elaine H., 84
Kim, Eunjung, 113–14, 123–4, 125
Kim, Han Sang, 95
Kim Heung-man, 19
Kim Hong-joon, 4, 157
Kim Hui-gap, 25
Kim Hyeong-geun, 19
Kim Jee-woon, 3, 147, 152–3, 157, 158, 159
Kim Jong-mun, 26–7, 29
Kim Ki-duk, 157, 158
Kim Ki-young
  academic studies of, 4
  awards and accolades, 8, 73
  background, 6
  'Best' list of own films, 52
  BIFF retrospective, 2, 146–7, 150–7, 159–60
  death, 3, 156–7
  documentaries on, 2, 157–8
  education, 6
  films *see individual titles*
  film production company, 10, 11, 137, 152
  independence, 7, 11
  influence, 3, 108, 148, 157–8
  in Japan, 6, 54
  medical training, 6–7
  National Policy Films, 11, 104, 129–42
  pictured, 1, 7
  published scripts, 2, 62–3
  student theater, 6–7, 28, 101
  work for USIS, 7, 20–5, 29, 30, 108, 150
Kim Ki-Young (BIFF), 156
Kim Seok-jin, 6
Kim Soyoung, 25, 97
Kim Su-yun, 55, 56
Kim U-jin, 6
Kim Un-ha, 56

Kim Won, 92
Kim Yeong-gwon, 20
Kim Yeong-jin, 5–6, 158
Kim Yong-ui, 36, 37
Kim Young-sam, 51, 151
Kim Yu-bong, 7, 7, 11
Kinoshita Keisuke, 34, 36, 38–40, 44–8
Klein, Christina, 35–6, 65, 66
Kobayashi Masaki, 54
Korean Film Archive (KOFA), 5, 62, 150–1, 153, 156, 158
Korean Film Commission, 4, 131, 150
Korean Film Council (KOFIC), 52, 150–1
Korean Film Directors: Kim Ki-young (Korean Film Council), 4
Korean Film Producers Association (KFPA), 54
Korean Motion Picture Promotion Corporation (KMPPC), 134, 150
Korean Sign Language (KSL), 119–20
Korean War, 5, 7, 12, 18–20, 25, 29, 52, 56, 65–7
Kurosawa Akira, 34, 54

labor, 40–1, 46, 104–5, 106
Lacan, Jacques, 75–84, 88
Lady Vengeance (2005), 157, 158
Langloise, Henri, 149
Lee Chang-dong, 148, 152, 157, 158–9
Lee, Nikki J. Y., 93, 95–6, 99, 147
Liberty News, 21–2
Liberty Productions, 21–2, 27, 29
Lie, John, 65
lighting, 23–5, 26, 28, 153, 159
Lippit, Akira Mizuta, 102
Locarno Film Festival, 148
London Korean Film Festival, 154
Lorentz, Pare, 23
Love of Blood Relations (1976), 131, 132

Macbeth (Shakespeare), 34
McNair, Wesley, 23
Madame Freedom (1956), 36, 87
male gaze, 110, 118
Man on a Tightrope (1953), 28

March of Fools, The (1975), 130
March of Time, 21, 23
Marxism, 39
masculinity, 56–8, 64, 74–5, 81, 83, 87, 91–2, 95, 97, 104, 110, 112, 116
masochism, 52, 58, 60
meaning, 118
media, 97, 151, 154
melodrama, 51, 52, 61, 104, 141
Memories of Murder (2003), 158
metaphysics, 99–100
Mijoguchi Kenji, 2
military coups, 8, 53, 150
Minari (2020), 107, 152
modernism, 6, 36, 99
modernity, 34, 44–8, 52–3, 74–5, 78, 80, 83–6, 88, 97
modernization, 39, 43, 45, 74, 96–7, 104–5, 133
morality, 36, 37, 39–40, 42, 43, 45, 47–8, 104
Mother (1977), 134, 139
Mother and a House Guest (1961), 88
Mother and Child Health Act, 113–14
motherhood, 92, 95–6, 109, 113–14, 118, 124, 134–5, 139, 140
Motion Picture Law, 8, 130–1, 133, 134, 150
Mulvey, Laura, 110, 118
music, 23, 25, 98

narrative structure, 8, 75–7, 101
nation-building, 18, 21, 26, 30, 55, 56, 104
National Archives and Records Administration (NARA), 21, 25
national cinema, 3, 5, 17–18, 20, 22, 30, 67, 148, 155
National Deaf Center, 122
National Film Production Center (NFPC), 130–1
National Policy Films, 11, 104, 129–42
National University Theater, 6–7, 101
nationalism, 6, 45, 48, 55, 73, 104, 110, 133, 150
naturalism, 40, 137

nature, 36, 41, 46, 137
necrophilia, 9, 130
neo-realism, 8, 26, 28
Netflix, 155
Neumi (1980), 9, 108–9, 117–25, **120**
New Korean Cinema, 43, 153, 155
New Village Movement, 133–6, 138–40, 142
New Wave movement, 147, 153, 155–6
newsreels, 7, 18, 21–2, 23
Nietzsche, Friedrich, 105
Ninotchka (1939), 27–8
normativity, 8–9, 39, 41, 43–4, 46, 92, 104, 108–12, 115, 119, 122, 124
North Korea, 6, 18, 25, 65

O Yeong-jin, 6, 7, 27–8, 29
objectification, 110, 118, 122, 123
Oedipus complex, 95
Office of Public Information (OPI), 20, 21
Office of War Information (OWI), 23
Oldboy (2003), 148, 157
Ostrowska, Dorota, 149
Otherness, 35, 79, 96–7, 119
Outstanding Korean Film Award, 8
Ozu Yasujiro, 2

pain, 58, 60
Pak U-seong, 80
Pak Yu-hui, 138
Palme d'Or, 146
Paquet, Darcy, 153
Parade of Wives (1974), 134
Paramount News, 21
Parasite (2019), 146, 148, 154, 158
Paris Film Festival, 154
Park Chan-wook, 3, 74, 147, 148, 152–3, 157, 158, 159
Park Chung Hee, 8, 34, 51, 53, 55, 66, 104, 129–42, 150
Park Geun-hye, 55
Park Jung-bum, 146
Park Kwang-su, 74, 147, 153
patriarchy, 51, 63, 81–2, 84, 85, 88, 95, 136, 140

Patterson, Kevin, 123
performativity, 100, 109, 111, 124
Petrunik, Michael, 110
phallic function, 81, 86
phallic symbols, 85–6
photogénie, 103, 105
Platonic ideals, 93, 99
Poetry (2009), 148
Polanski, Roman, 34
police, 65
popular culture, 35, 51, 57, 136
Portrait of Shunkin, A (Tanizaki), 38
postcolonial, 6, 10, 29, 34–5, 56, 65, 84, 110, 125
power, 53, 56, 79, 82, 86, 108, 109, 118–21, 123
premodernity, 39, 43, 45, 48, 52, 74–5, 85, 97
Presidential Advisory Council on Science and Technology, 151
Prix Un Certain Regard, 148, 149
production companies, 10, 11, 21, 130–1, 137, 150, 152; *see also* film studios
Promise of the Flesh (1975), 92, 152, 153
Promotion Project Plan (PPP), 155
propaganda, 11, 18–25, 28, 29–30, 36, 108, 131–6, 141
Pyeongyang, 6

rape, 42, 46, 135
Rashomon (1950), 54
"Rat Man" case, 98
rats, 9, 41–2, 75, 77–81, 91, 97, 98, 101–2
Raymond, Marc, 157
real order, 75, 76–8, 80–1, 82–4, 86, 87
realism, 22, 39, 73, 74, 101, 152–3, 159
Renoir, Jean, 149
repetition, 8, 92–3, 98–101, 104
repression, 8, 9, 11, 77, 82, 83, 87–8
reproduction, 9, 42, 43, 80, 92, 97, 104–5, 113–14
revival, 92, 93, 99
Revivre (2015), 152
Rhee Syngman, 43, 51, 53, 65, 87
Richard, James Havis, 152
Ridgeway, William G., 19–20, 25

ROK Army, 19, 20, 24, 65
romance, 51–67
Rotterdam Film Festival, 150
rural development, 133–9
rural–urban migration, 133

Sacred Mother figures, 36, 40, 47
sacrifice, 29, 38–40, 44–5, 47, 95, 112–13, 134, 136, 139
sadism, 52, 53
St Pierre, Joshua, 123
San Francisco International Film Festival, 8
San Sebastian Film Festival, 150
Sangnam, 18–19, 21
Schoonover, Karl, 155
Screen International, 159
Sea Knows, The (1961), 10, 34, 51–67, 59, 61, 66, 150
Second World War, 23, 38, 65–6
Seong Chun-hyang (1961), 88
Seoul, 6–7, 74, 84, 87, 98
Seoul National University, 6–7, 101
sexual enslavement, 52, 67
sexual fantasy, 56, 58, 60, 118, 156
sexuality, 3, 8–9, 41, 46, 52–3, 56–63, 79, 82–3, 86–8, 91–6, 102, 108–9, 114–17, 125, 130, 132, 135–6, 139–40, 153, 156, 158
sexuation, 81
Shakespeare, William, 34
Shearing, Clifford D., 110
Shim Ae-gyoung, 65, 130, 131
Shimanaka Hōji, 38
Shin Sang-ok, 11, 22, 131, 152, 159
Shinoda Masahiro, 40
silence, 110, 115, 123
Silver Bear Extraordinary Prize, 154, 159
Sinhan Munye Film, 11, 137
smell, 75, 96, 158
smoke, 75, 83, 85, 86, 88
social norms, 8, 9, 39, 43–4, 46, 109–12
Soil (1978), 11, 131, 132–6, 140
Soil (Yi), 133, 136
Soviet Union, 5
spectrality, 82

Spider House (2022), 3
squirrels, 78, 102, 105
State Street (1950), 28
sterilization, 113–14
Straits of Joseon (1943), 29
streaming, 4, 155
Stringer, Julian, 93, 95–6, 99, 147
student activism, 5, 47, 53, 65, 74, 87
student theater, 6–7, 28, 101
stuttering, 109–17, 137, 139–40
sublimity, 36, 39, 40, 44, 47
subtitles, 4–5, 22
suicide, 47, 86, 87, 94, 102, 106, 123–4, 135, 136
Sundance Film Festival, 155
superego, 83
Surrogate Woman, The (1986), 147
symbolic order, 75, 76, 78, 81, 82–4, 86, 87
Sympathy for Mr. Vengeance (2002), 157

taboos, 9, 85, 130
Tale of Two Sisters, A (2003), 157
Tanizaki Jun'ichirō, 38
Taylor-Jones, Kate, 56, 64
technology, 83–4, 104
television, 84, 131
Telluride Film Festival, 150
territorial disputes, 52, 67
theater, 6–7, 28, 100–1
Thirst (2009), 158
This is America, 23
Thomas, Carol, 112
time, 45, 52, 76, 86, 98
topology, 75, 76–8
Toronto Film Festival, 150
totalitarianism, 8, 38
Totem and Taboo (Freud), 81
Touch-me-not, A (1956), 7, 11, 150
tradition, 10, 35, 36–8, 47, 48, 97, 104
Train to Busan (2016), 148
trains, 75, 85–6
Transgression (1974), 10, 130
transnationality, 5, 6, 10, 147
triadism, 75–88

Truffaut, François, 149
Tuition (1940), 55

uncanniness, 6, 79, 81, 101, 103
unconsciousness, 76–8, 80, 95
United Nations Korean Reconstruction Agency (UNKRA), 30
United States
  Academy Awards, 35, 107, 146, 152, 154, 158, 159
  anti-communism, 36, 53
  attempts to reconcile Japan and Korea, 53
  cinema audience numbers, 146
  economic aid to Korea, 87
  film festivals, 8, 155
  film production in Korea, 7, 18–25, 28, 29–30, 108, 150
  and hegemony, 36
  Hollywood, 3, 22, 28, 30, 36, 54, 131, 133, 136, 155
  propaganda, 18–25, 28, 29–30, 36, 108
  and the Vietnam War, 138
United States Information Agency (USIA), 21, 28, 29
United States Information Service (USIS), 7, 18–25, 28, 29–30, 108, 150
universality, 64, 81–2, 83, 88, 99–100

vampirism, 97, 99, 102
Venice International Film Festival, 35, 147, 148, 149–50, 154
Vietnam War, 109, 110, 112, 137–9
violence, 2, 42–3, 46–7, 91, 97, 124, 129
vitality, 80, 99–104
voice, 107–25

waesaek controversy, 54, 65
Wang, Ben, 39
Ward of Affection (1953), 21
Wasson, Haidee, 150
Water Lady (1979), 9, 11, 108–17, **115**, **116**, 124–5, 131, 132, 136–40, **138**, **139–40**
Welles, Orson, 34
western dress, 85, 98

Westerns, 45
Woman of Fire (1971), 8–9, 51, 91–6, 97–9, 101, 102, 104, 107, 157, 158
Woman of Fire '82 (1982), 51, 92–6, 97–9, 101, 102, 107, 153, 158
Wong, Cindy Hing-Yuk, 156

Yangsan Province (1955), 10, 21, 150, 153
Yasumaru Yoshio, 39–40
Yecies, Brian, 65, 130, 131
Yi Dong-jin, 154
Yi Du-yong, 159
Yi Gwang-su, 133, 136
Yi Gyeong-sun, 18
Yi Hyeong-pyo, 20
Yi Hyo-in, 6, 44, 52–3, 74
Yi Kyeong-sun, 19
Yi Man-hui, 22, 129, 130, 131
Yi Sun-jin, 22
Yi Ye-chun, 61
Yi Yeon-ho, 6, 34, 52
Yi Yeong-il, 18, 22, 73, 132
You and I (1941), 54–5
Youn Yuh-jung, 107, 152, 154, 158
youth culture, 105
Yu Du-yeon, 26
Yu Hyeon-mok, 11, 22, 129, 131, 152
Yu Jang-san, 18
Yu Ji-hyeong, 131
Yun Posun, 53
Yushin System, 8, 10–11, 104, 129, 131, 133, 141, 150

Žižek, Slavoj, 82

EU representative:
Easy Access System Europe
Mustamäe tee 50, 10621 Tallinn, Estonia
Gpsr.requests@easproject.com

www.ingramcontent.com/pod-product-compliance
Lightning Source LLC
Chambersburg PA
CBHW051128160426
43195CB00014B/2383